Mar. 2012

The Official Guide to

ancestry.com℠

The Official Guide to

⚘Hancestry.com^{SM}

by George G. Morgan

⚘Hancestry publishing™

Library of Congress Cataloging-in-Publication Data

Morgan, George G.,
The official guide to Ancestry.com / by George G. Morgan.—2nd ed.
    p. cm.
ISBN-13: 978-1-59331-319-7 (alk. paper)
ISBN-10: 1-59331-319-5 (alk. paper)
1. Ancestry.com (Firm) 2. Genealogy—Computer network resources—Handbooks, manuals, etc. 3. United States—Genealogy—Computer network resources—Handbooks, manuals, etc. I. Title.

CS21.5.M672 2008
025.06'9291—dc22

2008032560

Ancestry.com
An imprint of Turner Publishing Company

200 4th Avenue North, Suite 950
Nashville, TN 37219

445 Park Avenue, 9th Floor
New York, NY 10022

www.turnerpublishing.com

First Printing 2008
10 9 8 7 6 5 4 3 2

ISBN: 978-1-59331-319-7

Printed in the United States of America

Contents

Introduction xvii

What Is Ancestry.com? xviii

What This Book Will Do for You xx

What's New in the Second Edition? xxi

Chapter 1
Getting Around the Site 1

Logging In 1

    Account Information 3

Navigating the Site 5

    Quick Links 5

The Tabs 6

    Home 6

Search 8

    Print and Share 9

    Community 11

    DNA 12

    Learning Center 13

    Store 14

Summary 14

Contents

Chapter 2
Searching for Your Ancestors 17

The Search Basics 18

Add Names 20

Add Dates.. 21

Add Places 21

New Search Overview 22

Searching 24

Finding a Specific Database Title 29

Search Strategy 32

Summary 33

Chapter 3
Working with Digitized Image Collections......... 35

How to Access a Digital Image............................ 35

View Record... 37

View Image 40

The Toolbar 41

View in Full Page Mode 42

Drag 42

Zoom 42

Image Size 43

Magnify.. 44

Options 44

Image Number, Previous, and Next 47

Print 47

Save 48

Share 49

Help 50

Summary 50

Chapter 4
Family Trees..51

Creating a New Family Tree................................ 52

Starting a Tree from Scratch 52

Upload a GEDCOM 55

Working with Your Family Trees 56
    Overview 57
    People 59
    Family Tree 63
    Photos 65
    Stories 66
    Audio 66
Summary 67

Chapter 5
Working with Census Records 69
United States Federal Census Records 70
Searching the Census Records 71
U.S. State and County Census Records 77
    The Nebraska Census, 1854–1870 Records 78
    Maryland Records 79
UK Census Records 80
    Searching the Census Records 82
    The Scotland 1841 Census 86
Canadian Census Records 87
Summary 91

Chapter 6
Birth, Marriage, and Death Records 93
The Major Record Types 94
The Social Security Death Index (SSDI) 96
A Sample Marriage Database: Maryland
    1655–1850 101
Banffshire, Scotland: Parish and Probate
    Records 103
England & Wales, FreeBMD Birth Index:
    1837–1983 103
Summary 106

Contents

Chapter 7

Military Records..**107**

Early American Military Databases 109

American Civil War Records 111

World War I Draft Registration Cards,
     1917–1918 113

U.S. World War II Army Enlistment Records,
     1938–1946 115

WW II United News Newsreels, 1942–1946 116

Summary 118

Chapter 8

Immigration Records **121**

Immigration Records at Ancestry.com 121

Searching the Collections................................123

Sample Immigration Databases and Titles..............128

Summary 134

Chapter 9

Pictures, Newspapers, and Maps.....................**135**

Searching for Pictures 136

Member Photos 139

     Private Photos.......................................142

     Other Great Image Collections 142

Searching Newspapers and Periodicals 144

     The United States Obituary Collection..........146

Maps, Atlases, and Gazetteers 149

     An Introduction to Cartography 150

Working with the Maps, Atlases & Gazetteers
     Collection 153

Summary 155

Chapter 10

Stories, Memories, and Histories......................**157**

Searching and Browsing the Collection 158

Exploring Different Types of Books from the

Collection 161

A Family History 162

A Local History 164

American Genealogical-Biographical

Index (AGBI) 165

Slave Narratives 167

Dawes Commission Index.........................169

Summary 170

Chapter 11
Directories and Member List Records 173

Searching a City Directory 175

U.S. School Yearbooks.....................................177

U.S. Public Records Index 178

UK and U.S. Directories, 1680–1830...................179

British Phone Books 1880–1984 181

Summary 183

Chapter 12
Court and Land Records 185

Searching the Databases.....................................187

Summary 190

Chapter 13
Reference and Finding Aids 191

Searching the Reference and Finding Aids

Records 192

Searching Books..194

The *Periodical Source Index* (*PERSI*) 196

Summary 200

Chapter 14
Printing and Sharing 201

Getting Started...202

Making a Family History Book............................203
Working with Your Project 205
    Workspace...205
    Thumbnails and Main Toolbar 206
Editing Page Elements 208
Previewing and Ordering................................211
Sharing Projects 212
Printing Records 212
Summary 214

Chapter 15
Ancestry Community............................. 215

The Components of the Ancestry Community 216
My Public Profile 218
Message Boards...221
    Format..221
    Searching the Message Boards.....................224
Member Connections 233
The Member Directory 233
Summary 235

Chapter 16
DNA... 237

Testing at Ancestry.com 239
The DNA Homepage......................................239
Your DNA Test 240
Looking at Your Test Results...........................241
DNA Groups 246
Summary 247

Chapter 17
The Learning Center 249

Welcome to the Learning Center 250
Find Answers...256
Build a Tree..260

Join the Community 262

Discover More 264

Keep Learning 266

Searching the Archive 272

Summary 273

Chapter 18
The Ancestry Store 275

Books 276

Records 277

Software 278

Photos 278

Maps 279

Gifts 279

Ordering 280

Summary 281

Chapter 19
Putting It All Together 283

Traditional versus Electronic Evidence 284

Using the Help Tool at Ancestry.com 285

    Ask Ancestry 286

    Email Ancestry Support 287

    Videos 288

    Webinar 289

Happy Hunting 290

Dedication

This book is dedicated to my favorite aunt, Mary Allen Morgan (1905–1969). She provided me with the loving guidance, mentoring, and education that made me appreciate words, books, and learning, and she helped me connect those things to a love of family history. She was also my first and best adult friend. She gave me homemade lemonade, peach cobbler, blackberry cobbler, "angel" sourdough rolls, candied citrus peel, and a wealth of family stories and traditions along the way. She was better than all those around her and deserved so much more in her life. I'm glad she was such a vital part of my life and I a part of hers. She is very much missed and still very much loved.

Acknowledgments

Ancestry.com has been and remains an almost overwhelming experience. Each time I use it, I discover something new. The people in content acquisition and program development at The Generations Network, Inc., who generate, manage, and support each functional area, are truly amazing. They are enthusiastic and creative, and it is their hard work that makes Ancestry.com in all of its geographies positively sing.

There are many people who helped make the second edition of this book become a reality. What makes this edition so special is the addition of new chapters about DNA and about MyCanvas (previously called AncestryPress), the great new online publishing tool at Ancestry.com. A complete revision of the Learning Center has been launched in the interim between editions of this book and it is an exciting, multi-media, online library! In addition, the new search function at Ancestry.com is the embodiment of the search engine we've wanted for years. The names of all those who contributed to these developments are too numerous to list. Likewise, the support desk personnel who keep things running from day to day and help *all* of us are some of the greatest in the industry!

Acknowledgments

You really cannot imagine what it is like to try to write a book about a highly dynamic site such as Ancestry.com *while it is being redesigned*. Functionality, screen shots, and data content/organization were all changing over the months this book was being written. Keeping the communication links open and sharing visions was a challenge. However, as the developers turned out new content and tested it, I had input in the process when I found changes that needed to be made and processes corrected. Everyone worked as a team and the result was a better product *and* a better guidebook.

I'd especially like to thank the wonderful people at Ancestry Publishing for their faith in my ability to create the second edition of this book. Jennifer Utley is a consummate professional whose advice is always good. She is a visionary who knows what will and will not work, and she is always helpful in surmounting any difficulties that arise.

Paul Rawlins worked diligently on editing the manuscript and creating the index, learning from the process and making my work look so much better. Matthew Rayback, the editor of the first edition, also participated in the editorial process and remembered *how* I write and how to make my writing look and feel consistent. I cannot thank you both enough. We three make a great team!

Finally, I would like to thank the many thousands of users of Ancestry.com for acknowledging its superior content through their continued use of the service. It is my deepest hope that this book will help make you a better researcher and extend your research to new levels. I'm learning and discovering every day, just as you are.

Introduction

My genealogical research began when I was ten years old. That was back in the early 1960s when everything a researcher did involved either visiting a records repository in person or writing lots of letters. You submitted queries to magazines and to genealogical society newsletters and journals. You waited for responses to those letters and queries, which were agonizingly slow. If you were fortunate, you got something back that helped further your research; if not, you started over again in another direction.

As electronic communications came of age, many of us used slow, dial-up modems to connect to genealogy Bulletin Board Services (BBSs) and, later, to genealogy groups through early online services: Compuserve, GENie, Prodigy, and others, all of which were text-based facilities. The entry of America Online into the field intensified commercial competition with its expanded range of electronic resources. The Genealogy Forum on America Online became a leader in online genealogy, offering articles, graphical materials, message boards, scheduled online chats, a file cabinet for uploading and downloading of GEDCOM files, and other resources.

With the appearance of what we know as the modern Internet and the introduction of the first Web browsers that supported graphics (first Netscape, then Internet Explorer, and then others), worldwide communications exploded. E-mail and Web pages quickly changed the way we communicated, and it was not long before genealogy became one of the foremost uses of the Internet.

What Is Ancestry.com?

Among the earliest genealogical database resources on the Internet was Ancestry.com. I've used Ancestry.com for so long that it has become second nature for me to immediately turn to it for how-to articles and advice, databases, message boards, books and CDs, and much more. Most genealogists are well aware of Ancestry.com and have used it in some way. Ancestry.com is essentially a subscription database service; however, it also happens to contain a wealth of *free* material accessible to anyone.

Ancestry.com is the largest online genealogy database collection in the world. It is one of a large family of genealogy-related companies that make up The Generations Network, Inc., a company located in Provo, Utah, which includes:

- **Ancestry.com**—Ancestry.com is the world's #1 online source for family history information, containing the Web's largest collection of family history records—including databases, message boards, and digitized books and newspapers, to mention just a few—and helping genealogists organize and save their family trees.

Over the years, The Generations Network has expanded into a variety of countries and now offer sites specific to international locations including the United Kingdom (Ancestry.co.uk), Canada, (Ancestry.ca), Germany (Ancestry.de), Australia (Ancestry.au), Italy (Ancestry.it), France (Ancestry.fr), Sweden (Ancestry.se), and China (Jiapu.cn).

- **Genealogy.com**—Genealogy.com is a vast collection of family and local histories, vital records, military records, and much more.

- **RootsWeb.com**—RootsWeb.com is a thriving, free genealogy community on the Web, providing a robust worldwide environment for learning, collaborating, and sharing for both the expert and the novice researcher alike.

- **MyFamily.com**—MyFamily.com is a website at that allows anyone to easily create and maintain a private, unique family website.

- *Family Tree Maker*—*Family Tree Maker* is the number-one-selling genealogical database software on the market, providing the user with everything needed to create, grow, and publish his or her family tree.

- **Ancestry Publishing**—Ancestry Publishing is the publishing imprint of The Generations Network, Inc. With more than sixty books in its catalog—including such landmark titles as *The Source: A Guidebook to American Genealogy* and *Red Book: American State, County, and Town Sources*, both in their third edition—Ancestry Publishing is the most prestigious publisher in the genealogy marketplace. In addition, it publishes *Ancestry* Magazine, a bimonthly publication dedicated to family history.

These subsidiaries complement one another by providing a comprehensive collection of family history resources for learning, researching, documenting, collaborating, and sharing genealogical information.

What This Book Will Do for You

As Ancestry.com has grown, and with the introduction of the various worldwide sister sites, there are more than 26,000 databases and titles of varying types and sizes available, as of August 2008. New content is added every month and the user interface continues to be examined, improved, and streamlined. So many databases and different types of browse and search capabilities exist that it can be confusing to move from one database or resource or another.

The purpose of this book is to help you access the power of the many Ancestry.com databases. You will learn how to navigate the site, how to browse, and how to use all of the search functionalities to maximize your use of the entire site. You will learn how each of the major content areas are organized and presented and what is included in each area. Sample searches will be described, the appropriate database search templates and search results will be illustrated, and practical suggestions will be offered for using the results to continue and further your research.

This book focuses on the experience of a user in the United States and works with the Ancestry.com database offerings, including both free and subscription content.

In addition to access to all the databases, Ancestry.com provides a powerful and dynamic family tree tool that allows you to build one or more of your own family trees online, add photographs and stories, and invite other authorized people to view and comment on it. The Ancestry Community

contains the largest genealogical message board facility in
the world, and it allows you to search for and connect with
other researchers working on the same family lines that you
are. Further, the Learning Center provides access to a whole
library of published articles, columns, how-to materials, and
more to help you become a savvy genealogical researcher.

This book is not intended as a guide to doing your family
history. Though I give tips and suggestions throughout, you
should consult a guide to genealogy if you have any questions
about methodology. For example, you might consider my own
book on the subject:

Morgan, George G. *How to Do Everything with Your Genealogy*.
Emeryville, CA: McGraw-Hill/Osborne, 2004.

What's New in the Second Edition?

Since I wrote the first edition of this book, major changes and
additions have been made to Ancestry.com. While you can
certainly use many of the research tips and ideas in the first
edition, this second edition addresses many of the new changes
and additions, including the following:

- The new search function

- MyCanvas (previously called AncestryPress)

- AncestryDNA

- The updated Learning Center

- Enhancements to Family Trees

It is important to remember that Ancestry.com is a dynamic
resource that is constantly changing. While it is impossible
for a book like this to accurately reflect all aspects of the
site into the future, the fundamentals contained herein will
remain valuable, even as the site changes. Some of the features

discussed in this book may look different than shown here, but you can still use those examples to help you learn.

This guide will coach you through using the full range of the Ancestry.com international family of databases and other electronic resources. In no time at all, you will have become a pro in making the online content at Ancestry.com an essential part of all of your research. You will be navigating and searching the data quickly and effectively, *and* you will be better prepared to apply what you find to improve the quality and efficiency of your research at Ancestry.com and across the Internet.

Happy Hunting!

George G. Morgan
Odessa, Florida
August 2008

Chapter 1

Getting Around the Site

Ancestry.com is easy to use once you learn the ropes for navigating the site and using the various search tools. In this chapter, you will learn these essential skills. With more than 26,000 databases online with different record types and content, the way you work with the search forms will differ from database to database. Don't let this intimidate you. The way you search will essentially look similar and act the same, regardless of the database.

I encourage you to enter the examples shown in the figures in the chapter and then practice each step with one of your own ancestors. Doing so will help you become more comfortable using Ancestry.com.

Logging In

Let's begin at the beginning with the Ancestry.com homepage <www.ancestry.com> (see figure 1.1 on the next page). At the top, notice the fields marked "Member Login." As a subscriber

Figure 1-1: The Ancestry.com homepage before login

to Ancestry.com, you enter your username and password here. There are free areas on Ancestry.com, but a subscription to either the U.S. Deluxe Membership or the World Deluxe Membership provides you access to the full range of databases that Ancestry.com has to offer. If you are not yet a subscriber, click the "Subscribe" link to view the two subscription plans and pricing plans available. If you are already a subscriber, enter your username and password and click **Login**. If you have forgotten your username and/or password, you can click the "Forgot Password?" link for help.

Even if you are not logged in, you can start a Family Tree or begin searching the Ancestry.com database collections. If you are not a subscriber, you can still register and access a number of features such as family trees, parts of the Ancestry Community, the publishing tool, and the Learning Center, which has online multimedia tutorials and reference resources. You cannot, however, access the premium databases without a subscription. The easiest way to register is to start your own Family Tree by clicking **Start your tree**. Follow the instructions to create your tree and sign up for free membership.

The gray bar across the top of the page consists of tabs, or links to different main sections of the site. Later in this chapter we'll go through each of these in detail.

From the bottom section of the homepage, you can browse all the collections at Ancestry.com. The "Recent Buzz" section provides access to recent press articles about Ancestry.com and its parent company, The Generations Network, Inc. In addition, descriptions and links to recently added databases can be read in the "New & Coming Soon" section. Upcoming additions are also announced here. As is common on websites, you can also find a variety of useful information in the page's footer.

Account Information

After logging in, you should see your username in the upper right, followed by links that allow you to log out of Ancestry.com, view and work with "My Account" settings, and access the "Help" facility online.

On the "My Account" page, you can view or modify your current subscription or manage your account settings, using the options in the "My Account Information" section (see figure 1-2 on the next page). The options include the following:

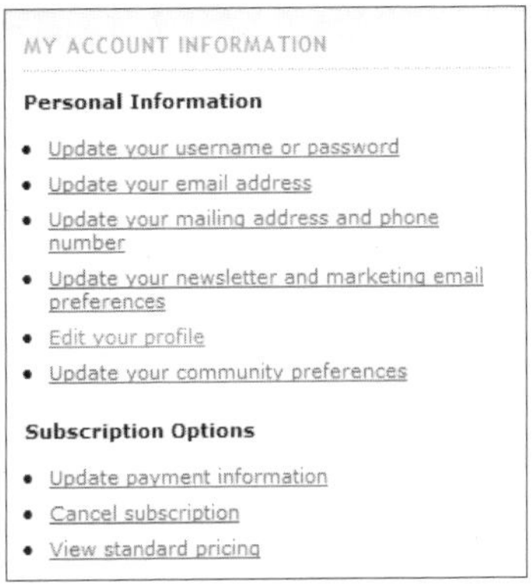

- **Update username or password**—You may change your login information at any time. Be certain that

Registering

As Ancestry.com grows, more and more free features will be available to users by following a simple registration procedure. This will give you a username and a password you can use to sign in with on return visits.

MY ACCOUNT INFORMATION

Personal Information

- Update your username or password
- Update your email address
- Update your mailing address and phone number
- Update your newsletter and marketing email preferences
- Edit your profile
- Update your community preferences

Subscription Options

- Update payment information
- Cancel subscription
- View standard pricing

Figure 1-2: "My Account Information" section of the "My Account" page

you write your new username and/or password down in a safe place for future reference.

- **Update e-mail address**—It is important to maintain your correct e-mail address for your account so that Ancestry.com administrative staff can contact you. The e-mail address is also used in other areas of Ancestry.com to provide a means for other members researching the same ancestral lines to contact you.

- **Update your mailing address and phone number**—This information is accessible only by you and the Ancestry.com account management team and Help Desk staff.

- **Update your newsletter and marketing e-mail preferences**—This page allows you to define the types of information you receive from Ancestry.com:

  - **Ancestry Newsletter Subscriptions**—Subscribe to the monthly newsletter, the weekly, or both.

  - **Ancestry Product Watch**—Request regular updates about products, promotional offers, and discounts on family history books, software, and other items.

  - **Special Offers**— Select "From Ancestry" and/or "From Ancestry's Trusted Partners."

  - **E-mail Format**—Specify whether the e-mails sent to you are formatted in HTML with pictures and text or as text-only messages.

You can also update your credit card information for subscription billing purposes or cancel your account from the "Subscription Options" section.

The "Need Help?" section contains answers to common questions concerning your account. The "more…" link takes you to the Knowledge Base, where you can find more answers.

Navigating the Site

Once you've signed in, you can access any of the site's features and information. As we explore the various sections of the site, follow along and do the examples shown so you get the experience of actually moving through the site and working with the features discussed.

Quick Links

In working through the "My Account" pages, you should have noticed a string of links like those shown in figure 1-3. These are called Quick Links, and they help you navigate the site more efficiently.

In figure 1-3, you can see a line that reads as follows: You are here: <u>Home</u> > <u>My Account Options</u> > Newsletter & Marketing Email Preferences

Quick Links

Quick Links are often called "bread crumbs."

This indicates that you have moved from the homepage to another page titled "My

Figure 1-3: Quick Links

Account Options" and then to another page titled "Newsletter & Marketing Email Preferences." As you navigate through Ancestry.com, you'll see these lines of links. You can use them to navigate quickly through recently viewed pages without using your browser's **Back** button. For example, if you had landed on "Update your newsletter and marketing email preferences" following the route described above, you could simply click the "My Account Options" link to move back to that page. Likewise, if you click the "Home" link, you will move to the Ancestry.com homepage. This can be very convenient when you are working in other areas of Ancestry. For example, I searched the 1850 census for my great-great-grandfather Jesse Holder in Gwinnett County, Georgia (see figure 1-4 on the next page).

Search > Census > U.S. Census > 1850 United States Federal Census > Georgia > Gwinnett > **Cates**

Figure 1-4: Quick Links on 1850 census image page

I can click on any of the underlined links to move backwards, one link at a time, or leap back to "Census" and begin another general census search. In other words, these Quick Links make it simpler and faster to move around the Ancestry.com site.

Also, from just about anywhere in the site, you can click the Ancestry.com logo in the upper left of the page, and this will take you back to the Ancestry.com homepage.

The Tabs

Let's look now at the different tabs available on the homepage.

Home

After signing in, you'll see significant changes to the homepage (see figure 1-5 on the next page). The logged-in homepage works as your command center when using the site. From here, you can access your trees, search, return to recent searches, and so on. If you're familiar with Ancestry.com, you'll recognize many of these features from the old "MyAncestry" page.

Family Trees

We'll talk about Family Trees in greater detail in chapter 4, but essentially, Family Trees on Ancestry.com are the best way to store, view, and search for information on your family. In this first section of the homepage, you can view activity on and information about on your trees. More importantly, you can go to any of your trees by clicking the "My Trees" drop-down. Trees are a fundamental part of how Ancestry.com functions, so if you do not have one, you should consider starting one.

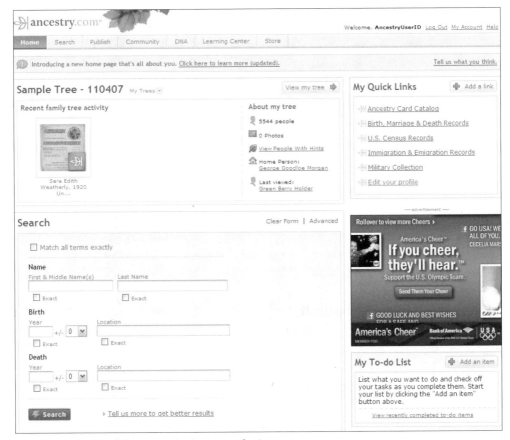

Figure 1-5: A portion of the Ancestry.com homepage after login

Searching

The search form allows you to search *all* of the Ancestry.com databases. If you want to narrow your search by providing more information, click "Tell us more to get better results." We will discuss searching on Ancestry.com in great detail and provide examples in chapter 2.

Other Features

Below the search form, you'll find "What's Happening at Ancestry.com," which provides you access to descriptions and links to recently added databases and news about the company.

Notice the section called "Recent Activity." This feature allows you to continue working with the people, places, and records that you've already been researching from one online session to another. This feature is, without doubt, one of the most convenient tools available. Even before you begin active searching, you can set up and keep track of people and places that you want to research. You can also save records to your Shoebox, and then, after additional consideration, you can link them to individuals in your Family Tree. If you've been with Ancestry for a while and you had people saved in the old "People I'm Looking For" feature, you'll find a link to those here as well.

Search

The primary reason you have subscribed to Ancestry.com is most likely to search the wealth of databases available there. The "Search" page is the main place on the site for conducting your searches.

The search function at Ancestry.com has undergone a number of revisions in recent years. A complete rewrite of the search function was introduced in 2008. It features a more robust search engine and even gathers information from your Family Tree to fill in fields automatically and eliminate a great deal of manual data entry.

The top portion of the "Search" page (see figure 1-6 on the next page) contains the same search form you saw on the homepage, which allows you to search all 26,000+ databases and the more than 6 billion records in them. You also have links to some excellent tutorials and "how-to" references for searching.

Below the search form in the "Go Directly to Specific Databases or Collections" section is a link to the Card Catalog (see figure 1-7). Here you can browse for databases and filter them by keyword (using the Keyword box) or browse by collection. We will talk more about using the Card Catalog and on specific search strategies in chapter 2.

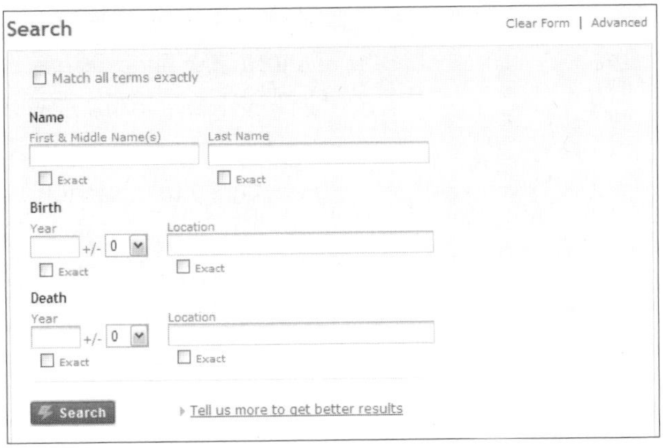

Figure 1-6: The main "Search" form

Print and Share

Ancestry.com has recently introduced a professional-quality publishing feature, which you can access on the **Print and Share** tab. You can use this feature to create books, albums, cookbooks, posters, and more, all using data and images from

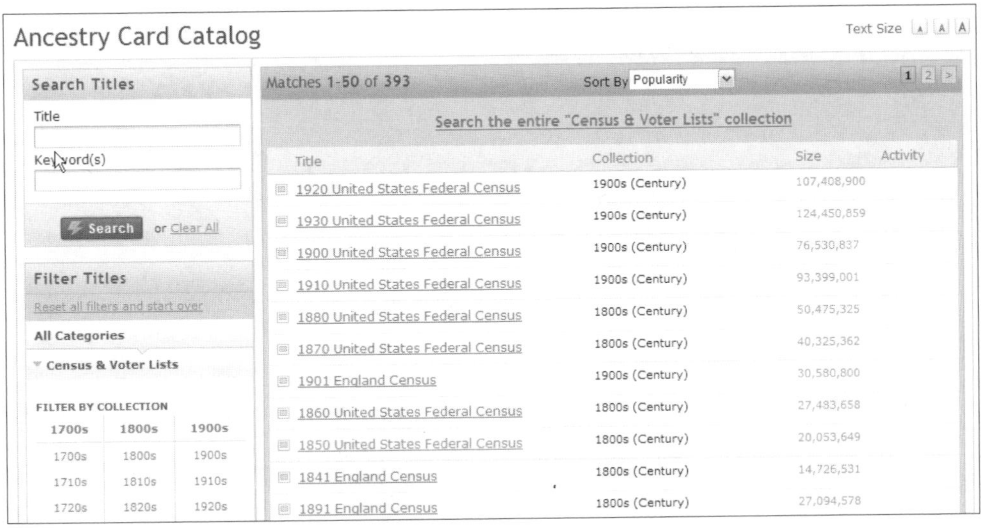

Figure 1-7: A portion of the Card Catalog

your Family Tree at Ancestry.com or by manually uploading and including photographs, text, and other data. Professionally developed page forms provide beautiful backgrounds, and complimentary clip art, flags, script, and other embellishments can be added to create just the visual effect you want.

Your projects and their contents are completely private until you are ready to share them. Your project can be printed in handsome book form to preserve the information for posterity, or you can generate beautiful posters for gifts or to use at family gatherings. An example of just one page format for a family heritage project is shown in figure 1-8.

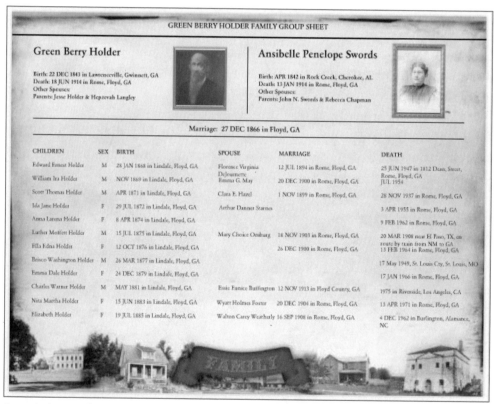

Figure 1- 8: A page from a publishing project

We will discuss the publishing feature in chapter 14, and you will see how easy it is to create stunning, professional-looking results with this easy-to-use publishing tool.

Community

The Ancestry Community (see figure 1-9) is where you make connections with other researchers at Ancestry.com. You can access it through the **Community** tab. There are three important components of this area.

The message boards combine the power of both the Ancestry.com and RootsWeb message boards to create a place where you can post and read information and queries about surnames, individuals, locations, ethnic and religious groups, international research and locales, institutions, record types and other resources, genealogical software, and many other topics. This collaboration with other researchers may give you information and clues that help extend your research.

Figure 1-9: Profile box on the "Community" page

The message boards allow you to customize your experience by defining your "Favorites"—those message boards that you want to track and read frequently—and set up notifications to be sent to you via e-mail when someone posts a new message or a reply. We will discuss how to set up your preferences for message boards and how to get the most from them in chapter 15. You can also search the boards from the "Message Boards" section of the "Community" page or browse using the links given.

In the "Members Connections" section, you can make contacts with other people researching the same individuals or lines as you. Go exploring in this area to see what the connection service is like.

The "Member Directory" lets you connect with other people who share your interests in a particular surname and/or location. We will discuss this feature, too, in a later chapter, but, as you will see, you can search the directory from the Ancestry Community.

DNA

Genetics and the use of DNA in genealogical research are hot topics these days. Thousands of genealogists are having their DNA tested, both paternal and maternal where appropriate, to prove existing research and to identify matches with other researchers who are genetically related.

At Ancestry.com, your test results are added to a massive and growing database of others' test reports and to your Ancestry.com profile. Your results are then compared against other Ancestry.com members and subscribers to determine if there are other close matches, and e-mail notifications are sent to you and potential matches so you can investigate further and contact one another if you choose.

Click the **DNA** tab.

The resulting "DNA" page has a great deal of introductory information for you (see figure 1-10). The panel at the right will introduce you to DNA as it relates to genealogy and then continue with discussions about paternal and maternal DNA testing, a link to the DNA blog, and a list of frequently asked questions. There's even a recorded interview conducted by National Public Radio with DNA genealogy expert Megan Smolenyak that provides excellent insights into the subject.

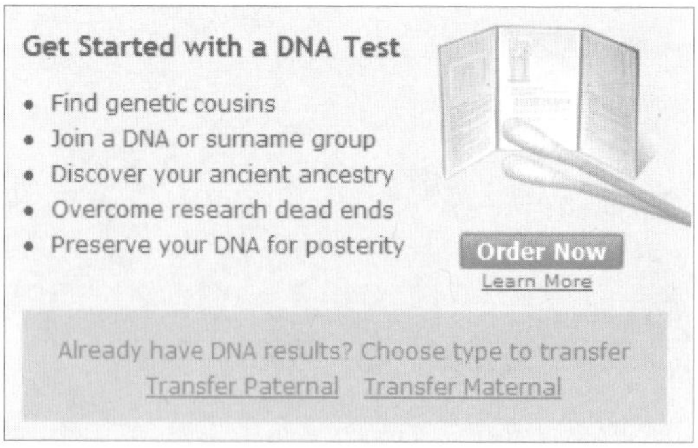

Get Started with a DNA Test

- Find genetic cousins
- Join a DNA or surname group
- Discover your ancient ancestry
- Overcome research dead ends
- Preserve your DNA for posterity

Order Now
Learn More

Already have DNA results? Choose type to transfer
Transfer Paternal   Transfer Maternal

Figure 1-10: Ordering a DNA test on the "DNA" page

DNA is definitely a growing part of genealogical research, and Ancestry.com is ready to help you get started. We'll discuss DNA Ancestry more in chapter 16.

Learning Center

The Learning Center is a tremendous resource, providing access to a wealth of reference materials (see figure 1-11). Access it by clicking the **Learning Center** tab.

The library contains all of the articles that have appeared in *Ancestry* Magazine and the now defunct *Genealogical Computing*, as well as the columns and articles published in the *Ancestry Daily News*, the *Ancestry Weekly Journal*, the *24/7 Family History Circle* blog, and much, much more.

The Learning Center has been completely redesigned in the last year, and the homepage features a video window, again with Megan Smolenyak. There are more than twenty helpful and instructive videos in the Learning Center. You will also find entire sections on how to search different types of records,

Figure 1-11 Portion of the Learning Center homepage

how to create your own Family Tree at Ancestry.com, how to join and participate in the Ancestry Community, how to expand your research beyond the basics, and more. The articles and columns featured in the Learning Center are written by the very best genealogical experts of our time and provide insight into all aspects of genealogy. Best of all, these resources are browseable *and* searchable.

We'll cover the Learning Center in chapter 17. There is so much here, you will find yourself using it all the time.

Store

At the Ancestry Store (accessible through the **Store** tab), you can discover some of the best genealogical publications and software titles (see figure 1-12). Ancestry is a leading publisher of authoritative genealogical reference books. These include *The Source: A Guidebook to American Genealogy*; *Red Book: American State, County, and Town Resources*; *They Became Americans*; and many more. The company also produces *Family Tree Maker* and other genealogy software. You will find more than 10,000 high-quality items in the Ancestry Store. We discuss the Ancestry Store in greater detail in chapter 18.

Summary

Now that you know how to navigate the Ancestry.com site and have had an overview of the way it is

Figure 1-12: Staff favorites on the "Ancestry Store" page.

organized, we'll dive into how to really use the search facilities in the next chapter. Then we'll talk about how to use what you've found and how to create and work with Family Trees. Then it's on to different record types, lots of practical examples and research strategies, and the rest of the Ancestry.com site.

Here we go!

Chapter 2

Searching for
Your Ancestors

As you've seen, Ancestry.com has many components, functions, and tools. For most users, however, the primary focus of their work at Ancestry.com is to search the more than 26,000 databases and 6 billion names on the site.

If you are a longtime Ancestry.com user, you have seen the evolution of searching from a simple name-date-location search to one with advanced features like exact searching and wildcard searches. In 2007, Ancestry.com began rebuilding the search function from the ground up to enable users to more effectively search and locate what they are looking for.

In early 2008, user testing began on the new search. As of this writing, the default at this time is the new search, but you can opt out and use the old search if you want. As such, this chapter (and indeed the book) deals only with the new search. If you use the old search still and have questions, you can find the search chapter from the first edition of this book at <www.ancestrystore.com> as a free PDF download.

Searching in Other Locations

This book focuses on Ancestry.com for U.S. users, but we will also explore a number of the databases for other geographies. If you access other collections (such as the UK, Canadian, Australian, or German collections), you should be able to apply what you learn in this chapter to those database collections.

We will use specific examples, and I encourage you to follow along, step by step, and do the searches using the criteria I use in the examples. Please recognize, however, that Ancestry.com is continually adding new content and updating existing databases. As a result, the search results you see when you replicate my examples may differ from those shown here. Don't let that confuse you. Just take the time to examine the search results and click on links to view sample records. In this way, you will become familiar with a great many databases and their content. You can then consider them potential resources for your own research.

In later chapters, we will address many of the records that you can search, exactly how to search each type, what information you will discover, and how it applies to your research. As you work through the examples, you will become more proficient at creating effective searches and get the most out of Ancestry.com.

The Search Basics

We search for information in a database by entering search criteria, such as first name, surname, location, or time period. You will enter your criteria on search forms. Your search is often referred to as a query.

You saw the generic search form in chapter 1 (see figure 2-1 at the top of the next page). In general, this (or a variation of it) is the same form you will see throughout the site. It's important to keep in mind, however, that though the search form may be the same, the information you are looking for may differ. It's important to keep track of what you're actually looking for and consider these criteria when you are forming your query.

Consider, for example, that the information in the U.S. federal census is completely different from that in the Social

Security Death Index (SSDI), the Irish Records Index (1500–1920), or the Baden, Germany Emigration Index (1866–1911). Thus, as you are searching these different databases, you will want to structure your query based on the information you think you might find. Note that German census database records are in German, and therefore, for best results, you should search using words entered in German.

Figure 2-1: The standard search form

A good general search strategy is to type in as much information as possible. If you're not sure about some information, take an educated guess. As long as you're close, it can help. Try these general suggestions to improve your results:

- Add a middle name if you can

- Add a birth and/or death year

- Add a birth and/or death place

After completing your initial search, you might want to narrow your search results to those found only in a particular category or database. You can always do this using the content panel to the left of the results panel. Simply click on the desired category or database listed to the left of the search results to narrow your results. This will modify your result to reflect the new filters or information you've applied.

As you narrow your search to a particular category or database, some of your search options on the left may not apply because you've narrowed down to content that does not contain that type of information. For example, if you narrow down to the Census & Voter Lists, you will not be able to add death information, since censuses and voter lists records do not have death information.

You can also add or change information in your search at any time by adding more or different information to the form and then clicking **Search**.

Add Names

Type in as much of your ancestor's name as you can. The more information you can give, the more focused your results will be. Ancestry.com automatically looks for common nicknames, abbreviations, and other alternate spellings for you. For example, a search for "Bill Smith" might return "William Smith," "Wm. Smith," "Bill Smyth," or "B. Smith." This is particularly helpful because names are often be misspelled or mistranscribed in the original records or indexes. Therefore, looking for alternate spellings can sometimes help you find a good match, even though the name may look completely wrong to you.

You can also add a woman's maiden name to search for both her married and maiden names, or you can do two different searches, one with her married name and one with her maiden name. Try as many combinations as you can imagine, such as the following:

• Mary Elizabeth Williams Smith

• Mary Elizabeth Williams

• Mary Elizabeth Smith

Note that as you begin to type a name, Ancestry will often prompt you with names from your Family Trees (see figure 2-2 on the next page). If the person you are searching for is indeed one of these people, simply select it from the list, and that person's information will be auto-filled in the search form.

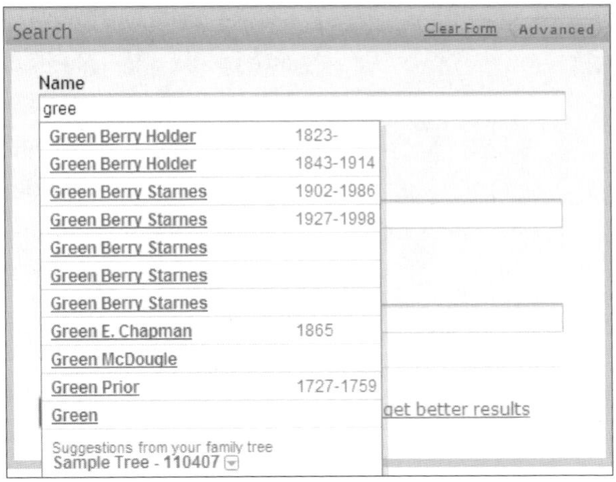

Add Dates

Adding birth and/or death dates can really help your search. It's much easier to find your Elizabeth Smith knowing she was born in 1872 than it is to find her among all the possible Elizabeth Smiths on Ancestry.com. You're even more likely to find her if you know she was born in 1872 and died in 1937.

Figure 2-2: The "type-ahead" feature on the search form

What if you are unsure about the exact date? Take an educated guess. As long as you're within a few years, you'll get much better results than if you leave a date field blank. Ancestry.com automatically looks for close dates, just in case the record is wrong or your guess was a little off.

Unless you know exactly what you're looking for, it's often wise to search a range of years around the date you've entered. To do this, use the +/- drop-down on the search form by a date field (like a birth date) and select the desired range (see figure 2-3). Note that the ranges are only available with the advanced searching feature (more on that later). For example, you might enter a birth year of 1852 and then indicate a +/- range of 0, 1, 5, 10, or 20 years. This is especially useful in searching census records or when you are unsure of the actual year of birth.

Figure 2-3: The year range drop-down

Add Places

Be as specific as you can when it comes to entering a place. If you know the city, start with that, but if not, enter the county, state, or country. Beyond birth or death location, be sure to add other places of residence if your ancestor spent a significant amount of time there. As you type a placename, Ancestry will prompt you from its list of placenames. If the placename you are looking for is on the list, simply select it, and the name will be auto-filled into the field.

Now, let's explore the new search function.

New Search Overview

Since the search function at Ancestry.com has recently been changed, many users are still unfamiliar with it. Some of the highlights of the new search include the following:

- **Site-wide Search**—Search all of Ancestry.com at once without sacrificing a thing. You can simultaneously find historical records, newspapers and periodicals, histories and stories, and photographs and maps, and they will all be shown on the same page in a much simpler, easier-to-read layout.

- **Type-ahead Tools**—Type information into a search field, and Ancestry.com will anticipate what you are typing and fill in the remaining fields based on information already in your Family Tree (see figure 2-2). Once you select a name from the type-ahead list, the names, dates, and additional information will be filled into the other fields on the form. You can then add other search criteria, or you can change or delete information that was pre-filled for you.

- **Advanced Search Options**—Narrow your search with advanced search options that make sure your results exactly match the terms you've specified.

- **Powerful Filters**—Browse database titles by filtering a title's category, location, and/or date simultaneously.

- **Sorting**—Sort the list of database titles that you're interested in alphabetically, by the date they were added or last updated, by popularity, or by size.

- **Keyword Search**—Locate databases that have a common subject or word.

- **Refine Search**—Refine your search more easily by adding or removing information directly in the content panel to the left of the results panel, instead of having to scroll to the bottom of the page.

- **Reorganized Categories**—Find databases more easily in new categories and subcategories that have been regrouped to better help you narrow your search.

- **Matching Person**—Get the best matches possible from Family Trees on Ancestry.com.

- **Record Preview**—Hover your curser over a search result to preview more detailed information without having to click on and actually open the result. This helps you more quickly check a result to see if it is really the one you want.

- **Image Snapshots**—View sections of newspaper and journal images highlighting your search terms to see whether a match is relevant.

- **Photo Results**—See thumbnails of photos and other image searches in your search results.

- **Record Counts**—See how many matches you have in each category in your search results and then refine, filter, and narrow your searches more efficiently.

The new Search offers a great many advantages in how you enter your search criteria, how the results are displayed, how you can refine your search, and how you work with the actual results.

Searching

The top portion of the new "Search" page is shown in figure 2-4. Note the search form and the "Featured" and "Learning Resources" sections.

Most often, you'll begin by filling in the "Name" field in the search form. If you have a Family Tree on Ancestry.com, an existing name in the tree will be suggested. If there are multiple individuals with the same name, you will see their names and dates and can select one.

At the top of the search form, you'll find the **Advanced** button, which expands the form to reveal some additional options (see figure 2-5 on the next page). Advanced searching gives you the ability to constrain the search to match some or all of your search criteria exactly as you entered it. For example, if you are not sure of an ancestor's exact name, but you know for sure when he or she was born, you can select

Figure 2-4: The "Search" page

"Exact" for the "Birth" field but leave the others blank. Your results will then include only people born in the year you indicated.

With advanced searching, you can also use the range drop-down beside the birth and death year fields (refer back to figure 2-3). As I said before, these can be used when you aren't quite sure of the year and want to specify a range of years. Figure 2-6 shows the advanced search form with several of these options selected. Note also the type-ahead feature in the "Location" field.

The search shown in figure 2-6 yielded six matches (all except one of which were exactly correct) for my great-grandfather, Green Berry (or Greenberry) Holder, who was born in 1843 and died in 1914. (One match was not correct because I did not mark the first name to be an exact match.) You can see where using the year and +/- range can be especially useful in narrowing a search.

Figure 2-5: The advanced search form

Figure 2-6: The advanced search form with various options

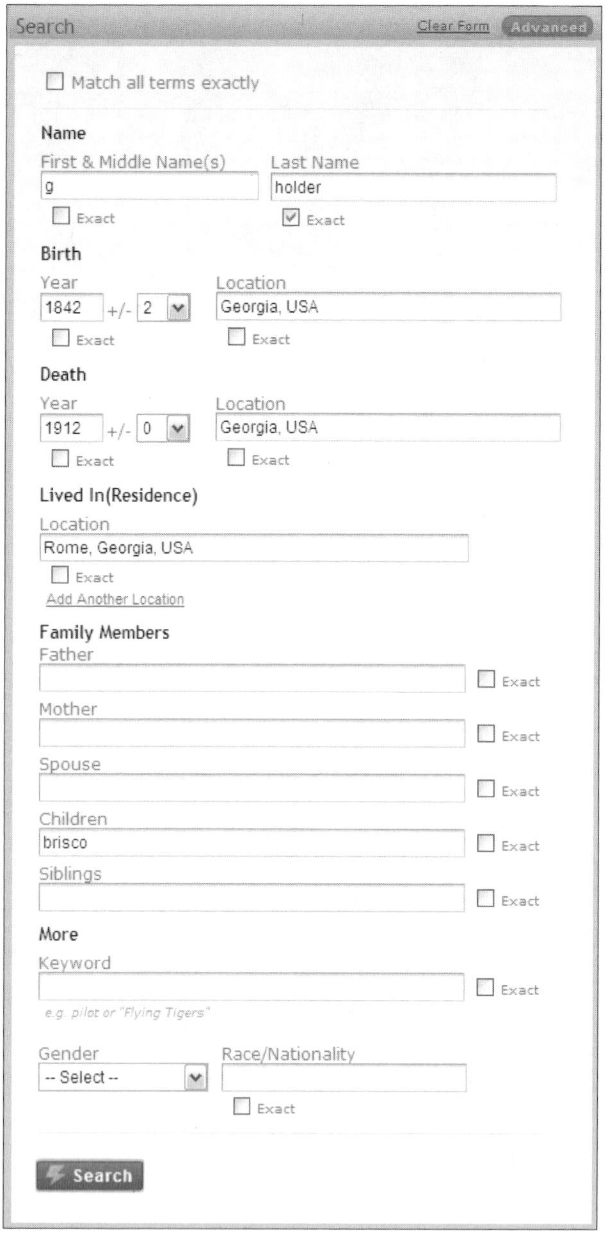

Figure 2-7: The expanded search form

Another way to enhance your search is to click "Tell us more to get better results," which is located at the bottom of the form. When you click this link, the search form expands substantially, as shown in figure 2-7. If you allowed the form to pre-fill the name and information from your Family Tree, other additional fields will be filled as well. You can also apply advanced searching features like "Exact" to this expanded form.

Remember that not every record will have contents to match every one of these fields. You may be better off starting your search with the "Exact" option deselected for most or all of the fields. You can focus in later by selecting that option as you become more sure of what you're looking for.

If you are using the expanded form shown in figure 2-7, you can also narrow your search by using the "Keyword" field on the search form. Note that there is no "Exact" option for this field. Therefore, your search results may be very large and contain few helpful matches if you use just the "Keyword" field (my search yielded 459,659 results!).

When your search has yielded results, you will be brought to a results page like that shown in figure 2-8. Note the content panel on the left, which includes the "Refine Search" section and options to filter your search by different categories, and the results panel to the right, which shows the results of your search. In the results panel, the yellow stars indicate the relevancy of the match to the data you have entered. A five-star match is likely to be very relevant, while a one-star match is probably not so good.

The yellow triangles shown in some searches indicate alternative information, usually suggested by other users. By moving your mouse over the triangle, the alternative information will appear.

Keyboard Shortcuts
⊰≫

At any time while you are searching, you can type "r" on your keyboard to refine your search. You can also type "n" to start a new search.

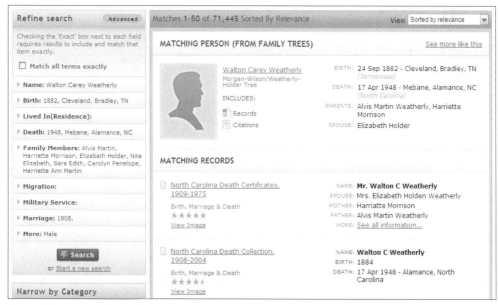

Figure 2-8: A portion of a results page

If you want to refine your search results, use the "Refine Search" section in the content panel. You can refine your search for many of the fields by clicking on the information you want to change, which will expand the form, allowing you to make changes or add new information. If you want to make part or all of your search exact, click **Advanced** at the top, which enables advanced searching as described previously. When you have made all the changes you'd like, click **Search** to conduct a new search of all the databases using your new criteria.

You can also refine your search by focusing on specific databases or groups of databases. To do this, scroll down and find the "Narrow by Category" section (see figure 2-9). Notice again that the databases have been regrouped in an effort to make them more intuitive.

The results shown in figure 2-8 were taken from the search I performed for Walton Carey Weatherly. Notice in the "Narrow by Category" section the small gray number by each category. These indicate the number of matches that were found in each category by my search.

To narrow your search to one category, click the link for that category. You'll get a new list of search results, this time only from the category you selected. In my case, I clicked on the Birth, Marriage & Death category. Let's look at the results area that I received. Keep in mind that I did not use "Exact" on any of the fields for my search.

Figure 2-10 (on the next page) shows the most relevant results for my search. The first match is absolutely the right person and is shown as a 5-star match. I can click the link labeled "North Carolina Death Collection, 1908–2004" to see more information from that source or click "View Image" to see the digitized image of the resource online. The remaining results appear because they match some of

Narrow by Category	
▼ **All Categories**	
Census & Voter Lists	5,000+
Birth, Marriage & Death	5,000+
Military	5,000+
Immigration & Emigration	5,000+
Newspapers & Periodicals	5,000+
Pictures	1,063
Stories, Memories & Histories	2,392
Directories & Member Lists	5,000+
Court, Land, Wills & Financial	2,619
Reference Materials & Finding Aids	167
Family Trees	5,000+

Figure 2-9: "Narrow by Category" section

my search criteria (remember I did not use the exact search feature). These top matches consist of multiple pages, as indicated by the numbered boxes in the upper right corner. You can click on the next number in sequence or click the box containing the > symbol.

📄 North Carolina Death Certificates, 1909-1975	NAME: **Mr. Walton C Weatherly**
	SPOUSE: Mrs. Elizabeth Holden Weatherly
Death, Burial, Cemetery & Obituaries	MOTHER: Harriatte Morrison
★★★★★	FATHER: Alvis Martin Weatherly
View Image	MORE: See all information...
📄 North Carolina Death Collection, 1908-2004	NAME: **Walton C Weatherly**
	BIRTH: 1884
Death, Burial, Cemetery & Obituaries	DEATH: 17 Apr 1948 - Alamance, North Carolina
★★★★	
View Image	
📄 North Carolina Death Certificates, 1909-1975	NAME: **Robert Dudley Weatherly**
	SPOUSE: Melba Lewis
Death, Burial, Cemetery & Obituaries	FATHER: John W Weatherly
★★★	BIRTH: 30 Jan 1882 - Greensboro, North Carolina, United States
View Image	MORE: See all information...

Figure 2-10: Top search results for Walton C Weatherly in Birth, Marriage & Death records

Go back to the "Narrow by Category" section. When I chose to narrow my search to Birth, Marriage & Death records, notice that the category has also been broken into subcategories: Birth, Baptism & Christening records; Marriage & Divorce records; and Death, Burial, Cemetery & Obituaries records. You can click any of the subcategories to focus your search even further, or click "All Categories" to browse other categories.

Finding a Specific Database Title

Ancestry.com has more than 26,000 databases online, more than any other genealogical resource on the Internet. It also provides faster access to the genealogical data than any other genealogy site on the Web. You can browse through available databases from the main "Search" page.

Below the search form, you'll see a list of database titles that are available on Ancestry.com (at the time of this writing they are shown in a section called "Go Directly to a Specific

Go Directly to a Specific Title or Collection

Go to the Card Catalog

Census & Voter Lists

1930 United States Federal Census

1920 United States Federal Census

1901 England Census

1911 Census of Canada

See more...

Immigration & Emigration

New York Passenger Lists, 1820-1957

U.S. Passport Applications, 1795-1925

Border Crossings: From Canada to U.S., 1895-1956

See more...

Stories, Memories & Histories

Public Member Stories

Slave Narratives

Daughters of the American Revolution Lineage Books (152 Vols.)

See more...

Court, Land, Wills & Financial

U.S. General Land Office Records, 1796-1907

Texas Land Title Abstracts

Philadelphia County, Pennsylvania Wills, 1682-1819

U.S. Freedmen Bank Records, 1865-1874

See more...

Birth, Marriage & Death

Social Security Death Index

England & Wales, FreeBMD Marriage Index: 1837-1983

Texas Birth Index, 1903-1997

California Birth Index, 1905-1995

See more...

Newspapers & Periodicals

United States Obituary Collection

The Times (London, Middlesex, England)

Stars and Stripes Newspaper, Europe, Mediterranean, and North Africa Editions, 1942-1964

See more...

Maps, Atlases & Gazetteers

Historic Land Ownership and Reference Atlases, 1507-2000

U.S. County Land Ownership Atlases, c. 1864-1918

Lippincott's Gazetteer of the World, 1913

See more...

Reference Materials & Finding Aids

Source: A Guidebook of American Genealogy

Ancestry's Red Book: American State, County, and Town Sources

U.S. Military Records

See more...

Military

World War I Draft Registration Cards, 1917-1918

U.S. World War II Army Enlistment Records, 1938-1946

British Army WWI Medal Rolls Index Cards, 1914-1920

U.S. Civil War Soldiers, 1861-1865

See more...

Pictures

Public Member Photos

Library of Congress Photo Collection, 1840-2000

U.S. School Yearbooks

Historical Postcards Collection, c. 1893-1963

See more...

Directories & Member Lists

Massachusetts City Directories

New York, City Directories

Connecticut City Directories

British Phone Books, 1880-1984 Releases 1-4

See more...

Family Trees

Public Member Trees

OneWorldTree

Ancestry World Tree

See more...

Figure 2-11: "Go Directly to a Specific Database or Collection" section of the "Search" page

Database or Collection"; see figure 2-11). Click any of these databases (like "1930 United States Federal Census") or collections (like "Census & Voter Lists") to go to a search form tied directly to that resource.

A more precise way to browse records is to use the Card Catalog, which you can access by clicking any of the links labeled "Go to the Card Catalog." Notice that the Card Catalog is designed similarly to the results page (see figure 2-12 on the next page). Now you can use the filter options on the content

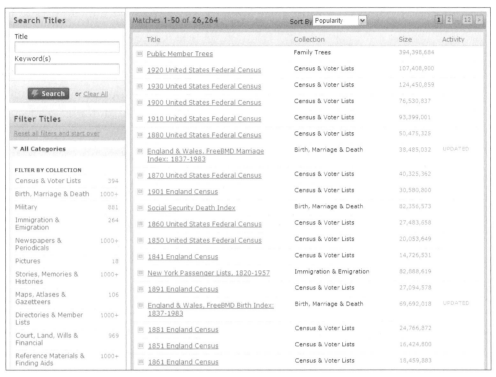

Figure 2-12: A portion of the Card Catalog

panel to narrow choices to the type of database in which you
are most interested. Those filter options include:

- **Category**—We have already discussed the categories and
  subcategories and how they can be used to narrow a search.
  When browsing, you are simply narrowing the scope of
  your browsing to those areas.

- **Location**—The locations available include Australia,
  Canada, Europe, and the USA, or you can search or browse
  databases for all geographies.

- **Dates**—You can also filter your browsing by century (pre-
  1600, 1600s, 1700s, 1800s, 1900s) and then decade from
  the beginning of the1600s through the 1990s.

At the top of the results panel, you will also see options to sort the list by popularity or database title or to conduct a search of the entire database list by keyword.

Once you find a database of interest, you can click on it to be taken to its search page, which includes a description of the database and a search form that searches only for records from that particular database.

Remember that you can keep refining the search criteria by clicking on the category, location, and/or date filters at the left of the search results list. You also have the option at any point to begin a new search.

Search Strategy

When conducting your research, your best search strategy may be to start simple and then add additional search criteria. For example, let's say you enter one of your ancestors, James Walsingham. If you also enter the years of birth and death and the locations, chances are good that you won't get any matches. You may be inordinately fortunate to have matched with a database—perhaps a printed family history—that includes all of the criteria you entered, but that is unlikely. After all, how many records contain all of these pieces of information? I can think of only one that may possibly have them all—a death certificate—and even that may not have them all.

I entered an exact search for the name James Walsingham and found almost 2,300 search results—far too many for me to deal with, especially as they are all over the world. I can narrow the search by entering a year of birth or death or a location for either or both of those events, or I can limit my search to a specific record type, such as Birth, Marriage & Death. Now, there are only eighty-five search results presented.

Summary

This chapter should have provided you with an overview of the search feature at Ancestry.com. The best way to become familiar with searching is simply to try your own searches and explore the many options Ancestry provides.

In the chapters that follow, we will examine different record types and how to become more effective with searching, interpreting, analyzing, and using them. We will look at both searches as we proceed. I urge you to work through the examples and explore different links, different search strategies, and different filtering options. Before you know it, you will be searching Ancestry.com like a professional.

Chapter 3

Working with Digitized Image Collections

When you access a database that includes a digitized image, it is important to be able to view it, analyze the information on it, and have the options to print it, save it, share it, or even connect it to one of your personal Family Trees.

The purpose of this chapter is to explain how to access images and how to use each of the functions associated with them. By the time you finish reading this chapter and performing all the functions you read about, you should be an expert in working with any of the Ancestry.com collections online. In addition, when we talk about these collections in later chapters, you will already know how to effectively work with them.

How to Access a Digital Image

For the examples in this chapter, I will use the "1850 United States Federal Census" database. It includes an every-name index and images of each census population schedule.

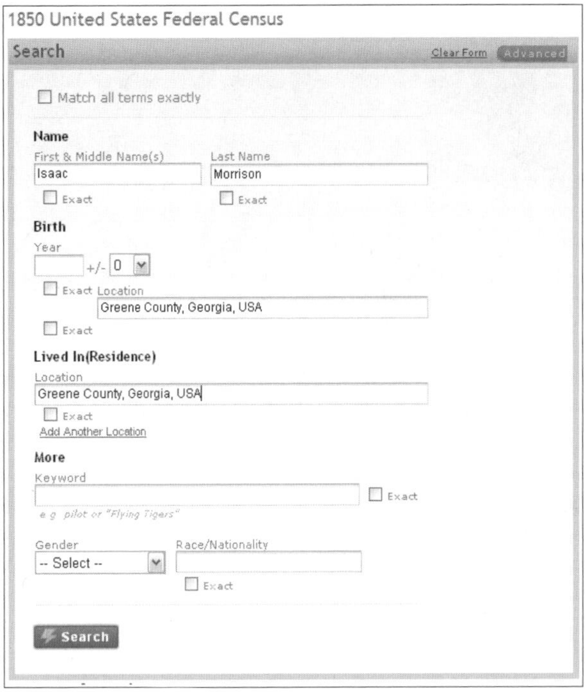

Figure 3-1: Completed search form for the 1850 U.S. Federal Census

The object of my query is my second great-grandfather, Isaac Morrison, of Greene County, Georgia; his wife, Rebecca; and their family.

The best way to search for a specific database is to find it in the Card Catalog. Go the "Search" page, click "Go to the Card Catalog," and click "Census & Voter Lists" in the content panel (on the left). You should be able to find the 1850 United States Census in the results panel, so click, and we're ready to conduct our search (see figure 3-1 for the completed search form). Notice that I did not click the "Exact matches only" option (for more on this option, see page 28).

The search results list shows multiple Isaac Morrisons, as you can see in figure 3-2. However, only the first one satisfied my search criteria that he (1) live in Greene County, Georgia, in 1850 and that (2) he be born in Georgia. I think I'm on the right track. Remember that you can narrow the number of matches on the results page by refining your search from the content panel (in the "Refine Search"

View Record	Name	Home in 1850 (City, County, State)	Estimated Birth Year	Birth Place	View Image
View Record ★★★	Isaac Morrison	District 143, Greene, GA	abt 1813	Georgia	

Figure 3-2: A portion of the results for Isaac Morrison

section). Simply add or remove information and click **Search**.

From the search results list in figure 3-2, I have two options for accessing the digitized image of the census on which Isaac appears: "View Record" and "View Image." Let's explore the differences.

View Record

Click the "View Record" link.

As you can see, what is displayed is not the full image of the census document. Instead, this page shows various information. Note that throughout Ancestry.com, the term "record" refers to pages like these (which often include simply indexed information, without original images), rather than the image of the record itself.

In the main section, you'll find details about Isaac Morrison taken from the actual census population schedule, which we will examine a little later in the chapter (see figure 3-3). There is a link labeled "View original image," which would take you directly to the image itself (though this isn't available for all records).

There is also a link labeled "View blank form." If you click this link, assuming that you have the free

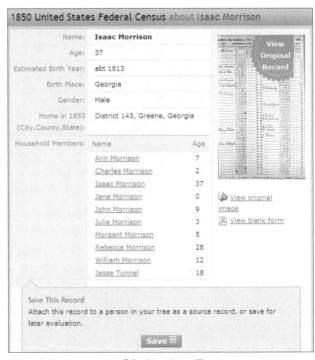

Figure 3-3: Main section of the "View Record" page

Adobe *Acrobat Reader* installed on your computer, a PDF file containing a blank transcription form for the 1850 census will open. You may want to print the form so you can read the column headings more clearly than you might on the less-than-crisp images of the population schedule itself. It also helps you follow along, column by column, when your ancestors are listed further down on a census page and the column headings are not in view when you are readying and analyzing the data.

Below these, you'll find the "Save This Record" section. Clicking the **Save** button allows you to save this record either to one of your trees or to your Shoebox. Once you've saved a record to your Shoebox, you can access it from the "Shoebox" section of the homepage.

You will also find this record's "Source Citation," which can be used for your own citation. Simply copy and paste it into your records. It might look like this:

> Image Source: Year: 1850; Census Place: District 143, Greene, Georgia; Roll: M432_71; Page: 72; Image: 145.

On this page, you will also see "Source Information" for the record and the database description. In the "Description," click "Learn more…" to see a more complete description of the database. The information in the "Source Information" section is also suitable for generating a source citation for your records. My source citation might read as follows:

> Ancestry.com. 1850 United States Federal Census [database online]. Provo, Utah: MyFamily.com, Inc., 2005. Original data: United States. 1850 United States Federal Census. M432, 1009 rolls. National Archives and Records Administration, Washington D.C. <www.ancestry.com>. Accessed 01 November 2006.

Please notice that I included text from the "Source Information" section. However, I also added the Ancestry.com URL and the date on which I accessed the data. This provides a record for me or for any other researcher of where and when I accessed the data.

The "Page Tools" section of the page gives you another way to connect this census record to your personal family tree or to your Shoebox (see figure 3-4). The link labeled "Comments and Corrections" takes you to the page shown in figure 3-5.

Here you have three options:

1. You can "Add an Alternate Name" that will appear attached to the record for anyone to see. This may be used to correct or clarify the record. The entry you add is anonymous.

2. You can "Add a Comment" to this record, to which other researches can respond in a way similar to a message board. This may help other researchers explain or correct confusing information in their genealogy database.

3. You can "Report an Image Problem" to the technical support team at Ancestry.com for their review.

Page Tools
🖨 Save record to someone in my tree
💾 Save record to my shoebox
✏ Comments and Corrections
✉ E-mail image to a friend
🖨 View printer-friendly

Figure 3-4: The "Page Tools" section of the "View Record" page

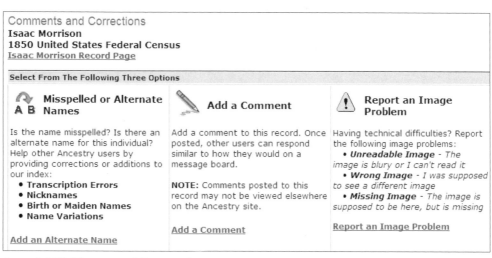

Comments and Corrections
Isaac Morrison
1850 United States Federal Census
Isaac Morrison Record Page

Select From The Following Three Options

A B **Misspelled or Alternate Names**	**Add a Comment**	**! Report an Image Problem**
Is the name misspelled? Is there an alternate name for this individual? Help other Ancestry users by providing corrections or additions to our index: • **Transcription Errors** • **Nicknames** • **Birth or Maiden Names** • **Name Variations** Add an Alternate Name	Add a comment to this record. Once posted, other users can respond similar to how they would on a message board. **NOTE:** Comments posted to this record may not be viewed elsewhere on the Ancestry site. Add a Comment	Having technical difficulties? Report the following image problems: • *Unreadable Image* - The image is blury or I can't read it • *Wrong Image* - I was supposed to see a different image • *Missing Image* - The image is supposed to be here, but is missing **Report an Image Problem**

Figure 3-5: The "Comments and Corrections" page

Back in the "Page Tools" section, you will see another link that allows you to "E-mail the image to a friend." I often use this feature to send interesting documents to family members or researchers. You can also view a printer-friendly version of the record and then easily print it. Note that this is not a printer-friendly version of the census image itself, but of the information shown on this page.

Below the "Page Tools" section is the "Make a Connection" section. This gives you access to the "Member Connection Service," allowing you to make connections with other people who share your interest in researching this person or family.

Finally, if you scroll down the page, you'll see your search template displayed again. Rather than having to go back in your browser to the previous page, you can refine your search and resubmit your query here.

View Image

You can go directly to the record image from the results page (shown in figure 3-2) by clicking on the icon of the magnifying glass and document in the "View Image" column at the right side of the entry you want to view. You are now ready to begin working with the image (see figure 3-6 on the next page).

You will notice two things at the top of the window. The first is a set of Quick Links (see "a" in figure 3-6). As you will recall, you can click on any of the underlined links to move backward (for more on Quick Links, see page 5).

There is also a link labeled "Having trouble viewing the image?" (see "b" in figure 3-6). If you are experiencing problems, click on this link, select the appropriate type of problem, and then provide some descriptive text for the support personnel to locate and attempt to correct the problem. Please note, however, that some of the digitized

Loading Images

When the image appears, some browsers will show a small pop-up box that reads, "Press SPACEBAR or ENTER to activate and use this control." This is not a problem; simply press either of the keys.

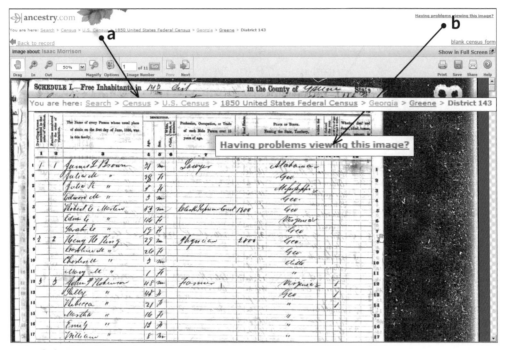

Figure 3-6: Census page

images may appear very faintly written and difficult to read. This is caused by microfilming problems, and Ancestry.com may have produced the most enhanced image possible for visibility.

The Toolbar

We are now going to focus on each of the tools on the toolbar, which is shown in detail in figure 3-7.

You will find that the toolbar is similar in all the image databases, although the **Drag** tool and other options may not

Figure 3-7: The toolbar in Image Viewer

always be available. The intent of this chapter is to show you how *all* the possible controls operate. So let's get going!

View in Full Page Mode

You want to be able to see as much of an image as possible in your Web browser. Ancestry.com has provided a tool to help you do just that. Look on the right side of the blue line that reads "Image About: Isaac Morrison" and you will see a link labeled "Show in Full Page." Click on the link, and your browser's menu bar, button bar, and all other header bars will be hidden from view. This will provide more room for the page content to be displayed. Click on the same area again to reverse the action and to make your browser's header bars reappear.

Drag

In many image collections, you will see a small hand icon on the toolbar labeled **Drag**. This tool allows you to click and drag the image more efficiently than by using the scroll bars. To activate it, simply click **Drag** and then move your mouse over the document. Your cursor should change from an arrow pointer to the hand icon.

Click-and-hold your left mouse button, and the hand changes to a grasping image. If you continue to hold the left mouse button down, you can drag the image on the page in any direction until you see a location on the document that you would like to examine. To "let go" of the image, simply release the left mouse button.

Zoom

If an image is too small for you to read, you can enlarge the document for closer inspection. This can be done in two ways.

On the toolbar, to the right of **Drag** button, you will find two buttons: **In** and **Out.** The **In** button has a magnifying glass marked with a "+", while the **Out** button's icon is a magnifying glass marked with a "-". These buttons allow you to zoom in or out on the image. The different digitized image collections have different levels of magnification. Clicking **In** increases the size of the document for easier viewing, all the way up to the highest magnification. Clicking **Out** reduces the image size.

For example, when I zoomed in once, I was able to more closely examine the age written down for William Morrison. Comparing the second digit of the number listed by William's name with the fractional age of ½ listed for the youngest child, Jane, I determined that William was twelve years old at the time of the 1850 census. It turned out that the enumerator sometimes made unusual strokes for the number 2, and a comparison on this page helped clarify the entry for William's age.

Image Size

The second method of changing the size of the image display is to use the drop-down list that contains the standard control settings. All of the image collections online provide settings based on a percentage of the original size of the document. Some also include "Fit Image," "Fit Width," and "Fit Height." These cause the image to be displayed to fit the browser window. If the collection you are viewing provides the **Drag** tool, the function will not work in the "Fit Image" and "Fit Height" settings because there will be nowhere to move. **Drag** does, however, operate on the "Fit Width" setting, where the full width of the original document is displayed, but you can only drag the document up and down.

Magnify

Sometimes you will want to take a closer look at an area of an image, just as you would with a physical document. The **Magnify** tool is the answer.

Click **Magnify** in the toolbar. Now move your mouse over the document image. You will see a square box with dotted-line crosshairs. Position the crosshairs over the center of the area you want to magnify and then press-and-hold the left mouse button. That area will be magnified by about 3×. While holding the left mouse button down, you can move the magnifier around the document page. However, if you want to move the page, you will need to click **Drag** to activate that tool again.

You will find the magnify function exceptionally helpful for examining and analyzing handwriting.

Options

Now that you know how to access and manipulate images, it's time to consider the options for viewing the images in different ways.

Click **Options** on the toolbar, and the window shown in figure 3-8 is displayed. This window controls the quality of the digitized images you can view. Once you set the options, they will become the default settings on your account for working with all image collections.

There are four view options settings that you can change. Let's define each one.

View Options

Image enhancing: ⊙ Enhanced images (usually more readable)
○ Original scans

Image compression: ⊙ High-quality images
○ Standard-quality images (faster)

Image thumbnail: ☐ Show thumbnail window

Image viewer: ⊙ Enhanced Image Viewer
○ Basic Image Viewer

[OK]   [Cancel]

Figure 3-8: "View Options" window

Image Enhancing

Ancestry.com is responsible for the digitization of a large percentage of the images in its collections. This includes the censuses, ship passenger lists, and World War I draft registration cards, to name a few. Most of the digitization was done using microform images, and during the process, Ancestry.com "cleaned up" the images by adjusting lightness, darkness, and contrast and by despeckling problem images. The intent was always to make the images more readable and therefore more useful to the researcher.

As a result of all of this work, some of the digitized collections offer you the option of also viewing the original scanned images. In most cases, the enhanced images produced are superior to the original image. However, you many want to view the original scanned image of a document, particularly if you are having difficulty reading the enhanced image, to see if the original is more legible.

Image Compression

Ancestry.com provides users with "standard quality images" as a default. These are quite crisp and readable, and, more important, they are easy and quick to download for users without high-speed connectivity.

There is, however, another version of the images. These higher quality images contain more pixels and are often of a slightly higher resolution—thus they take longer to download, especially for subscribers using dial-up connectivity. You can experiment with these options and see what works best for you.

Image Thumbnail

A "thumbnail" is a very small version of a full-size image. Thumbnails are commonly used in graphics software and photographic editing programs. Ancestry.com allows you to turn on or off a thumbnail view of the currently displayed document. When this option is on, it overlays a small area in the upper right-hand corner of the document displayed in your browser window (see figure 3-9). If you look at the thumbnail view, you will see that a small rectangular area is highlighted yellow on the thumbnail, which indicates where your browser window is currently located and what area is being viewed.

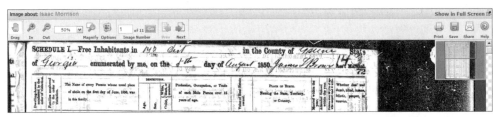

Figure 3-9: Census record in Image Viewer with Thumbnail Image displayed at the top right

Click **Drag** and move the hand over the highlighted area in the thumbnail image. Now, click-and-hold the left mouse button and drag the highlighted area over the thumbnail image. You will see that the image in your browser follows right along and is moved just as the highlighted area in the thumbnail moves. This is yet another way to move around the document image.

Image Viewer

Over the years, Ancestry.com has used several types of image viewer software for its digital collections. The viewers are and have always been available to download from Ancestry. com. While some users still use the Basic Image Viewer, Ancestry.com upgraded to an Enhanced Image Viewer quite a while ago. It provides sharper images, faster download speeds through enhanced data compression, and access to some additional features, such as the Thumbnail View and the ability to view both the enhanced and original scans that we discussed above.

You may select which viewer you prefer, but downloading and installing the free Enhanced Image Viewer will insure that you have the best experience at Ancestry.com.

Image Number, Previous, and Next

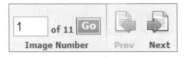 This section of the toolbar allows you to go to and move between images. The white box indicates the number of the image that you are currently viewing. The number to the right indicates the total number of images in this batch. This example of this census document is page 1 of 11. This means that there are a total of 11 documents for Greene County, Georgia, in District 140, for the 1850 United States Federal Census. This area allows you to move between document images in two ways.

- Highlight the number of the document in the white box and change it, and then click the **Go** button in order to move to that page. This provides a quick way to move between noncontiguous document pages.

- Use the **Prev** or **Next** buttons. If movement in that direction is possible, the arrow will be green. If movement is not possible in one or the other direction, the arrow in that direction will be grayed out.

Print

 The **Print** button on the toolbar is the only way to ideally print an image from Ancestry.com. It provides you with two options: normal print and custom print. In this chapter, we'll discuss normal printing. We'll talk about custom printing in chapter 14.

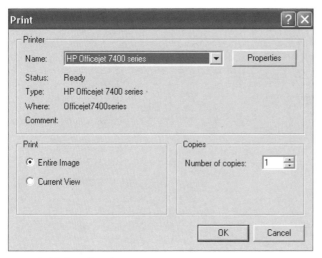

Figure 3-10: "Print" window

When you select "Normal print," a print window will open on your computer (see figure 3-10). Be aware that different printers behave in different ways, and the options they offer may influence how you print your document copies.

Note that I have two options in the "Print" window: to print the entire image or just the current view. The current view option may be appropriate, for example, if I have zoomed in to enlarge an area.

If an original document is in landscape orientation, you will need to change your printer's orientation setting. Otherwise, you will end up with a truncated image. To change the orientation of your printer to accommodate original documents in landscape mode, click the **Properties** button in the "Print" window, and there should be a setting to define portrait or landscape-oriented printing. (Don't forget to change this back for other print jobs later!)

Save

There will be many times that you will want to save a copy of an image you have discovered on the site. You have three methods to do this. Figure 3-11 on the next page shows the window that is displayed when you click the **Save** button on the toolbar.

Your first option is to save the file to the record of someone in your personal Family Tree. Simply click the **Attach to someone in my tree** option.

The second option is to save the record to your Shoebox on Ancestry.com. To do this, click the **Save to my Shoebox** option. Once you have saved it to your Shoebox, you can access it again later in the "Shoebox" section of the homepage.

The third option is **Save to your computer**. Many

Figure 3-11: "Save Options" window

genealogists save a copy of the image and link to a multimedia/photo area on their computer. Others save the file and then e-mail it to others later.

After you have selected your option, click **OK**. If you have opted to save the record to your computer, you will be prompted to supply a name for the file and a location where it will be saved. The image will, by default, be saved as a JPEG file.

Share

If you are like me, you get excited when you make a find. I am likely to send a copy of the record to another member or two of my family. You can also send a copy of the record to someone else who is researching the same family line or specific members.

Sharing a record with someone else is very simple. All you have to do is click the **Share** button, and a window appears that is similar to the one shown in figure 3-12.

Enter an e-mail address and, if you

Figure 3-12: The "Share" window

like, edit or add text to your message. The image will be e-mailed as an attachment with your name and return e-mail address (as shown in your account profile).

Help

The **Help** button on the toolbar provides access to some helpful information about using the Enhanced Image Viewer. When you click the button, a new window opens that includes a number of Frequently Asked Questions and a list of each of the tools we have discussed in this chapter with some descriptive information about them. This is a good place to get refresher information.

Summary

We have covered a great deal so far. By now you should be an expert in searching for information in databases, and if the content includes digital images, you should know exactly how to work with them.

In the next chapter we will discuss Family Trees. Once we have that under our belts, we will explore each of the major record groups and discuss the practical application of that data.

Chapter 4

Family Trees

One of the most important features of Ancestry.com is the ability to create and manage your own Family Trees. Family Trees have been a part of Ancestry.com for a long time, and they remain an active and vibrant feature of the site.

Creating a Family Tree allows you to organize your research, share it with others, and create a dynamic, interesting mini-site for your family or the family you are researching. In addition, Ancestry.com uses the information you enter into your Family Trees to help you further your research.

You access your Family Trees from the top section of the homepage. This section will look different depending on whether or not you have created your own Family Tree. Once you have created a tree, this section will be labeled with the title of one of your Family Trees and will be the place where you manage all the trees you've created. We'll discuss managing your trees in more detail later in this chapter, but first, let's look at how you create a tree.

Figure 4-1: Creating your first Family Tree

Creating a New Family Tree

You can create your first Family Tree either before you've registered with Ancestry.com or from your logged-in homepage. Fill in your name in the "Start your free family tree" section of the homepage. If you don't have any trees, this section appears whether you're logged out or in. Once you've filled in your name, click "Start your tree." On the next page, which is shown in figure 4-1, click either "Add Father" or "Add Mother."

When you've added information about either your father or mother, you will prompted to name your tree, select privacy preferences (which we'll discuss later) and save your tree. If you are new to Ancestry.com, you will also be prompted here to register. When you have saved your tree, you can immediately edit it, adding new information if you wish.

Note that to start a tree, you can also click "Upload a GEDCOM" to upload a file from your computer (any kind of family tree file works, not just GEDCOMs).

Once you've started your first tree, you can create other trees whenever you want. As with your first tree, you can do so from scratch or by uploading a file.

Starting a Tree from Scratch

To start a new tree from scratch, click the "My Trees" drop-down in the "Family Trees" section of the hompage. Select "Create a new tree." Next, follow the prompts, beginning on

Why Start a Family Tree on Ancestry.com?

If you've done any family history research at all, you likely have your family tree saved in some other program, such as *Family Tree Maker* or *Personal Ancestral File*. It's important to keep in mind, however, that Family Trees are an important feature of Ancestry.com and having one and using it will greatly enhance your experience on the website.

For example, Ancestry.com is constantly searching its databases for members of your Family Tree. Every time you see a leaf icon beside the name of someone on your tree, it means Ancestry has found possible matches to your family member. Click the leaf to see a results page of these matches. You can then attach the record to your tree, if you find that it is correct.

In addition to this, having a Family Tree helps you use the new search function as well. When you are filling in the search form, it can be auto-filled using information from your tree (see chapter 2).

the "Start Your FREE Family Tree" page (see figure 4-2). Enter your name, gender, birth date and place, and then click **Next**.

Once you have entered your own information, you will be asked for information about your father and your mother, including information about their deaths, if applicable. If you don't have some or all of this information at the time you create the tree, don't worry. You can click **Next** even if the form isn't entirely filled out, or you can click the "Skip this page" link at the top to move to the next page.

In the last step, you will be prompted to name your Family Tree (don't stress over this, you can always

Figure 4-2: "Start Your FREE Family Tree" page

A History of Trees

Throughout its history, Ancestry.com has tried various kinds of online family trees. Ancestry World Tree is a collection of GEDCOMs submitted by users. OneWorldTree features uploaded information from users, but it also includes a search functionality that compares submitted information to information in other submitted trees and online databases to help users enhance their research.

For all intents and purposes, the information from these trees is now treated like any other database on Ancestry.com. For more information about databases like Ancestry World Tree and OneWorldTree, see chapter 2.

change it later). In addition, you are given the option to make your Family Tree public or private.

The decision to make your Family Tree public or private ultimately determines how effective your tree is as a research tool. If you designate your tree as private (by deselecting the "Allow others to see my tree" option), no one except people you invite can see all the details of your tree. Others searching on Ancestry.com will be able to see basic information (such as a birth date) about the member of your tree they are searching for, as well as the contact information you have provided in your Member Profile. They can then contact you to view more of your tree. In addition, information about individuals that Ancestry.com believes are living (based on information about them in your tree) will never be shown to others without your explicit permission.

Living Relatives

A person in a tree is considered living if there is no death date indicated and he or she is younger than eighty-five years old.

If you set your tree as public (by selecting the "Allow others to see my tree" option), it will be available to anyone searching the Family Trees database to view. Remember that even if you designate your tree as being public, only you and people you invite can contribute to or change information on your tree. Also, you can change this designation at any time.

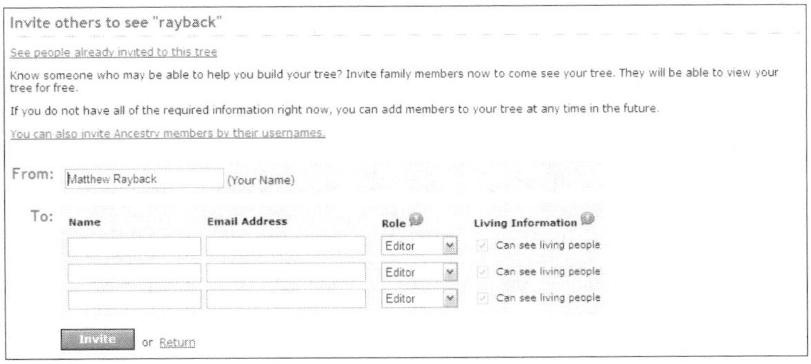

Figure 4-3: The "Invite others to see" page

Next, you will be given the chance to send an e-mail to family members or friends, inviting them to your tree (see figure 4-3). For each person you want to invite, provide a name and an e-mail address and decide what role you want them to have and whether or not they can see living people in your tree.

A person's role on your tree determines what actions they can take in your tree. You can see a chart detailing which roles can perform which functions by clicking the blue "!" above the

	Guest	Contributor	Editor*
View your tree	✓	✓	✓
Leave comments	✓	✓	✓
Add stories and photos		✓	✓
Add and edit people			✓

Roles in your tree

People you invite to see your tree can participate in varying degrees. You can choose from the following roles for your invitees:

*Note: The Editor role can always see information of Living People in the tree.

Figure 4-4: An explanation of the various roles available to members of your tree

word "Role" (see figure 4-4).

Upload a GEDCOM

The other way to start your first tree is to upload an existing file. You can upload any kind of family tree file. Click the

File Types

You can upload the following file types:

.ged

.ftw

.fbk

.paf

.fdb

.leg

.gedz

"My Trees" drop-down in the "Family Trees" section of the homepage. Select "Upload a GEDCOM file."

In the "Choose file" field on the resulting window (see figure 4-5), enter a file name or click **Browse** to locate a your family tree file on your hard drive. Enter a name in the "Tree Name" field and decide whether you want your tree to be public or not. Enter a description in the "Description" field if you want. For example, you could use this field to list specific surnames on your tree.

Once you have finished making the decisions about the file you are about to upload, click the "Submission Agreement" link and read the agreement. If you agree, click the "I accept the Submission Agreement" check box; then click **Upload**. You can now begin to work with your new tree.

Working with Your Family Trees

Once you have created your first tree, you can manage it (and any others) right from the homepage. You can see mine in figure 4-6. Notice that the Family Tree manager shows the tree I have most recently worked with—in this case, "Sample Tree— 110407," which was created by uploading a GEDCOM file on that date. Since that time, I have added to and edited it. I also have another tree, which I

Upload a Family Tree

When you upload a GEDCOM file, all of the people in it are placed into a new tree on Ancestry. The name you choose to give your tree will be visible to your guests and other Ancestry members. How do I upload my tree?

Choose file		Browse
	Find the GEDCOM file on your computer. Maximum file size is 100MB.	
Tree Name		
	Give your new tree a name	
	☑ Allow others to see my tree as a public member tree and allow my tree information to be compiled into OneWorldTree What does this mean?	
Description		
	Enter surnames, years, etc., to help people understand what your tree is about. (optional)	
	☐ I accept the Submission Agreement	
	Upload or Cancel	

Figure 4-5: The "Upload a Family Tree" page

Sample Tree - 110407 My Trees ▾   View my tree ➡

Recent family tree activity	About my tree
Sara Edith Weatherly, 1920 Un...	👤 5544 people
	🖼 0 Photos
	🔍 View People With Hints
	🏠 Home Person: George Goodloe Morgan
	👤 Last viewed: Green Berry Holder

Figure 4-6: The author's Family Tree manager on the homepage

can access using the "My Trees" drop-down and selecting it.

You can think of each Family Tree you create as a personal website for that family. When you click the name of a tree in the "My Trees" drop-down, you are brought to a page that acts as a "homepage" for that tree. This is the "Overview" page. Figure 4-7 shows this page for the first tree in my list, "Sample Tree—110407."

You will notice that the "Welcome" page of your Family Tree is different from other areas of Ancestry.com. The normal Ancestry.com tabs have become links along the top of the "Overview" page.

From this "Overview" page, you can easily manage and navigate through your Family Tree. Just as on the Ancestry.com homepage, the easiest way to navigate your Family Tree is by using the tabs at the top of the main section.

Overview

The "Overview" page takes you to the default page of your tree, which gives an overview of your tree and lets you manage its various features (see figure 4-7). On this page, you can perform many useful actions to manage your tree, as well as review recent additions and changes.

Figure 4-7: The **Overview** tab for "Sample Tree—110407"

Recent Content

The main section of the "Overview" page allows you to view and add content (such as photos or audio clips) to your tree.

We will discuss working with these kinds of content later in this chapter, as most of them have their own tabs. In each case, to add content from the **Overview** tab, click the appropriate **Add** button.

Recent Video

You can record videos to help tell your family stories. At the time of this writing, the "Recent Video" section is one of two places where you can add videos to your tree (the other is on the "People" page), which is why we're discussing it now. In this section, you can view and record videos.

To record a new video, click "Record a Video Story." Make sure your webcam is plugged in; then follow the prompts for the video recording process. You can record up to twelve minutes of video. When you're satisfied, click **Save** and add a title and descriptive information.

Other Homepage Actions

There are a few more actions you can take on the "Overview" page. In the "People in this tree" section, you can view people attached to this Family Tree. You will see the tree's "Home Person" and the "Last Viewed" person on your tree. You can even see an alphabetical list of everyone on the tree by clicking "See full list of people." In the "Tools" section are three links that help you control the settings of your Family Tree:

- **Manage my tree**—This link leads to a page (see figure 4-8 on the next page) that lets you take many actions to manage your tree, including deleting it.

- **Change tree privacy**—In making this decision, use the

information in the "What does this mean?" sections to help you decide. When you're done, click **Save**.

- **Change home person**—The home person of your tree is the person around which the tree is built. Generally your home person should be you, but if you are working on a tree that doesn't include you, you can use this feature to decide which person should be the home person.

Tree Name	ggm - 100406
Tree Description	
	Update
Management Tools	✖ (delete tree)
# of Users Invited	0 (invite others to see your tree)
Is Tree Public?	No (change/more info)
Date Last Modified	3/19/2007
# of People in Tree	5338
# of Photos Attached to Tree	0
Home Person	George Goodloe Morgan (change) (set to none)
Who is "me" in this Tree	George Goodloe Morgan (change) (set to none)

Figure 4-8: The "Manage" page

After clicking the "Change home person" link, enter the name of the person you want as the home person into the field, indicate whether you are the home person or not, and click **Select** (see figure 4-9).

- **Publish and Print**—This link takes you to MyCanvas to create a family history book from your tree. For more on MyCanvas, see chapter 14.

It is recommended that you select yourself as the Home Person. If you are not in this tree, you can select a primary person you are researching.

Home Person: George Goodloe Morgan (1952 -)
or Browse the list of everyone in your tree

☑ I have selected myself as the Home Person.

Select or Cancel

Figure 4-9: The "Select a Home Person for this family tree" page

People

The **People** tab is where you see more detailed information about all the members of your tree. When you click on a person's name in most places on your Family Tree, you are brought to his or her "Person" page on the **People** tab, the main portion of which is shown in figure 4-10 (on the next page). Notice that there, you can see a summary of all the various content you have attached to that person.

The features on the **People** tab allow you to view and modify people in your tree. In the main section, you'll see

Figure 4-10: The main section of the **People** tab

information about the person in question. From here, you can add photos, stories, audio recordings, videos or comments (using the respective "Add" buttons).

In this main section, you can also search for records in the Ancestry.com databases that relate to this person and add them to your Family Tree. If you click "Search for historical records," you will be presented with a search results page (see figure 4-11). You can go through the list and determine which of the results, if any, are connected to your family member and then add those records to your tree as documentation just as

Figure 4-11: A portion of the search results page for a search done from a Family Tree

you would if you had found the record in a normal search.

You can also add comments to the person you are viewing on the **People** tab by clicking "Add a comment." You might want to add a comment to give other viewers more information about this person, explain your research, or for a variety of other reasons.

Another main feature of the **People** tab is the "Timeline" section, which helps you outline major events in that person's life. A portion of a

Figure 4-12: A portion of a "Timeline"

timeline is shown in figure 4-12. To add an event, click "Add event" in the "Timeline" section. Select an event from the dropdown list; then fill in the subsequent fields and click **Submit**. Possible events include "Arrival," "Description," "Residence," and more.

Once an event is included in the "Timeline," you can modify it by simply clicking the title of the event. On the resulting page, you can change information as necessary, add records to support this event, provide alternative information, and so on.

The sections on the right side of the **People** tab provide a variety of options. These include the following:

- **Family Members**—This section allows you to view and navigate to members of the person's immediate family. Click on any of the names shown, and you will be taken to that person's "People" page. You can also click "Family Group Sheet" to go to a page resembling a family group sheet (see figure 4-13 on the next page).

- **Tools**—The links in this section provide you with a number of familiar options, including searching for source records and inviting family members to contribute. The "Find

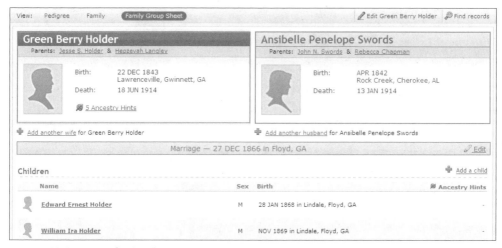

Figure 4-13: "View more family information" page

Famous Relatives" link lets you search Ancestry.com for famous people who might be related to you. You can also review research notes compiled by you and others about this person by clicking "View research note."

- **Source Records**—In this section, you can see how many sources are associated with this person. If you click the "View all source citations" link, you can view each of these sources. In this section, you can add additional sources or learn more about sourcing in general.

- **Community**—As you might expect, this section provides a link to the **Ancestry Community** and helps you find other people who are interested in this person.

From anywhere on your Family Tree you can move to the
"People" page for anyone on your tree. Click "Home Person,"
or enter a name in the "Find a person in tree" field. Notice
that as you enter a name in this field, Ancestry.com tries to
anticipate who you might be searching for and provides a list of
people in the tree who might match your query.

Family Tree

If you want to view
your Family Tree,
click the **Family Tree**
tab (see figure 4-14).
Here you will find five
generations of your
family organized in
a pedigree chart. If
this is your first time
to the **Family Tree**
tab, the person in the
first position will be
your home person
(probably you). If

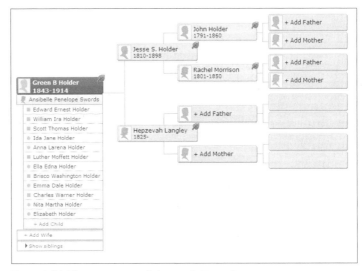

*Figure 4-14: The main section of the **Family Tree** tab*

you are returning to your Family Tree, the person in the first
position will be whoever it was the last time you visited. If you
go to the **Family Tree** tab directly from the **Person** tab, the
person in the first position will be the person whose page you
were just viewing.

To view information about any member of the tree, roll
your mouse over that person's name, and his or her full birth
and death dates will appear, as well as the option to search for
records for that person, view him/her from the **Person** tab, or
edit his or her information.

Notice that you can switch between several common family tree views: pedigree, family, and family group sheet. You can switch easily from one view to another by clicking the view you want.

In the pedigree view, you'll see another way to search Ancestry.com from your Family Tree (as mentioned previously). Notice that next to some of your family members' names, you'll find a green leaf. This indicates that Ancestry.com has found some records that may be related to that family member.

When you hover over the leaf icon, you will see an indication of the number of records Ancestry.com has found that might enrich your tree. If you click one of the possibilities (such as "1 possible Source Record found"), you will come to a search results page showing those records.

You can find hints similar to these throughout your Family Tree. Whenever you see the green leaf, you'll know that Ancestry.com is suggesting search results for that family member.

If your tree is larger than five generations, use the arrows to the right of the page to navigate through the generations. If you want to move forward in time, click the name of the spouse or child you would like to see in the primary position.

On the **Family Tree** tab, you can also edit the information for the person in the first position by hovering over his name and click "Edit."

Finally, you can print a copy of your five-generation pedigree chart on the **Family Tree** tab. You can choose to print it at home by clicking "Printer friendly" or you can publish it as a family history book using MyCanvas by clicking "Publish and Print." For more information on MyCanvas, see chapter 14. If you click "Printer friendly," a new window opens, giving you a preview of what the printed copy will look like. If you are satisfied with how it will look, click **Print this page**.

Photos

As the name suggests, the **Photos** tab allows you to view all of the photos you have uploaded to your Family Tree. To add a photo, click "Add a new photo," either on this tab or on any of the other tabs.

Next, enter the location on your computer where the photo is saved, or click **Browse** to search for it on your hard drive. Click the "Content Submission Agreement" link. If you agree with the submission agreement, select the "I accept" option and then click **Upload**.

You will be prompted to give the photo a title and description, as well as to indicate where and when it was taken (see figure 4-15). You can also declare what type of photo it is and attach the photo to someone on your tree. When you have finished, click **Save**. If you want, you can save your photo without attaching it to someone.

Once you have uploaded your photo, you can view it by simply clicking it on the **All Photos** tab. This will give you an expanded view of the photograph, as well as allow you to add or review

Figure 4-15: The "Photo Information" page

comments made about the image. From this view, you can also print the picture or remove it from your tree using the buttons at the top.

If you have lots of photos, you can download the enhanced photo upload tool from Ancestry.com on the photo upload page (in the "Got Lots of Photos?" section). The enhanced photo upload tool allows you to upload up to 500 pictures.

Stories

Every family has stories. Stories can enhance your family history by preserving memories and anecdotes related to your family members, which helps you understand your family better. You can add stories to your Family Tree from the **Stories** tab or by clicking any of the "Add a new story" links on the other tabs.

Next, decide whether you want to compose the story on Ancestry.com or upload it from your computer, and select the appropriate option.

Give your story a name; then compose it in the browser (see figure 4-16) or follow the instructions to upload it from your hard drive. Add a description, location, and date for your story. As with photos, you can now attach this story to a specific member of your family. When you have finished, click **Save**.

You can view and modify your story in exactly the same way you view and modify photos (see page 65).

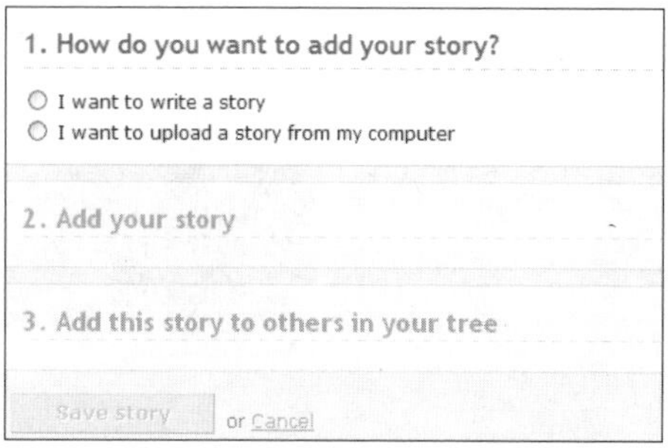

Figure 4-16: "Adding a story" page

Audio

Ancestry.com allows you to record audio stories as well. Figure 4-17 on the next page shows the **Audio** tab. Here you can listen to the last several audio stories you have recorded, view a list of all your audio recordings, or record a new audio story.

Audio Stories	Added by	Added on	Duration	This recording is attached to:
🔊 New Audio Storytelling Service from Ancestry	Megan Smolenyak	Tuesday, March 27, 2007 4:06:12 PM	0:32	

You have not added an Audio Story.
Bring the memories and experiences of your ancestors to life by adding their stories.

- Add new audio story

Figure 4-17: ***Audio*** *tab*

When you click "Add a new audio story," the pop-up window shown in figure 4-18 is displayed.

You have the option of recording your story on your own computer using a microphone or recording the story over the telephone using a toll-free number provided by Ancestry. com. Also on this window, you can invite your family members to record their own stories.

After you select an option, an intermediate window will appear. There are categories for conversation, such as "All about Me," "Growing Up," School," and "For Fun," and each of these includes questions to prompt the person recording the story. These can be a real help when trying to decide what to say.

Figure 4-18: "Record Your Family History" pop-up window

Summary

Family Trees are an exciting way for you to organize and save information about your family history and to collaborate with others in your family to enrich and expand your family experience. As we discuss various database types throughout this book, keep your Family Tree in mind. Look for ways to use it, whether by attaching a record to an individual in your tree or by helping you decide who to research next. If you are not making use of your Family Tree, you are not taking advantage of the full power of Ancestry.com.

Working with Census Records

Census records are the most frequently used records among genealogists. This has been proved again and again by statistics gathered by the National Archives and Records Administration (NARA) in the United States, The National Archives (TNA) in the United Kingdom, other countries' archives, the LDS Family History Library in Salt Lake City, and Ancestry.com.

Census documents are a strong resource for locating a person at a specific geographical location at a given point in time. Based on that information, it is then possible to search for other records and evidence in the same area.

Ancestry.com databases include many census documents. The focus of this chapter is on the census collections for the United States, the United Kingdom, and Canada. The vast majority of these collections include full indexes and digitized images. There are additional databases that consist of indexes only, including many of the American state and county censuses, the 1841 Scotland census, and certain areas of Germany. We will discuss the census materials that are available as we address some of the large geographical census collections available at Ancestry.com.

United States Federal Census Records

The United States has taken a population census every ten years beginning in 1790 and continuing to present times. From 1790 through 1840, the censuses list only the name of the head of household, with some information about others in the household. In 1850, the first every-name census was taken, and in 1880, the census started including the relationship of every individual to the head of household. At various times, additional census documents, or schedules, have been completed to provide detailed information about certain population and economic trends.

Ancestry has digitized and completely indexed by name all the available microfilmed federal census records from 1790 to 1930. These records include the following:

- **Population Schedules**—1790 to 1930, including the few surviving fragments of the 1890 census, which was destroyed in the Commerce Department fire in Washington, D.C., on 10 January 1921

- **Mortality Schedules**—1850 to 1880

- **Slave Schedules**—1850 and 1860

- **Veterans Schedules**—1890 (Surviving Soldiers, Sailors, and Marines, and Widows, and so on)

- **Census of Merchant Seamen**—1930

Ancestry.com has not digitized some of the other United States federal census schedules, such as Agricultural Schedules; Industry/Manufacturing Schedules; Social Statistics: Delinquent, Dependent and Delinquent Classes Schedules;

The Census and Privacy

The United States federal government's Privacy Act dictates that census information cannot be released to the public for seventy-two years from the date of the census enumeration. Thus, the most current available federal census data is that of the 1930 census.

Indian (or Native American) Schedules; or the Enumeration District (ED) Maps.

Listed below are four excellent books that provide in-depth information about the United States federal censuses. You can also use the Ancestry.com Library to locate other reference materials and articles that may aid your research.

Dollarhide, William. *The Census Book: A Genealogist's Guide to Federal Census Facts, Schedules and Indexes.* Bountiful, UT: Heritage Quest, 2000.

Hinckley, Kathleen W. *Your Guide to the Federal Census.* Cincinnati, OH: Betterway Books, 2002.

Morgan, George G. *How to Do Everything with Your Genealogy.* Emeryville, CA: McGraw-Hill/Osborne, 2004.

Szucs, Loretto Dennis, and Matthew Wright. *Finding Answers in U.S. Census Records.* Orem, UT: Ancestry, 2001.

Searching the Census Records

You have already seen that there are several ways to access the search forms for specific databases at Ancestry.com. If you are not comfortable with these options, go back to chapter 2 to reread and work through the examples. Here is a refresher on a few of the quickest ways to get there:

- **Search Results**—Use the main search form on the homepage. On the search results list, you can refine your search and/or use the filters in the column at the left of the page to narrow your search results.

- **Browse**—Use the "Go Directly to a Specific Title or Database" section on the "Search" page.

- **Card Catalog**—Use the Card Catalog by clicking "Go to the Card Catalog" anywhere on the "Search" page. In the

Figure 5-1: Census databases in the Card Catalog

Card Catalog, you can filter the databases you want to search in the following ways:

- **Filter by Collection**—Click the link labeled "Census & Voter Lists" to narrow the list of databases to only that collection of materials (see figure 5-1).

- **All Locations**—Select a location, such as USA. In that case, only those databases for the United States or specific states will be shown in the list.

- **All Dates**—Allow all databases to be listed, or narrow your listing to a specific time period. For example, you could click "1800s" to limit the list to only those census and voter lists that cover the period from 1800 to 1899. Alternately, you could select "1880s" to limit the list to only those databases in this category from the period 1880 to 1889.

Remember, if you have a Family Tree, the "type-ahead" feature will anticipate your data by searching names in your Family Tree and presenting a list of possible individuals below the field. You can click on a name to select it, and that person's data will automatically be entered in the form. Chapter 2 discusses the search feature at Ancestry.com in full detail.

Once you've arrived at the search form, fill in the fields with your search criteria and then click **Search**. Remember, you can click **Advanced** to search for exact search terms. As you work with census forms for individual censuses, you'll note different fields on each, reflecting the information on the actual census form. Remember that you can start with simple search criteria and later narrow your search by completing other data fields on the search form.

Figure 5-2 shows a 1900 census form I completed for a family member, Alvis M. Weatherly, the son of Amos M. and Hattie. In this example, all of the information provided comes from my Family Tree.

Note how I spelled Alvis's surname in the search form: "Weatherly." When I get to the search results page, however (see figure 5-3 on the next page), I find an Alvis M. Weatherley

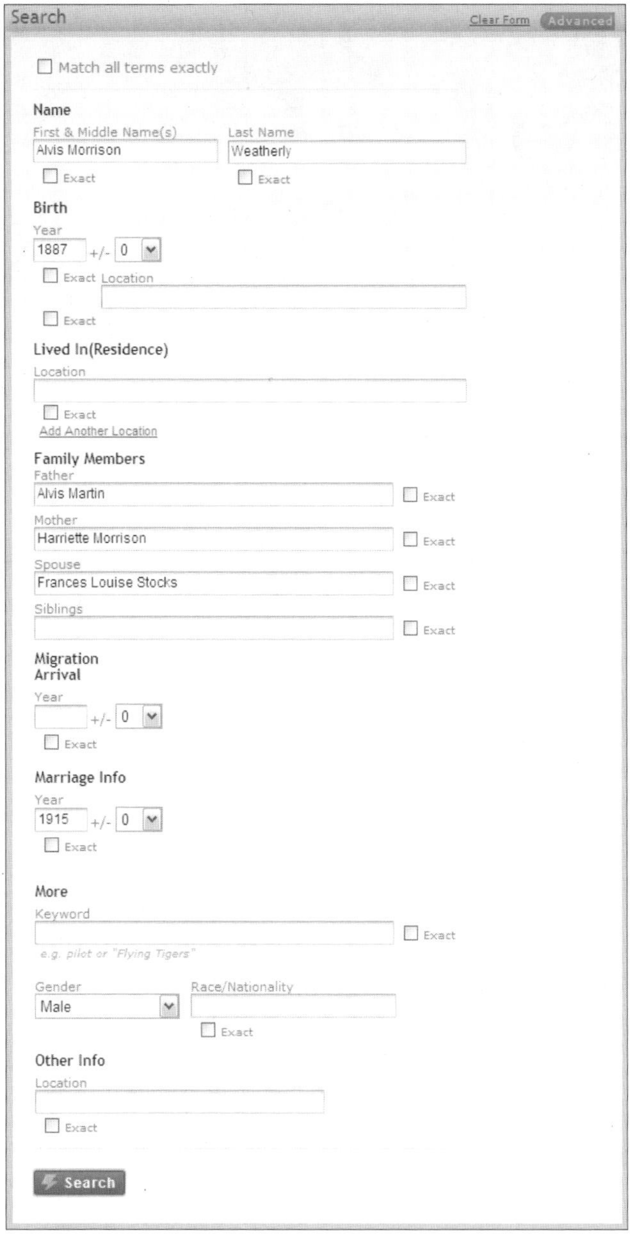

Figure 5-2: Search form for the 1900 census

View Record	Name	Parent or spouse names	Home in 1900 (City,County,State)	Birth Year	Birthplace	Race	Relation
View Record ★★★✩	Alvis M Weatherley	Amos M, Hallie	Rome, Floyd, Georgia	abt 1888	Georgia	White	Son

Figure 5-3: Results from the 1900 census

(note the difference in spelling). If I search using the "exact" option, I get no results. A quick look suggests that Mr. Weatherley is indeed the right man, though here his mother is listed as "Hallie." Why all the mistakes? An examination of the actual image offers an easy explanation (see figure 5-4).

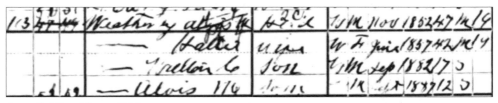

Figure 5-4: Detail from a 1900 census image

The enumerator's handwriting is very poor. Mr. Weatherly's surname is not quite legible, but his first name is an almost unreadable mess. His wife's name does appear to be "Hallie" but is, in fact, Hattie (short for Harriette), and one son's name is spelled as "Welton" when it should have been "Walton." You can see a combination of reasons why there were problems with the index: the enumerator's writing was very sloppy, the microfilmed image was faint, and there were spelling errors. As I said, if I had performed an exact search, I would have missed this helpful (if error-filled) record.

Notice that beneath the name is a second name (spelled the way I spelled it in my search) in brackets on the "View Record" page (see figure 5-5 on the next page). This is an alternate spelling that I suggested. If you click the icon beside that name, you are brought to a page explaining who suggested the alternate name and why alternate names sometimes exist.

At some point, someone has viewed the record for the index entry and has entered a comment or correction for the name. This helps you and other researchers locate the correct record because that information is considered in the search process.

When I view the record, I can save it to one of my Family Trees or to my Shoebox. I can use the "Page Tools" to perform these tasks and to make additional comments and corrections. And if I click on the link labeled "View printer-friendly," a clean copy of the record is presented that I can send to my printer (see figure 5-6 on the next page).

Figure 5-5: The "View Record" page for Alvis M. Weatherley

Since I found a number of errors in the index for this record, I want to make some changes and corrections, so I click "Comments and Corrections" in the "Page Tools" section.

I click on "Add an Alternate Name" and get the "Add a Correction" form (see figure 5-7 on the next page). After I've filled in the form and selected a reason for my submission from the drop-down list, I click **Submit Correction**. If you submit a correction, you will see a confirmation message, your submission will result in a correction to the Ancestry.com

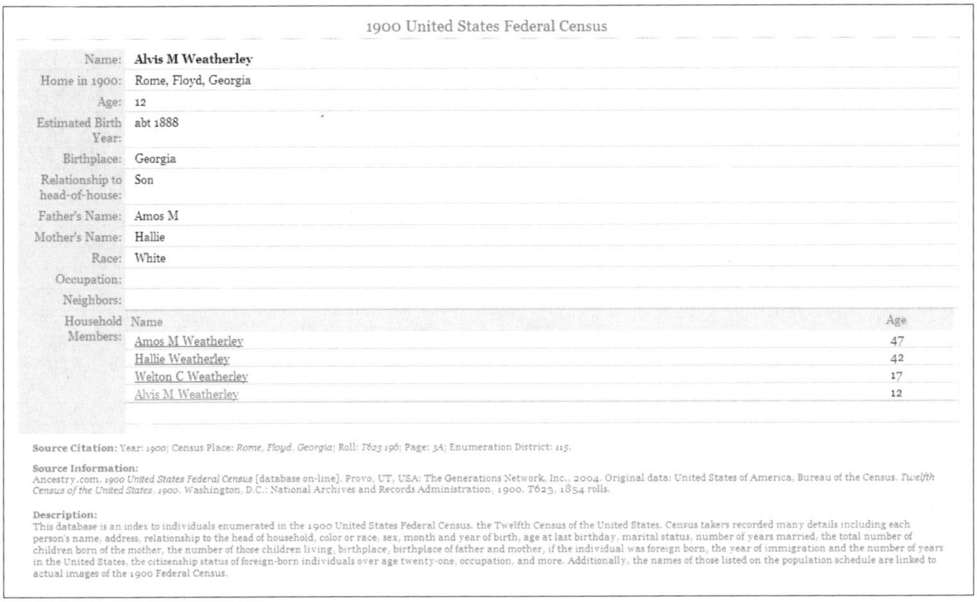

1900 United States Federal Census

Name:	**Alvis M Weatherley**
Home in 1900:	Rome, Floyd, Georgia
Age:	12
Estimated Birth Year:	abt 1888
Birthplace:	Georgia
Relationship to head-of-house:	Son
Father's Name:	Amos M
Mother's Name:	Hallie
Race:	White
Occupation:	
Neighbors:	

Household Members:

Name	Age
Amos M Weatherley	47
Hallie Weatherley	42
Welton C Weatherley	17
Alvis M Weatherley	12

Source Citation: Year: 1900; Census Place: *Rome, Floyd, Georgia*; Roll: *T623 196*; Page: *3A*; Enumeration District: 115.

Source Information:
Ancestry.com. *1900 United States Federal Census* [database on-line]. Provo, UT, USA: The Generations Network, Inc., 2004. Original data: United States of America, Bureau of the Census. *Twelfth Census of the United States*, 1900. Washington, D.C.: National Archives and Records Administration, 1900. T623, 1854 rolls.

Description:
This database is an index to individuals enumerated in the 1900 United States Federal Census, the Twelfth Census of the United States. Census takers recorded many details including each person's name, address, relationship to the head of household, color or race, sex, month and year of birth, age at last birthday, marital status, number of years married, the total number of children born of the mother, the number of those children living, birthplace, birthplace of father and mother, if the individual was foreign born, the year of immigration and the number of years in the United States, the citizenship status of foreign-born individuals over age twenty-one, occupation, and more. Additionally, the names of those listed on the population schedule are linked to actual images of the 1900 Federal Census.

Figure 5-6: Printer-friendly version of the record

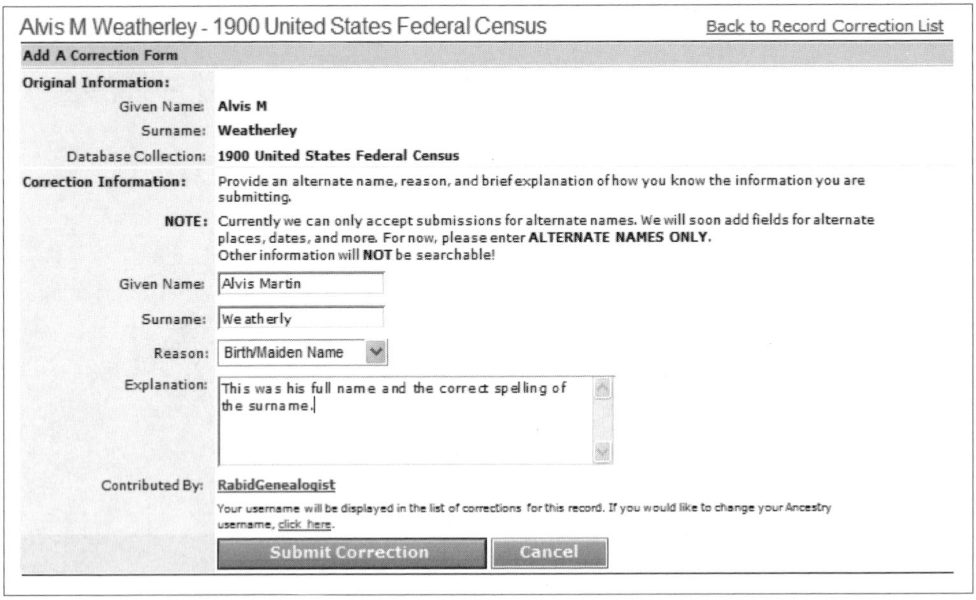

Alvis M Weatherley - 1900 United States Federal Census
Back to Record Correction List

Add A Correction Form

Original Information:

Given Name:	**Alvis M**
Surname:	**Weatherley**
Database Collection:	**1900 United States Federal Census**

Correction Information: Provide an alternate name, reason, and brief explanation of how you know the information you are submitting.

NOTE: Currently we can only accept submissions for alternate names. We will soon add fields for alternate places, dates, and more. For now, please enter **ALTERNATE NAMES ONLY.** Other information will **NOT** be searchable!

Given Name:	Alvis Martin
Surname:	Weatherly
Reason:	Birth/Maiden Name
Explanation:	This was his full name and the correct spelling of the surname.
Contributed By:	**RabidGenealogist**

Your username will be displayed in the list of corrections for this record. If you would like to change your Ancestry username, click here.

Submit Correction | Cancel

Figure 5-7: Completed "Add a Correction" form

index for that database, and any alternate names will show on the record as we've seen.

You may also want to add a comment to this record. Click "Add a comment" and then "Post New Comment" on the resulting page. Complete the form and click **Post Comment** (see figure 5-8 for an example).

If you experience a problem with the image itself—it is illegible or missing, the index links to a wrong image, and so on—you can report this by clicking "Report an Image Error." Complete the form with a description of the problem and as much information as possible,

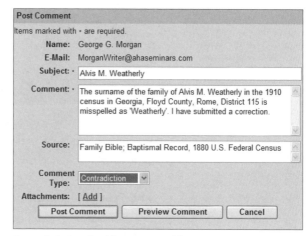

Figure 5-8: Completed "Post Comment" form

including pasting the Quick Links for the image page and the image number, and click **Submit**. Be aware that a correction may take some time.

U.S. State and County Census Records

Ancestry.com also has databases of United States' state, county, and a few local census records. There were censuses performed in 1885 in Colorado, the Dakota Territory, Florida, Nebraska, and the New Mexico Territory that were jointly funded by the federal and state governments. Copies of the surviving census schedules became part of the NARA collection and were therefore microfilmed. These documents, too, have been digitized and every-name indexes made available by Ancestry. com. You will work with these just as you have the other federal census images we have already discussed.

Other state, county, and local censuses, as well as other pertinent census-related records, have been collected into databases and are available to search at Ancestry.com. There are even some pre-federal, colonial census record collections. Most of these do not consist of digitized images, but rather are transcribed records from other indexes. Remember that these are secondary, derived sources of evidence when you weigh them with other evidence. However, they are no less important contributions to the body of evidence you are collecting.

To find these censuses, browse through the "Census & Voter Lists" category in the Card Catalog, as described earlier in this chapter or in chapter 2.

The Nebraska Census, 1854–1870 Records

The Nebraska Territory began taking territorial censuses when it became a territory in 1854. Territorial censuses were taken in 1854, 1855, and 1856, and county censuses were taken in 1867, 1874, 1875, and 1878–1879. This database covers the years 1854 to 1870.

When you arrive at the search form for this database, click **Advanced** and select "Match all terms exactly"; search for the first name "conrad" and the last name of "smith"; then click "View Record" for either result. In this case, the database is an index only, and there is no digitized record to access and see, though you have all the options of other "View Record" pages available here (see figure 5-9).

Nebraska Census, 1854-70 about Conrad Smith	
Name:	**Conrad Smith**
State:	NE
County:	Otoe County
Township:	Nebraska City
Year:	1856
Page:	015
Database:	NE 1856 Territorial Census Index

Save This Record
Attach this record to a person in your tree as a source record, or save for later evaluation.

Save ▾

Figure 5-9: Record from "Nebraska Census, 1854-1870"

Please notice the index entry that refers to Conrad Smith in Otoe County and Nebraska City in the 1856 NE Nebraska Territorial Census and that he appears on page 15. If you are looking for any information about the status and location of any state census, the best reference books on the subject are the following:

Dollarhide, William. *Census Substitutes & State Census Records* (2 volumes). Bountiful, UT: Family Roots Publishing Company, 2007.

Lainhart, Ann S. *State Census Records*. Baltimore, MD: Genealogical Publishing Co., 1992.

Maryland Records

Let's look at another example of a state census, whose search results may look different to you. In the Card Catalog, enter "maryland records" into the "Filter by Keyword" field and click **Search**. Locate and click on the link titled "Maryland Records Colonial, Revolutionary, County, and Church from Original Sources Vol. I." The next page contains a search form, source information, and a link at the bottom of the page that you can click to learn more about this specific database. Click that link for a complete list of the contents of the database.

Return to the form and enter "rachel" in the "First Name" field, "alexander" in the "Last Name" field, and click **Search**. See figure 5-10 on the next page for the results.

What you have found is a book that includes "Marriage Licenses Issued at Upper Marlborough, Prince George's County, Maryland—1777 to 1801." There are two entries: one from the bride index and the other from the groom index. Click the asterisk following the name of the type of records on the page and an additional Quick Reference Window will open that includes some additional information about the transcriber

Maryland Records Colonial, Revolutionary, County and Church from Original Sources

Marriage Licenses Issued at Upper Marlborough, Prince George's County, Maryland--1777 to 1801.*

Name: William Hayes
Spouse: Rachel Alexander
Marriage Date: 05 Sep 1795
Comment:

View Full Context

Maryland Records Colonial, Revolutionary, County and Church from Original Sources

Marriage Licenses Issued at Upper Marlborough, Prince George's County, Maryland--1777 to 1801.*

Name: Rachel Alexander
Spouse: William Hayes
Marriage Date: 05 Sep 1795
Comment:

View Full Context

Figure 5-10: Search results for Rachel Alexander in "Maryland Records Colonial, Revolutionary, County, and Church from Original Sources Vol. I"

http://search.ancestry....

Carefully transcribed and compared with the original records by Mrs. Amos G. Draper, Washington, D. C. Alphabetically arranged by the compiler of this volume.

Figure 5-11: Additional "Quick Reference" window

and source (see figure 5-11).

The two search results reflect the same marriage entry data for Rachel Alexander and William Hayes, who were wed on 5 September 1795. Click on the link labeled "View Full Content" to view a full list, in alphabetical order by surname and then first name of the bride or groom, of marriages.

As you can see, there are different types of materials in these databases, and their format and content differ. However, all of these materials help place your ancestor into geographical context at a specific point in history.

Let's move overseas to the United Kingdom and examine their censuses.

UK Census Records

Great Britain began taking a census in 1901, and individual censuses were taken for England, Wales, the Isle of Man, and the Channel Islands. The census was taken on one specific date, known as "census night." All persons spending the night under that roof were to be recorded at that location as of that date. The forms were typically collected the next day, and any missing residences or information were proactively collected and listed. The data was then compiled onto the census forms we see today.

The UK censuses were taken, as in the U.S., every ten years. Earlier censuses from 1801, 1811, 1821, and 1831 were statistical, with only the name of the head of household and the numbers of males and females listed. An every-name census was not created until 1841, and since that time, the census has become much more useful for tracing one's ancestors.

Parliamentary law protecting the privacy of individuals' information dictates that the United Kingdom's census images may not be released for 100 years. However, several bills introduced into Parliament between 2005 and 2007 attempted to amend the time to 90 years so the 1911 census could be released. The 1911 census will be available as early as 2010.

There are a number of excellent books that address these topics:

Bevan, Amanda. *Tracing Your Ancestors in the National Archives: The Website and Beyond*. Kew, London, England: The National Archives, 2006.

Colwell, Stella. *Family Records Centre: A User's Guide (Public Record Office Readers Guide)*. Kew, London, England: Public Record Office Publications, 2002.

Colwell, Stella. *The National Archives: A Practical Guide for Family Historians*. Kew, London, England: Public Record Office Publications, 2006.

Herber, Mark. *Ancestral Trails. The Complete Guide to British Genealogy and Family History*. 2nd updated edition. Baltimore, MD: Genealogical Publishing Co., 2006. *Note: A more recent edition of this book has been published in the U.K. but is not available in the U.S. at the time of this writing.*

King, Echo. *Finding Answers in British Isles Census Records*. Provo, UT: Ancestry, 2007.

Searching the Census Records

Let's search for and examine a specific English census record. Use what you have learned so far to find the search form for the 1861 England Census.

We'll perform a search of the 1861 England census for James Hyland. I know that he was born in Ireland and immigrated to England shortly after the Irish Potato Famine. I've already located him in the 1851 census but not in the 1841 census. I suspect that he is still living in the town of Oldbury, so these are the criteria I have entered into the search form in figure 5-12.

Because the search results list is so large, I refined my search by adding a birth year of 1813, as I believe it to have been, based on information I obtained in the 1851 census. However, I have decided to fudge it by two years +/- to try to catch any estimate made by the indexer.

This time I am rewarded with a better results list, and I find James Hyland, born in Ireland and living in Oldbury, Staffordshire, as the third entry in the list shown (see

Figure 5-12: Search form for James Hyland in the 1861 England Census

figure 5-13). His estimated birth year shown in the list is "abt 1814," so I was likely correct in entering his birth year as 1813 and adding a +/- variable to it.

I now have the options to either "View Record" or "View Image." In this case, I think I want to view the record. You'll see why when you look at figure 5-14 (on the next page).

The first thing you will notice is that the record is larger than others you may have seen. The same "Page Tools" and "Make a Connection" sections are here, and you have the options from the record box to click on links to view the original document and to view (and print) a blank census form. However, there are other links on the record of especial interest.

The most important links are those for the other members of the household.

Figure 5-13: "View Record" page for James Hyland

This information has been transcribed from the census document. Like James Hyland's record, the link takes you to

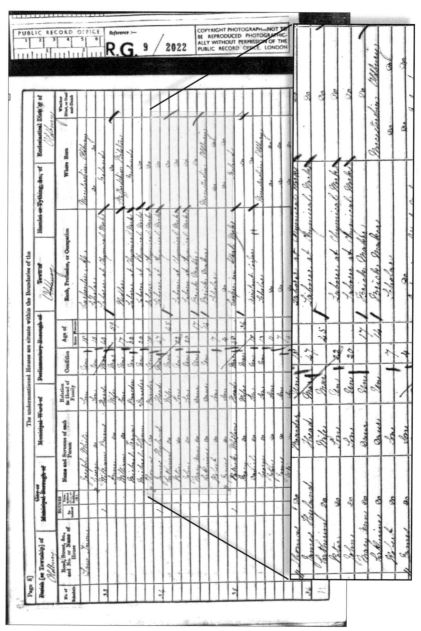

Figure 5-14: Census image highlighting James Hyland and family

a unique "View Record" page for the person shown. The next important link is the "View Image" link, which allows you to study the digitized original for yourself. Let's view the original image in the browser. I used the "Full Screen" option to view the image (see figure 5-14). The notice attached to the image on the right (at the top of the figure) is TNA's reference to the Record Group and Piece Number assigned to this document.

I zoomed in on the census image to 50 percent and captured the details about James Hyland and his family (see the highlighted section of figure 5-14). I now know the names and ages of his wife and his six children. I know that James and two of his sons were employed as labourers at the chemical works, while two of his daughters worked as brickmakers. Notice, however, the places of birth for each member of the family, and you will see that the parents and all but the last three children were born in Ireland. These last three were born in Worcestershire, Oldbury. This is important information because you may be able to find civil birth registrations as well as parish records for their christenings. Daughter Catherine is shown as 14 years old. If we subtract 14 years from 1861, we arrive at an approximate birth date of 1847. This is secondary evidence of the fact that the parents and older children left Ireland between then and the birth of an older child, Mary Ann, who is 17 according to the image. That means that the time of the family's arrival in England can be narrowed to the approximate period of 1844 to 1847, mostly within the period of the severe and infamous Irish Potato Famine. This is the kind of work that you must do, taking evidence and analyzing it in order to arrive at such hypotheses.

Returning to the "View Record" page, the final link is labeled "View others on page." While you can and will certainly manually read the other peoples' entries on the census form, a click on this link produces a results page linking to record pages for everyone else on the same page. What makes this valuable is that the list is in alphabetical order by surname and then forename, and it becomes easier to view patterns of relatives, friends, old neighbors from Ireland who may have traveled and settled together, and collateral lines. As with the study of any other census records, neighbors' information can be extremely useful from one census to another in tracing your own ancestors, their movements, their marriages, and other events.

The Scotland 1841 Census

The 1841 census taken in Scotland is also available in a database at Ancestry.com. It is, however, an index and not an image collection. Look at the database-specific search form I completed for Margaret Alexander of the County of Midlothian (figure 5-15).

Of all the results, the one I am interested in is the fifth on the list. When I click the "View Record" link, I am taken to the familiar page (see figure 5-16 on the next page).

However, there is no image option. You can obtain microfilm of the census througha Family History Center or the Scotland People's website <www.scotlandspeople.gov.uk>. However, in the meantime, the indexer has provided

Figure 5-15: Scotland 1841 search form

both a link to the list of other family members *and* all the other people who appear on the census page. Therefore, even though I do not yet have access to view the actual census page for myself, I can click on the link labeled "View others on page" and see a results page showing everyone on that census document. This can be invaluable in assuring that you have the "correct" Margaret Alexander.

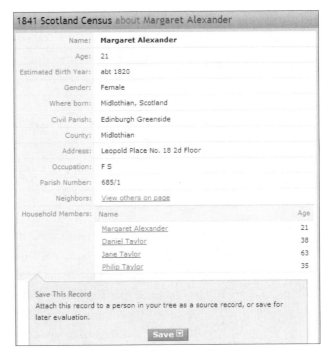

Accessing and working with the UK Census collection is, indeed, as simple as it is with the United States collection. You can trace

Figure 5-16 "View Record" page for Margaret Alexander

individuals' movements from decade to decade using the censuses. The information you obtain from the documents will provide you with other clues for other record types as well.

Canadian Census Records

Canada's long and rich history is woven throughout with French and British influence. It remains, of course, an officially bilingual country. Censuses have been taken in Canada for centuries, with the earliest having been ordered by Jean Talon in New France (Québec) in 1666. While other censuses were taken in various places, there are no others that survive from before the nineteenth century. Confederation in 1867 imposed the legal requirement that a census be taken regularly, and the first Dominion census was taken in 1871 and has continued every ten years since that time.

There are a number of books that can explain Canadian census history and content in more detail, including these:

Geyh, Patricia Keeney, Joyce Soltis Banachowski, Linda
K. Boyea, et. al. *French-Canadian Sources: A Guide for
Genealogists*. Orem, UT: Ancestry, 2002.

Baxter, Angus. *In Search of Your Canadian Roots: Tracing Your
Family Tree in Canada*. 4th ed. Baltimore, MD: Genealogical
Publishing Co., 2000.

For the purpose of this discussion, we will concentrate on the Canadian census databases available through Ancestry.com. These include the 1901 census, the 1906 census of the Northwest Territories, and the 1911 census of all of Canada.

By this time, you should be completely familiar with using the Card Catalog to browse databases and filter your list. In this case, clicking on the Census & Voter Lists category, Canada in the Location filter, and the 1900s decade area in the Dates filter should provide you with a short list of database titles, including the 1901 Census of Canada.

Note that below the form is a list of links to each of the provinces. When you click on a link, you will continue to be presented with new pages with other links to districts and subdistricts from which you can choose. When you click on a link to a subdistrict, the first page of the census Population Schedule or Tableau (table) will be displayed. You can then browse through the image pages using the tools on the toolbar. (See chapter 3 for information about working with digitized images.) You can also print one or more blank census forms to help you read all the columns and/or translate between English and French column headings. (Please note that there are separate census forms for each language where appropriate.)

When you return to the search form, you may note that there are additional search criteria in the Canadian census that we have not encountered in either the United States or United Kingdom forms. Let's conduct an exact search in the 1901 census.

I have chosen to search for Gilbert Flynn, an Irishman who I know was alive in 1901 and lived in the district of Addington in Ontario. I also know that his wife died several years before and that his son, daughter-in-law, and grandchildren shared his home with him. I therefore constructed a search in the new search form for Gilbert Flynn in Ontario, Canada. (As I typed in Ontario, the type-ahead feature presented me with a drop-down list of locations, including Ontario, Canada, which I clicked on to select and fill in the field.) Since I know so much about him, I also clicked "Match all terms exactly."

The results from the new search contained two listings: one was for Gilbert Flynn in Ontario, Addington District and Olden Sub-District; the other was for Gilbert Flynn in Ontario, Halton District and Trafalgar Sub-District. It was the first Gilbert Flynn in whom I was interested. The "View Record" page shows a lot of information, including the names and ages of all the members of the household. As you examine figure 5-17 (on the next page), please be aware that this is only the top portion of this page. Below what you see in the figure are source information and a detailed description of the contents of this database.

The excerpt from the actual census page on the "View original image" shows us a few things. First, the column headings are printed twice: first in English and then in French.

1901 Census of Canada about Gilbert Flynn

Name:	**Gilbert Flynn**
Gender:	Male
Marital Status:	Single
Age:	70
Birth Date:	16 Aug 1830
Birthplace:	Ireland
Relation to Head of House:	Head
Immigration Year:	1840
Racial or Tribal Origin:	Irish
Nationality:	Canadian
Religion:	Roman Catholic
Occupation:	Shoe Maker
Province:	Ontario
District:	Halton
District Number:	68
Sub-District:	Trafalgar
Sub-District Number:	I-5
Family Number:	88
Page:	8
Neighbors:	View others on page
Household Members:	Name Age
	Gilbert Flynn 70

View Original Record

View original image

View 1901 Form (English version)

View 1901 Form (French version)

Save This Record
Attach this record to a person in your tree as a source record, or save for later evaluation.

Save ☑

Figure 5-17:"View Record" page for Gilbert Flynn

We learn a great deal about Gilbert Flynn, including the fact that he was born in Ireland on 8 April 1837 and that he arrived in Canada in 1842. He is widowed, and he is of the Methodist faith. The family living with him does appear to include a son, a daughter-in-law, a daughter, and probably a granddaughter, although we would have to check this. In addition, there is a "Ferdine Pitman," who appears to be a live-in servant.

Let's look at a portion of the actual census document, which is accessible from the "View Record" page but not from the search results page in this case. Figure 5-18 (on the next page) shows details of the people living there. Without more information, we cannot assume that the relationships listed are the relationships of the family members to the head of household. Is Victoria the wife of Thomas or Gilbert? Is little Myrtle a daughter of Thomas or of Gilbert? While we may have our ideas, we really need to investigate more. Marriage records from the area may tell us whose wife Victoria is, and parish or civil registration records should tell us the names of Myrtle's parents.

Nom de chaque personne dans la famille ou la ménage, le 31 Mars, 1901.	Sexe.	Couleur	Relation de parenté ou autre avec le chef de famille ou du ménage.	Célibataire, marié veuvage ou divorcé	Mois et date de naissance.	Année de naissance	Age au dernier anniversaire de naissance	Naissance. Où c'est au Canada spécifiez la province ou territoire, et si-après "r" pour rural au "u" pour urbain, selon le cas.)	Année d'immigration au Canada.	Année de naturalisation	Origine, selon la race ou la tribu.	Nationalité.	Religion.
3	4	5	6	7	8	9	10	11	12	13	14	15	16
Flynn Gilbert	M	W	Head	W	8 April	1834	63	Ireland	1842		Irishm	Canadian	Meth
" Thomas	M	W	Son	M	10 August	1842	28	O	a		Irish	"	"
" Victoria	F	W	Wife	M	29 Sept:	1843	24	O	o		English	"	"
" Gertrude	F	W	Daughter	S	9 Jul	1882	18	O	o		Irish	"	"
" Myrtle	F	W		S	16 Mar	1898	2	O	a		Irish	"	"
Ulman Fredric	M	W	Domestic	S	6 Nov	1881	19	O	u		English	"	"

Figure 5-18: Portion of 1901 Canada census page

The census tells us the birth dates of each person in the household and their ethnic or national origin. However, it would appear that only Gilbert immigrated to Canada. The other people were most probably born in Canada. All are listed as Canadian citizens. We should probably investigate the census enumerators' instructions for this census. We can also look for immigration records for Gilbert, civil registration and ecclesiastical records in the Methodist churches in the area for the births of all the others, and for marriage records. We now have a number of leads that we can pursue.

Summary

The census collections we have explored and examined are impressive. Their availability at Ancestry.com makes your research much simpler, and certainly less expensive, than traveling to an archive to conduct research on site. Check the other Ancestry geographies' sites for more census collections and census substitutes. You will find that Ancestry.com will add more census materials as they become available to them, and you will see and hear them announced.

We have concentrated in the last several chapters on how to search for and through databases in great detail. We have covered the use of digital collections' images in extensive detail and you have seen an abundance of screen shots. In the following chapters on the different categories of records, we will concentrate on the types of databases, their content, and how to apply this to your research and a bit less on the "how-to" of locating the databases.

If you are still unsure how to search for databases and records and how to manipulate the digitized images, you will want to review the previous chapters and practice. Otherwise, we're off to discuss birth, marriage, death, and other related records in chapter 6.

Chapter 6

Birth, Marriage, and Death Records

Births, christenings, bar mitzvahs and bat mitzvahs, marriages, divorces, adoptions, deaths, and burials—and all the possible evidentiary records and materials that document these events—are the keys to building context for our ancestors. We want to know *who* they were; *where* they were born; whether they *immigrated* or *migrated,* as well as where they moved from; their *full names* and those of their *parents* and *siblings*; *who* and *when* they married; *where* they lived at every point in their lives; their *occupations*; if they performed *military service*; what *religious affiliation* they maintained; *where* and *when* they died; and *where* are they buried.

In this and the following chapters, we will look at the wide range of records on Ancestry.com that can help answer these questions. We will focus on birth, marriage, and death records in this chapter. Americans refer to these as "vital records" or "vital statistics." The English refer to them as "civil records" or "civil registration records."

You already know how to search for, view, and otherwise work with records. Therefore, we will concentrate from this point forward on representative Ancestry.com databases in each of the major record categories. We will explore what is available and how these records can be used to pursue your own research goals. Once you have delved into some of these databases, you should have little or no trouble working with others.

The Major Record Types

The Ancestry.com Birth, Marriage, and Death Records collection contains a broad variety of records. This section explains some of the types of records you might find:

- **Birth**—Birth records usually show the name of the child, gender, date and place born, parents' names, and sometimes other data, such as parents' birthplaces.

- **Marriage**—Marriage records usually show names of the bride and groom, date and place married, and sometimes other information, such as ages, place of residence, parents' names, officiating clergy or authorized government official, witnesses' names, and religious affiliation.

- **Divorce**—Divorce records document the dissolution of a marriage. They can place either or both of the individuals in a specific area at the time of the filing for divorce.

- **Death**—In addition to the name of the person, death records usually provide marital status (single, married, widowed, or divorced), the cause of death, the dates and places of death, name and location of mortuary, sometimes the burial location or disposition of cremated remains, and sometimes the occupation, date and place of birth, age, parents' names and birthplaces (usually state and/or country/province/parish), and other useful information. The more recent the death record, the more information you will typically find. There are some death indexes for specific locations that may help you pinpoint the date and location of a death, after which you may be able to trace a death certificate and other death- and burial-related records.

- **Church**—Church records contain information about baptisms, marriages, burials, and membership. In addition to the name of the person, church records often provide information about family members.

- **Cemetery**—The cemetery records included in the collection are tombstone inscriptions, burial permits, and death indexes. These records usually show names, birth and death dates, and occasionally additional personal information. Sometimes they also include information on surviving family members.

- **Social Security Death Index**—The Social Security Death Index (SSDI) is a database that contains the names of deceased persons who had applied for and were assigned Social Security numbers and whose deaths were reported to the Social Security Administration (SSA). These records usually include a full name, birth and death dates, and last known residence.

- **Obituaries**—The Obituary collection contains recent obituaries (2001 to the present) from hundreds of newspapers. In addition to names, dates, places of birth, marriage, and death, an obituary often identifies the deceased individual's relationships with other individuals, burial or memorial service details, and other details of a person's life events, affiliations, and achievements. We discuss obituaries in greater detail in chapter 9.

The information that you find in these records can provide important evidence or clues pointing you to original, primary source materials. Remember, however, that many databases are made up of indexes or transcripts, and you will want to obtain exact facsimile images of each record so that you can personally examine and analyze the data. Ancestry.com provides descriptive information and source citations for each of its databases, as you have already seen. This should provide you with sufficient information to track down the source materials and obtain the copies that you need to perform your scholarly research.

Let's examine some Ancestry.com birth, marriage, and death databases.

The Social Security Death Index (SSDI)

The SSDI is a compilation of information about deceased persons who had filed for and received Social Security numbers, who were paid Social Security benefits at some point in their lives, and whose deaths were reported to the Social Security Administration (SSA). There are several key points you should bear in mind.

Usually, a person whose name appears in the SSDI was employed, paid money into Social Security, and at some time applied for benefits of some sort. The two most typical benefits paid were old age pension or disability benefits. If the person paid into Social Security but never collected benefits, you will not find him or her in the file.

The spouse of someone who paid into Social Security, but who never worked and contributed to Social Security, will not be included in the file unless he or she received their spouse's benefits after the spouse's death, and even this is not always true.

People who worked for the railroads exclusively and did not work in another public sector will not be included in the SSDI. These people contributed to Railroad Retirement instead, a separate retirement security fund specifically for railroad workers, and collected benefits from that organization. Only if individuals also worked for a company not affiliated with the railroads will they appear in the SSDI, and they will appear with their unique number assigned to railroad workers (beginning with a 7).

If a person collected benefits at one time and his or her death was not reported to Social Security, that person will not be included in the SSDI.

The SSDI contains approximately 80 million records at the time of this writing (and the number increases every month), and the information in this database is, for the most part, reliable and accurate. Remember, though, that information concerning addresses and date of death may be incomplete or inaccurate, as it depends upon the person who reported the death.

Let's look at an example of a search of the SSDI. I searched for a record for Nora Cunningham, whose year of birth and state of residence I already knew. What I want to learn are the date of her death and the location so I can obtain copies of her death certificate, obituaries, burial location, will and probate records, and any other information that may be suggested by these source materials. My search was rewarded with a results page, shown in figure 6-1.

Two of the women shown at the top of the list were born in 1888, but because I know that the

View Record	Name	Birth Date	Death Date	Last Residence (City,County,State)	Order Record
View Record ★★★⯪	Nora Cunningham	21 Jul 1888	Jun 1980	Charlotte, Mecklenburg, North Carolina	🛒

Figure 6-1: SSDI results page for Nora Cunningham

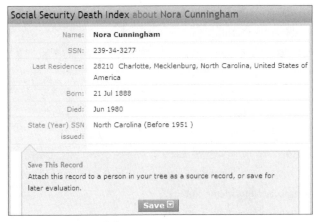

Figure 6-2: SSDI Search form

family lived near Charlotte, in Mecklenburg County, North Carolina, I chose the second entry on the list. You will notice the familiar "View Record" link on the left side of the record. However, on the right you will see a shopping cart icon in a column labeled "Order Record." Let's look at each of these.

When you click "View Record," you will see the familiar format of the record page (see figure 6-2). I did not know Nora's exact date of birth, but the record tells me she was born 21 July 1888. I now also know that her death date was in June of 1980. I can save the record to my Member Tree, or, if she was not in the tree, I could add her and the record to it. I also could save the record to my Shoebox for later review. There are, however, two important differences in the "Page Tools" section. The first is a link labeled "Order original certificate." In this case, The Generations Network has formed an agreement with a company named VitalChek that acts as an intermediary to order copies of birth, marriage, divorce, and death certificates for you, using your credit card. This is one method of obtaining an original copy of the primary evidentiary document. You can also contact the county directly to order a copy.

The other link in the "Page Tools" section is labeled "Request copy of original application." Clicking this link allows you to write a letter to the SSA to request a copy of the individual's original application for a Social Security number, which was done on a form numbered SS-5 (see figure 6-3).

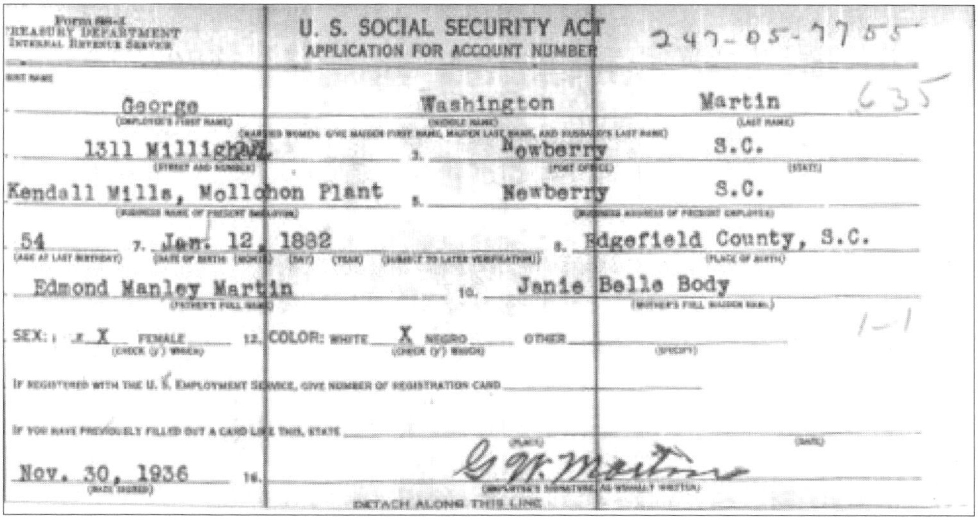

Figure 6-3: Sample SS-5 application form

The SS-5 contains information supplied by the applicant, including name, date of birth, parents' names, the person's place of residence, his/her employer's name and address, and the date the application was completed. It can provide details you may not otherwise have had or verify other evidence.

On the page is a link labeled "Click here to generate letter." This will generate a preformatted letter to the Freedom of Information Officer at the SSA requesting a copy of the SS-5 for the individual. There is a cost associated with the request.

As you can see, there are a lot of components to the SSDI record. Let me suggest some ways to use the SSDI information in your research:

- **Write Letters for SS-5 Form**—The most obvious activity is to use the letter-generation facility and send off for the SS-5 form.

- **Locate Lost Relatives**—I have had success locating lost branches of the family and information about them by using the SSDI. For example, I found a letter from my grandmother's brother from the 1940s in which he said he was moving his family to Dayton, Ohio. A search of his name and Dayton, Ohio, located a number of records, and by checking the birth date I was able to confirm his presence there and his date of death.

- **Confirming Dates**—I have often used the SSDI to search for a person whose name and place of residence I was uncertain of. When you locate his or her record, you can then check the birth date and compare it against what, if anything, you already have. You can also check the death date. If you need corroboration, you can write to the SSA for the SS-5 and/or to the vital records agency in the county in which the person lived and seek a copy of a death certificate.

- **Dates of Birth and Death**—You can use these dates to search for birth certificates, death records, obituaries, and other materials. Using the "Residence" and "Last Benefit" (if any listed) will help you home in on specific locations.

- **Residence**—I have often used the SSDI to locate the last residence of a specific relative, especially if I know his or her date of birth. I simply enter the surname and given name, along with date or year of birth, and execute a search. This usually provides me with records to help me isolate the last residence address in the SSA's files. If not, I broaden the search. (If you don't get a match the first time, there may be a given name problem where the person may have gone by a middle name. Leave the given name blank and try again. Likewise, try alternate spellings of surnames. "Johansson" may have been spelled "Johanson" or "Johannson" or some other way. Be persistent!) In addition, the residence information may point you to other materials in a specific geographic area, such as land records, tax rolls, voter registration rolls, licenses, court records, newspapers, school records, church records, employment records, probate records, death certificate, obituaries, and a variety of other record types.

- **Place Issued**—The state shown in the SSDI as the one in which the SSN was issued may be a surprise to you. A check of the person's SS-5 form will confirm the place where the application was made and the SSN was issued. I have one ancestor whose issued location was shown in the SSDI as Pennsylvania when I expected it to have been North Carolina. On receipt of his SS-5, I found that he was working in Pennsylvania in December of 1936 at the time he was required to obtain an SSN. This provided me with more details about his movements and employment history and pointed me toward research in another geographical area I would otherwise never have known to check.

If your ancestor or family member died before July 1963 when the SSDI was begun, he or she probably had an SSN. You can write a letter to request his or her SS-5. The cost is a little higher if you cannot provide the person's SSN. Be sure to include the person's full name (and any nicknames by which he or she was known), the person's birth date and location, the death date and location, and your full name and address.

A Sample Marriage Database: Maryland 1655–1850

I used the Card Catalog to locate the database titled "Maryland Marriages 1655–1850." Using the search form for this database, I searched for a female named Dorcas Alexander who married a man whose surname I believed was McCoy in

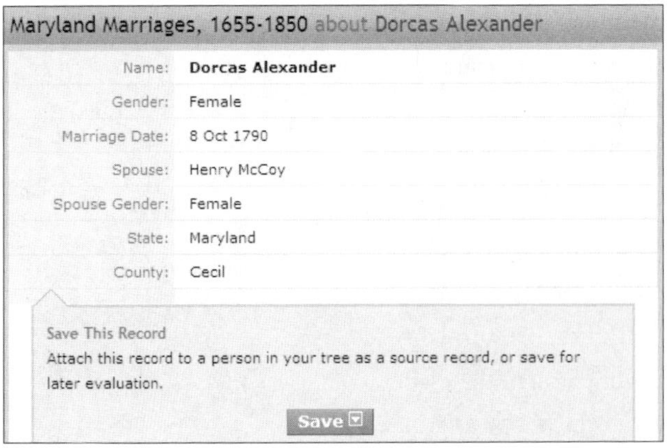

Maryland Marriages, 1655-1850 about Dorcas Alexander

Name:	**Dorcas Alexander**
Gender:	Female
Marriage Date:	8 Oct 1790
Spouse:	Henry McCoy
Spouse Gender:	Female
State:	Maryland
County:	Cecil

Save This Record

Attach this record to a person in your tree as a source record, or save for later evaluation.

Save ⊡

Figure 6-4: "Maryland Marriages 1655–1850" for Dorcas Alexander

Cecil County, on the Eastern Shore of Maryland. My search produced a match for a female named Dorcas Alexander in Cecil County, who married a Henry McCoy on 8 October 1790. I clicked on that and the record in figure 6-4 was displayed. Here I learned that the groom's name was Henry McCoy and that the marriage date was 8 October 1790. In addition, I have the information *and* the source citation information from the bottom of the page. According to the Source Information at the bottom of the page, the original marriage records should be in the county clerk's office. I can now make contact with the courthouse in Cecil County, located in Elkton, Maryland, and request a copy of any marriage records the courthouse has on file.

Under the "Description" is more information about the database. It is important that you always click on any "Learn more …" link you see because you can often find exceptionally valuable information. In this case, there is much more text and it includes the Family History Library microfilm reference numbers (FHL # 0013866) for the records in all the counties, including Cecil County, with marriage records referenced in this database. I now also have the option of visiting my local LDS Family History Center to obtain the film to see and print a copy of the original marriage record(s). This can save me either a letter to the Cecil County, Maryland, county clerk's office or a trip there or to the FHL Salt Lake City.

Banffshire, Scotland: Parish and Probate Records

There really are many different record types at Ancestry.com. If you have Scottish ancestors from Banffshire, one database of interest might be the "Banffshire, Scotland: Parish and Probate Records." It is part of a larger collection of databases of historical parish and probate registers from the countries of England, Wales, Scotland, and Ireland. More than 15 million names in this collection can range in date from the early 1500s to the mid- to late 1800s.

I selected the Banffshire database and did a search for James Macindoo. The search results list included the parish marriage record information for his marriage on 14 April 1600 to Jonet Paterson (see figure 6-5).

Lanarkshire, Aberdeenshire, Banff, Ayr, & Stirling: - Commissariot Record of Hamilton and Campsie, Register of Testaments, 1564-1800

Mac. Mc. contd. (Marriages)

The Commissariot Record of Hamilton and Campsie.

Register of Testaments, 1564-1800.

County: Banff

Country: Scotland

Paterson, Jonet, spouse to James Macindoo, in Cult of Jordanehill 14 Apr 1600

Figure 6-5: Record from the "Banffshire, Scotland: Parish and Probate Records"

England & Wales, FreeBMD Birth Index: 1837–1983

Civil Registration in England and Wales became law on 1 July 1837, shortly after Queen Victoria ascended the throne. It mandated that births, marriages, and deaths be registered with a civil office in the area where a person or family lived, though it took some time to gain full compliance by the population of all of England and Wales.

The ledgers containing registrations of each type of record are currently held at the Family Records Centre in

London. The original certificates of births, marriages, deaths, adoptions, and divorces are held by the General Register Office (GRO) and can be ordered in person at the National Archives (TNA) in Kew, Richmond, Surrey, or at the GRO website at <www.gro.gov.uk>.

The FreeBMD Indexes for Births, Marriages, and Deaths consist of transcriptions of alphabetical register ledgers at the GRO. These were compiled for each quarter of the year after all the registry offices provided copies of the certificates to the GRO. Therefore, there are separate registers for each type of record, organized into alphabetical sequence by year and quarter (for example, January/February/March). The FreeBMD Index database is searchable by name and quarter, district, county, and other criteria. The search results are presented in the familiar format with links labeled "View Record" and "View Image." You may certainly look at the record page, but be sure to also examine the image to verify the accuracy of the transcription.

Let's try an example. Using the Card Catalog, locate the database titled "England & Wales, FreeBMD Birth Index: 1837–1983." Click it and go to the search form. Now, exact search for Alice Maud Vinson and look at the results (see figure 6-6). You should see two people named Alice Maud Vinson. One was born in the third quarter of 1872 in St. Thomas, County Devon, and the other was born in the first quarter of 1880 in Islington in Greater London, London, Middlesex. Click the second entry.

View Record	Name	Year of Registration	Quarter of Registration	Mother's Maiden Name	District	County	View Image
View Record ★★★ ☆ ☆	Alice Maud Vinson	1872	Jul-Aug-Sep		St Thomas	Devon	
View Record ★★★ ☆ ☆	Alice Maud Vinson	1880	Jan-Feb-Mar		Islington	Greater London, London, Middlesex	

Figure 6-6: "FreeBMD Birth Index" results for Alice Maud Vinson

You see the information about Alice's birth, as well as a "Volume 1b" and "Page 459." The year, quarter, district, county, volume, and page number are all essential in order to order a copy of the birth certificate. Let's verify the accuracy of the information in the record box by viewing the image.

The image you see is the full page from the alphabetical birth registrations ledger for the first quarter of 1880. Scroll down the page until you find the surname Vinson, and then examine the entry for Alice Maud. Figure 6-7 shows the detail from that page. The entry shows the registration was made in Islington, and the volume and page number listed are, indeed, "1b" and "459." (A click on the link to "Page 459" will provide a list of all birth index entries on that page of the parish register.)

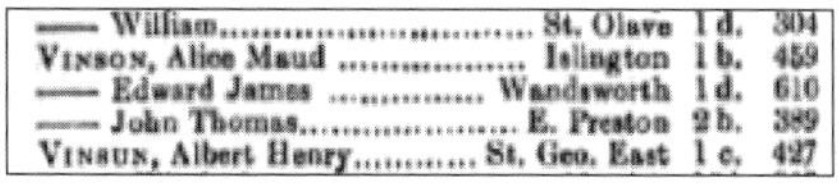

Figure 6-7: Detail from image in "FreeBMD Birth Index" for Alice Maud Vinson

Now, take a look at the options in the "Page Tools" section of the record page (see figure 6-8). There are three new options that you have not seen before.

- **Search for Alice Maud Vinson in the UK Census Collection**—You can click here to search the UK Census collection. You can then narrow your search to a specific census (see chapter 5 for information on searching census records).

- **Search for Alice Maud Vinson in the London *Times***—A click here will provide you with a list of links, by date, in the *Times* database. You may then have to search the digitized images of the newspaper to see if our Alice is mentioned in the text (see chapter 9 for information on searching newspapers).

- **Order Birth Certificate for Alice Maud Vinson**—A click on this link will take you to the General Register

Page Tools

🖨 View printer-friendly

🔍 Search for Alice Maud Vinson in the UK Census Collection

🔍 Search for Alice Maud Vinson in the London Times

🛒 Order Birth certificate for Alice Maud Vinson

Figure 6-8: Page tools in the "FreeBMD Birth Index" database

Office (GRO) website, where you may order a copy of Alice's birth certificate. (Your first visit to this site to order a certificate copy requires that you set up a free ID and password.) Be sure you have all the information mentioned before because you will be prompted to provide specific data in order for the GRO to locate the right record and copy it for you.

Summary

You should have seen, as we explored the birth, marriage, and death records, that these databases contain a wealth of information from many areas.

In each database, you've seen that as we find one record we may well find information that can lead us to one or many additional records of various types. The more you learn about available record types, the more creative you will become in locating multiple, independent types of evidence. Additionally, the more exploration you do of what databases and contents are available for a given area or record type, the more ideas you will get.

Spend some time practicing with different databases, whether you have ancestors in the area or not. Doing so will help you build your search skills and make you familiar with all the options available to you.

Chapter 7

Military Records

Armies, navies, and other martial forces have been part of
human history since ancient times, and military history is
the focus of immense publication and research. Huge bodies
of military records have been preserved in archives and
government repositories around the world. The National
Archives (TNA) in England, for example, maintains
documentary military records of the British Army from 1760
forward as part of its War Office (WO) record group, Royal
Navy records from 1667 forward in the Admiralty (ADM)
record group, and massive quantities of other military records
dating from the Civil War in England in the 1640s and back
into the twelfth century. Many of these have been indexed
at various levels and can be searched on site at TNA in Kew,
Richmond, Surrey. Other records are held by the respective
branches of the military and in collections of manorial
documents across the United Kingdom.

North American military records at all levels are maintained by the National Archives and Records Administration (NARA) in the U.S. and at the Library and Archives Canada, not to mention in state and provincial archives and libraries.

As genealogists, we should be intensely interested in military history and the related records produced over time. Military records are many and varied, including indexes to unit and service records, draft registration and enlistment records, military service records, death and casualty lists, pension files, and other associated documentary records.

Since this book concentrates on Ancestry.com rather than all the other Ancestry database collections in the UK and Ireland, Canada, Australia, and Germany, we will primarily examine different types of military records databases that exist for the United States and its colonial predecessors. However, we will also list some of the other geographies' military records that are available to World Deluxe subscribers.

Ancestry.com hosts searchable indexes to actual records and, in some cases, to digitized images of actual documents. As with all the databases at Ancestry.com, source information and descriptions of the contents of each collection are available for your reference. If you are searching for an actual record or a folder for an individual, you will want to contact the repository cited in the source to determine the availability of copies of documents. The source information will also provide you with the details you need to write a source citation to document the evidence you have located.

To follow along with the examples in this chapter, access the "Military Records" search form from the "Go Directly to a Database or Collection" section on the "Search" page.

Keep in mind as well that you can access some military information using U.S. census records:

- 1840—Included the names and ages of military pensioners

- 1850—Listed the occupations (including military service) of all males over the age of fifteen

- 1890—Collected a special census of Union veterans and widows

- 1900—Detailed separate military schedules and indexes for all military personnel

- 1910—Recorded survivors of Civil War service, including Confederate and Union forces

- 1920—Separately enumerated all overseas military and naval forces and many domestic bases; some bases are listed under state and county records

For more information on searching census records, see chapter 5.

Early American Military Databases

It is important to recognize that the earliest colonial documents for the American colonies may no longer exist. Some of the only reference material available may have been compiled and published in the form of family, local, and military histories. The information may have been culled from rare documents, journals, and colonial government records located in the U.S. and overseas. With that in mind, let's look at two databases for Revolutionary War–era military information.

In the Card Catalog, locate the database titled "Muster and Pay Rolls of the War of the Revolution." I performed an exact search for John Alexander, with no keyword information

View Image		Chapter	Page Number	Title
9 [Mch 23] 9 [Mch 23]	Robert White, 1st Lt...... John Alexander, 1st Lt...... John Alexander, 2nd Lt...... Andrew Irvine 2nd Lt......	Pennsylvania Troops	536	Muster and Pay Rolls of the War of the Revolution
Showing **4 of 4** matches found on this image. ★ ★ ✦				
	William Thompson................ Solomon Alexander................ John Smith..................... Richard Piles....................	Virginia Troops	628	Muster and Pay Rolls of the War of the Revolution
Showing **2 of 9** matches found on this image. ★ ★ ✦				

Figure 7-1: Results page from the "Muster and Pay Rolls" for John Alexander

entered. The results page contained several entries (shown in figure 7-1).

The information in this database was transcribed exactly as it was published. Again, notice how you can preview the image to help you narrow your search. In this case, I'll click the John Alexander from Pennsylvania and view the full record. Notice that you can then browse forward and backward to see other records in the database, or in this case, other records in the book. This may help you locate other personnel in the same military unit or activities relating to a particular time period.

Let's look at another Revolutionary War—related database: "American Revolutionary War Rejected Pensions."

View Record	Name	State	Location	Reason
View Record ★ ✦	Mary Patterson, widow of William	Maine	Edgecomb, Lincoln	No satisfactory proof that the vessels were public ones on board of which service was performed.
View Record ★ ✦	Robert Patterson (deceased)	New York	Erwin, Steuben	He did not establish six months' service before he died.

Figure 7-2: Results for "Patterson" in "American Revolutionary War Rejected Pensions"

This time I searched exactly for the surname of Patterson. I was rewarded with thirteen results (see figure 7-2).

The information in the "View Record" pages provides me with names, states, and locations, along with the reason for the rejection of the pension application (see figure 7-3 on the next page). The original pension applications are held at the National Archives and Records Administration if you decide you want to order copies to examine for yourself.

American Civil War Records

The American Civil War, or the War Between the States, stands as the bloodiest period in United States history. More has been written about this period and the participants than about any other topic in American history. Military regimental histories and

American Revolutionary War Rejected Pensions about Mary Patterson, widow of William

Name:	**Mary Patterson, widow of William**
State:	Maine
Location:	Edgecomb, Lincoln
Reason:	No satisfactory proof that the vessels were public ones on board of which service was performed.

Save This Record
Attach this record to a person in your tree as a source record, or save for later evaluation.

Save ▾

Figure 7-3: Record for Mary Patterson in "Rejected Pensions"

personal memoirs were published by the hundreds between 1865 and 1900, and along with magazine articles and dedicated periodicals such as the monthly *Confederate Veteran*, they recounted the campaigns, battles, and individual stories of men and women during this tumultuous period. In addition, there are literally millions of documents associated with military service; muster and pay rolls; casualties and deaths; hospitalization; pensions to veterans, widows, and orphans (including the surviving 1890 Federal Census special Veterans Schedules); military unit records; and many others.

Ancestry.com has compiled an excellent collection of databases and finding aids for American Civil War research.

Let's start with a search of my great-great-grandfather, Jesse Holder, in the "American Civil War Soldiers" database. My Jesse is the man whose residence was listed as Gwinnett County, Georgia. When I click the link to that record for him, the record shown in figure 7-4 (on the next page) is displayed.

This database is one that is growing, with more than 2 million soldiers' records entered of the more than 4 million soldiers who served in the war. This record tells me that Jesse Holder enlisted as a private in "Company F, 24th Infantry

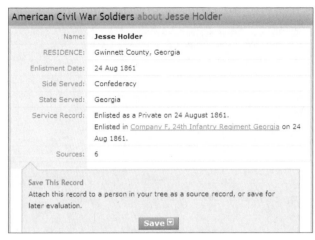

Figure 7-4: Record for Jesse Holder in the "American Civil War Soldiers" database

Figure 7-5: Results page for the "American Civil War Regiments" database

Regiment Georgia" on 24 August 1861. The link to the unit in which he enlisted can be clicked and takes me to a results page for the "American Civil War Regiments" database (see figure 7-5).

When I click the "View Record" link, there is a "Regimental History" in some cases and a list of battles and armed conflicts in which it was involved. A portion of the history record for the "24th Infantry Regiment GA" is shown in figure 7-6 (on the next page).

You will notice that some of the names of battles are links. They will present you with a descriptive record of the engagement and the name of the source from which the account was taken. You can also click "View Full Context" to see this account in context with the entire military history for that date.

Look at figure 7-6 again. At the top is another link labeled "List of Soldiers." When you click this link, you are presented with a results page for members of the entire military unit, starting with the highest ranking officer and working down to the privates. The "24th Infantry Regiment GA" had a total of 1,304 personnel.

What you have seen is an example of the interrelationship between these databases. You can see that you could begin with a name or a regiment, if you know one or both, and locate detailed information about an individual. The details about enlistment date, regiment, regimental history, battles and engagements, and rosters of all the unit personnel can help add a tremendous amount of context to your understanding of your ancestor's military life. Based on the knowledge of the regiment and the battles

American Civil War Regiments	
REGIMENT:	24th Infantry Regiment Georgia
Date of Organization:	30 Aug 1861
Muster Date:	9 Apr 1865
Regiment State:	Georgia
Regiment Type:	Infantry
Regiment Number:	24th
Regimental Soldiers and History:	List of Soldiers

Regimental History

Battles Fought
Fought on 6 May 1862 at Williamsburg, VA.
Fought on 31 May 1862 at Seven Pines, VA.
Fought on 31 May 1862 at Near Seven Pines, VA.
Fought on 18 Jun 1862 at Richmond, VA.
Fought on 29 Jun 1862 at Savage's Station, VA.
Fought on 1 Jul 1862 at Malvern Hill, VA.
Fought on 2 Jul 1862 at Malvern Hill, VA.
Fought on 30 Aug 1862 at 2nd Manassas, VA.
Fought on 14 Sep 1862 at Crampton's Gap, MD.
Fought on 16 Sep 1862 at Sharpsburg, MD.
Fought on 17 Sep 1862 at Sharpsburg, MD.

Figure 7-6: A portion of the regiment history for the 24th Infantry Regiment GA

in which it participated, you can study the engagement, the conditions, and other factors and really bring your ancestor to life. Perhaps you will then want to check the "Civil War Pension Index: General Index to Pension Files, 1861–1934" database for a pension application file at NARA and then order copies to add to your research. The "National Home for Disabled Volunteer Soldiers" database is another resource you might want to check. This is an exciting part of your family history research!

World War I Draft Registration Cards, 1917-1918

One of the most exciting collections on Ancestry.com is the "World War I Draft Registration Cards, 1917–1918" database. This database contains an index and images of

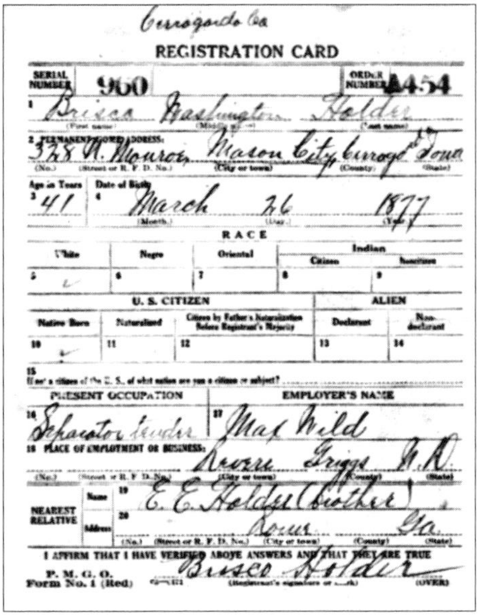

Cerrogordo Co

REGISTRATION CARD

SERIAL NUMBER 960 ORDER NUMBER A454

1 Brisco Washington Holder

(First name) (Middle name) (Last name)

2 PERMANENT HOME ADDRESS: 328 N. Monroe Mason City Cerrogordo Iowa

(No.) (Street or R. F. D. No.) (City or town) (County) (State)

Age in Years 3 41 Date of Birth 4 March 26 1877

(Month) (Day) (Year)

RACE

White	Negro	Oriental	Indian Citizen	Indian Noncitizen
5 ✓	6	7	8	9

U. S. CITIZEN Native Born	Naturalized	Citizen by Father's Naturalization Before Registrant's Majority	ALIEN Declarant	Non-declarant
10 ✓	11	12	13	14

15 If not a citizen of the U. S., of what nation are you a citizen or subject?

PRESENT OCCUPATION: 16 Separator tender

EMPLOYER'S NAME: 17 Max Wild

18 PLACE OF EMPLOYMENT OR BUSINESS: Revere Griggs N.D.

(No.) (Street or R. F. D. No.) (City or town) (County) (State)

NEAREST RELATIVE Name 19 E. E. Holder (brother)

Address 20 Rome Ga.

(No.) (Street or R. F. D. No.) (City or town) (County) (State)

I AFFIRM THAT I HAVE VERIFIED ABOVE ANSWERS AND THAT THEY ARE TRUE

P. M. G. O. Form No. 1 (Red) Brisco Holder (Registrant's signature or mark) (OVER)

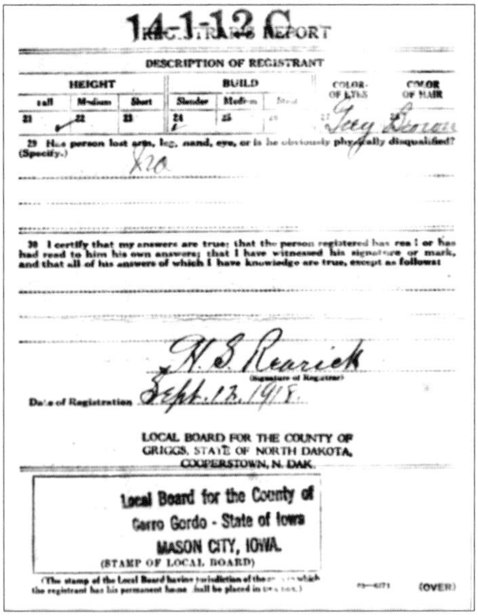

14-1-12 C

REGISTRAR'S REPORT

DESCRIPTION OF REGISTRANT

HEIGHT Tall	Medium	Short	BUILD Slender	Medium	Stout	COLOR OF EYES	COLOR OF HAIR
21	22 ✓	23	24 ✓	25	26	27 Grey	28 Brown

29 Has person lost arm, leg, hand, eye, or is he obviously physically disqualified? (Specify.) No

30 I certify that my answers are true; that the person registered has read or has had read to him his own answers; that I have witnessed his signature or mark, and that all of his answers of which I have knowledge are true, except as follows:

H. S. Rearick (Signature of Registrar)

Date of Registration Sept. 12, 1918

LOCAL BOARD FOR THE COUNTY OF GRIGGS, STATE OF NORTH DAKOTA, COOPERSTOWN, N. DAK.

Local Board for the County of Cerro Gordo - State of Iowa MASON CITY, IOWA

(STAMP OF LOCAL BOARD)

(The stamp of the Local Board having jurisdiction of the area in which the registrant has his permanent home shall be placed in this box.)

(OVER)

Figure 7-7: WWI draft registration card for Brisco Washington Holder (front and back)

World War I draft registration cards completed by approximately 24 million men living in the U.S. in 1917 and 1918. Information that may be found for an individual includes name, place of residence, date and place of birth, race, country of citizenship, occupation, and employer. Also included is the name and address of the registrant's nearest relative, which can be either a clue to connect an individual to the rest of his family *or* a confirmation that you have located a long-lost relative.

One of my most exciting genealogical finds came when Ancestry.com completed its digitization and scanning of these records. I had been desperately searching for a missing great-uncle, Brisco Washington Holder, who left home in Rome, Georgia, in about 1906. I entered his name in the search template as an exact search. Sure enough, a results page yielded a match.

This listing and the "View Record" page provided me with a middle name and a date of birth, neither of which I had known before. However, when I clicked the "View Image" link, even more information was revealed, as shown in figure 7-7.

The draft registration card was obviously completed by Brisco, based on a comparison of his signature and other handwriting on the card. From Georgia he had found his way to live in Mason City, Cerro Gordo County,

Iowa, and worked as a separator tender for Max Wild of Griggs, North Dakota. (Research for Max Wild in the 1910 Federal Census showed that he was in the grain business.) Brisco stated his age as 41 and listed his oldest brother, E. E. Holder of Rome, Georgia, as his nearest relative, which verified that I had the match I wanted.

The back of the card was almost as exciting as the front. The physical description of Brisco told me he was tall, slender, and had gray eyes and brown hair. I have only seen one photograph of Brisco, and these details help bring his appearance to life for me. The remaining information was completed by the registrar, H. S. Rearick, on 12 September 1918, which was the date of the third draft call in the U.S. for World War I. The stamps of the local draft boards of counties in both North Dakota and Iowa seems contradictory, but it is possible that the Griggs County, North Dakota, draft board prestamped cards and sent a supply to the Cerro Gordo County, Iowa, board for use in the third draft call. I may never resolve that discrepancy, but I did find Brisco on 12 September 1918.

U.S. World War II Army Enlistment Records, 1938–1946

A database of more recent military records is the "U.S. World War II Army Enlistment Records, 1938–1946." Figure 7-8 (on the next page) shows an example from this database, found using the search methods outlined in chapter 2.

As you can see from the example of Joe B. Mason, his year of birth and location are listed and his nationality noted. His enlistment date of 4 December 1942 at Camp Croft, South Carolina, as a private is also noted. He was six feet tall, weighed 137 pounds, had four years of college, and was married.

U.S. World War II Army Enlistment Records, 1938-1946 about Joe B Mason

Name:	**Joe B Mason**
Birth Year:	1914
Race:	White, citizen *(White)*
Nativity State or Country:	North Carolina
State:	North Carolina
County or City:	Almanc
Enlistment Date:	4 Dec 1942
Enlistment State:	South Carolina
Enlistment City:	Camp Croft
Branch:	Branch Immaterial - Warrant Officers, USA
Branch Code:	Branch Immaterial - Warrant Officers, USA
Grade:	Private
Grade Code:	Private
Term of Enlistment:	Enlistment for the duration of the War or other emergency, plus six months, subject to the discretion of the President or otherwise according to law
Component:	Selectees (Enlisted Men)
Source:	Civil Life
Education:	4 years of college
Civil Occupation:	Master, Ship or Mail Clerk (Clerk, postal or mail.) or Personnel Clerk or Traffic Rate Clerk or Dispatcher, Motor Vehicle
Marital Status:	Married
Height:	72
Weight:	137

Save This Record
Attach this record to a person in your tree as a source record, or save for later evaluation.

Save ▾

Figure 7-8: U.S. World War II Army enlistment record

The fact that an enlistment record exists would point to ordering a copy of any military service records from NARA. You might also want to check the Ancestry.com "World War II Prisoners of War, 1941–1946," the "WWI, WWII, and Korean War Casualty Listings," and the "World War II and Korean Conflict Veterans Interred Overseas" databases for any listing. These may confirm or refute any hypotheses that the person was taken prisoner, killed, or buried overseas.

WW II United News Newsreels, 1942-1946

One of the most exciting new additions to the military records collection is "World War II United News Newsreels, 1942–1946." Newsreels provided information and insight to a news-hungry American public. The newsreels in this collection provide the entire enthralling video content of each of these historic accounts. Note that there is also a version of this database available to nonsubscribers, but it is much smaller.

The search form for the newsreels collection, shown in figure 7-9, allows you to enter a keyword and to narrow your search to a specific year. You also can browse all the newsreel descriptions for a single year or the entire collection.

Figure 7-9:"WWII United News Newsreels, 1942-1946"search form

The results list, a portion of which is shown in figure 7-10, contains a description of each matching newsreel, including the names of people who appear in the film.

When you find a newsreel you want to view, click on the United News graphic at the left and a new page will open. A great deal of descriptive information is included at the bottom of the page.

The video window in the center of the page contains the United News logo, as shown in figure 7-11 (on the next page). It also contains a white arrowhead. Clicking on the arrowhead on the video or the black arrowhead at the bottom left will begin playing the newsreel video. The length

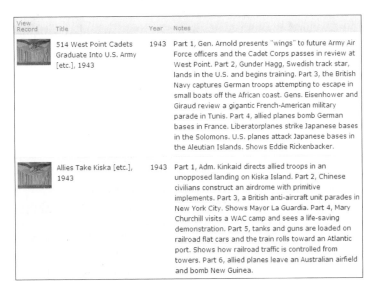

Figure 7-10: Newsreel results

Figure 7-11: "Newsreels" page

of the video is displayed under the video screen, and a progress bar will move as the newsreel plays.

You can change the size of the video window in a couple of ways. You can click on the bar beneath the video window labeled "Click here to see larger video format." Click on the bar again, which is now labeled "Click here to see smaller video format," and the window will be reduced to its original size. If you want to display the newsreel in full-screen mode, click the little icon to the right of the progress bar. This will expand the video area. You can exit full-screen mode at any time by pressing ESC.

You can control the volume using either your computer speakers or by clicking and dragging on the sound icon to the right of the full-screen mode icon beneath the video screen.

I expect that you will find these newsreels fascinating and compelling. They provide a multimedia experience that brings this historic time period to life.

Summary

If you've followed along and traveled through the Ancestry.com databases in this chapter, you've got a good sampling of the wealth of databases in the Military Records collection and how to work with them. We've focused on the American-related military records. However, there are military records in the other geographical areas of the Ancestry family:

- **Ancestry.co.uk**—The "Indian Army Quarterly List for 1 January 1912," "The Royal Irish Constabulary 1816–1921"; "British Army Pensioners Abroad, 1772–1899"; and others. The list continues to grow.

- **Ancestry.ca**—The "United Empire Loyalists"; "War of 1812: Miscellaneous Canadian Records"; and the "Rebellion of 1837, Upper Canada" databases are included, and there are more to come.

- **Ancestry.au and Ancestry.de**—Military records databases are being evaluated for addition to these two geographies.

Ancestry.com continues to be committed to expanding their military databases *and* the historical military reference materials to help you with your research. As you continue to hone your database search skills, you will be prepared to effectively use each new resource as it is added. In the meantime, continue to use Internet search engines and the libraries' and archives' collections on the Internet to expand your knowledge, and study political history, social history, and geography to place your ancestors in context and bring their military experiences to life.

Chapter 8

Immigration Records

Immigration is generally defined as the process of entering one country from another, often to take up permanent residence. The migration of a person from one place to another is a fascinating study. It involves the study of geography, history, social and physical conditions, and any number of other factors.

Immigration Records at Ancestry.com

The collection of immigration records databases at Ancestry. com is unequalled anywhere in the world. It includes indexed and digitized images of all readily available U.S. immigration passenger lists from 1820 to 1964; pre-1820 immigration references; available crew lists from post-1900; emigrant lists from parts of Germany; Canadian immigration records; denizations, naturalizations, and oaths of allegiance; naturalization stub books; and a variety of important reference books and other indexes.

In 1819, the U.S. Congress passed legislation requiring that the ship's master of each incoming ship carrying passengers provide a complete manifest of these passengers. The law was implemented in 1820, and these documents were presented to the customs officer at the port of arrival before any passenger disembarked. On a monthly basis, the customs officer was required to prepare a summary of all ship arrivals and a list of passenger arrivals. This report was sent to Washington, D.C. Ultimately, when the National Archives and Records Administration (NARA) acquired the massive collection of passenger lists, it also received the customs officers' reports.

NARA has microfilmed all available passenger lists. In cases where original manifests had not survived, the customs officers' reports were used as substitute documents for microfilming. Consequently, the collection of passenger list records is incredibly close to complete for the 140 years it spans.

Passenger lists provide invaluable details, such as names, gender, occupation, accompanying travelers, origin/port of departure, date and place of arrival, and others, all in the original handwriting. Later lists included much more detail, such as intended destination, place of birth, financial assets, and even the name of the nearest living relative in the country of origin.

An estimated 85 percent of Americans have an immigrant ancestor included in the Ancestry.com passenger list collection, which covers the height of American immigration. The passenger list collection records the arrivals of more than 100 million passengers and features printable images of 7 million original passenger list documents. The collection also contains approximately one thousand images of the actual ships immigrants traveled on.

Until the completion of this project, U.S. passenger list records could be found only on microfilm or in limited selections online at various dispersed locations, such as libraries and museums across the nation. For the first time, people can look to a single centralized source online to find all readily available passenger list records. More than a hundred American ports of arrival are represented in the compilation, including the entire collection of passenger list records from Ellis Island (1892–1957), a historic landmark and icon of immigration. The collection also accounts for popular ports in Boston, Baltimore, New Orleans, and the Angel Island receiving station in San Francisco. All of this content makes "jumping the pond" significantly more feasible.

Searching the Collections

There are such varied immigration materials on Ancestry.com that it makes sense for us to explore a number of different databases. First, here are some tips that you should consider when tracing your immigrant ancestors.

- **Search for your family members in U.S. records before looking in foreign records**—You are more likely to find an immigrant's birthplace or last foreign residence in American records. U.S. federal census records, beginning in 1850, include the names of everyone in a household and list each person's place of birth. Census records from 1880 and later indicate the birthplace of the individual and his or her parents. Census records from 1900 to 1930 include all this information, plus the year of arrival for a person who immigrated and whether they are an alien or a naturalized citizen or whether their naturalization paperwork process is in progress. Native language spoken is also a key clue in your research. Exhaust all

American resources before searching in sources from
other countries because the American records can contain
invaluable leads to point you to the country of origin.
Remember, however, that boundaries changed and that
you should consider the geopolitical and governmental
jurisdictions at the time a person was born, married, and
immigrated. The presence of different country names on
two U.S. federal censuses may be indicative of a boundary
change between the censuses and may not represent the
actual country from whence the person emigrated at the
time of his or her relocation.

- **Consider immigration patterns**—Your ancestors may not
  have boarded a ship in their home country. For example,
  the famous Von Trapp family was Austrian, but to escape
  the Nazis, they traveled to Italy before boarding a ship to
  America. Your ancestors may also have stopped in other
  countries on the way to America. These "layovers" may
  have been a day, a month, a year, or even generations.
  It is important to consider the different aspects of your
  ancestors' journeys and take into account any less common
  circumstances they may have experienced. Therefore,
  historical research into migration patterns and any
  recruitment programs or schemes to induce people to
  emigrate elsewhere may be invaluable to your research.

- **Look beyond Ellis Island**—Although the Ellis Island era is
  certainly the most famous time of immigration to the U.S.,
  immigrants have been making their way to America for
  hundreds of years. The main wave of immigrants that came
  through Ellis Island arrived in New York between 1892
  and 1924. You can narrow your search if you determine
  not only when your ancestors arrived but also if they came
  in through New York or some other port of entry. Again,

historical research into migration patterns and trends can greatly benefit your quest.

- **Consider other record types**—Other types of records may provide clues to your immigrant ancestors' origin and date and place of arrival. Voter registration records and military service and pension records may contain information about the national origin of your ancestor and his or her naturalization. Don't overlook the Family & Local Histories collection at Ancestry.com or at libraries and archives. These may include references to your ancestors, their families, and even some personal details about their immigration and where they settled. If your ancestors hailed from England, Ireland, Scotland, Wales, Isle of Man, or the Channel Islands from the nineteenth and twentieth centuries, the United Kingdom and Ireland Records collection—which includes censuses, parish records, and civil registration indexes—may provide significant help in your research. Keep an open mind about the different types of records that just may contain references to your ancestors' immigration details.

Some excellent books can help you research your ancestors' immigration and naturalization. Here are the bibliographic citations for five that are considered authoritative standards:

Colletta, John Philip, Ph.D. *They Came in Ships: A Guide to Finding Your Immigrant Ancestor's Arrival Record*. 3rd ed. Orem, UT: Ancestry, 2002.

Morgan, George G. *How to Do Everything with Your Genealogy*. Emeryville, CA: McGraw-Hill/Osborne, 2004.

Schaefer, Christina K. *Guide to Naturalization Records of the United States*. Baltimore, MD: Genealogical Publishing Co., 1997.

Szucs, Loretto Dennis. *They Became Americans: Finding Naturalization Records and Ethnic Origins*. Orem, UT: Ancestry, 1998.

Tepper, Michael. *American Passenger Arrival Records: A Guide to the Records of Immigrants*. Baltimore, MD: Genealogical Publishing Co., 1999.

You have already learned that the search forms vary for different databases and collections, depending on their content. This time we want to search all immigration records, so on the "Search" page, click "Immigration & Emigration" in the "Go Directly to a Specific Title or Collection" section.

Let's say that we want to search for physicist Enrico Fermi, who visited the United States on several occasions to attend conferences and deliver lectures. I performed an exact search for "Enrico Fermi" and found six results in the "New York Passenger Lists, 1820–1957" database. The results are shown in figure 8-1.

The detailed list allows me to view a record of the information. I can also view the original passenger list (or manifest) by clicking "View Passenger List." Figure 8-2 (on the next page) shows a portion of this digitized passenger list for his arrival on 16 June 1930. Note that the gender for Enrico Fermi in the record for this image is listed

View Record	Name	Arrival Date	Estimated Birth Year	Port of Departure	Ethnicity/ Nationality	Ship Name	View Ship Image
View Record ★★★	Enrico Fermi	16 Jun 1930	abt 1901	Naples, Italy	Italian (South) *(Italian)*	Roma	📷
View Record ★★★	Enrico Fermi	13 Jun 1933	abt 1901	Genoa, Italy	Italian (South) *(Italian)*	Conte Di Savoia	📷
View Record ★★★	Enrico Fermi	20 Jun 1935	abt 1901	Naples, Italy	Italian;Italian (South) *(Italian)*	Roma	📷
View Record ★★★	Enrico Fermi	2 Jul 1936	abt 1901	Naples, Italy	Italian;Italian (South) *(Italian)*	Conte Di Savoia	📷
View Record ★★★	Enrico Fermi	22 Jun 1937	abt 1901	Naples, Italy	Italian;Italian (South) *(Italian)*	Roma	📷
View Record ★★★	Enrico Fermi	16 Sep 1954		Paris, France			

Figure 8-1: Results for Enrico Fermi

Form 500 U. S. DEPARTMENT OF LABOR	List **6**						**LIST OR MANIFEST OF ALIEN PASSE**				
				ALL ALIENS arriving at a port of continental United States from a foreign port or a port of the insular possessions of the United States, and all aliens arriving at a p							
				S. S. "R O M A".		Passengers sailing from	N A P L E S				

1	2	3		4	5	6	7	8	9	10	11		12
No. on List	HEAD-TAX STATUS (This column for use of Government officials only)	NAME IN FULL		Age		Sex	Married or single	Calling or occupation	Able to—		Nationality. (Country of which citizen or subject)	† Race or people	Place of birth		Immigration Visa Number
		Family name	Given name	Yrs.	Mos.				Read what language (or, if exemption claimed, on what ground)	Write			Country	City or town	
1	TRANSIT	MOLINARI	BERNARDINO	50		m	M	longshoreman	Italian	yes	Italy	Italian S.	Italy	Roma	185 N.I.
2	TRANSIT	MOLINARI	MARIA	40		f	M	wife	Italian	yes	Italy	Italian S.	Greece.	Malta	184 N.I.
3		BATTAGLIA	GIULIANO	37		m	M	owner	yes	Italian	yes	Italy	Italian S	Italy	Paltima	129 N.I.
4		PLOWRIGHT	AIMIE	59		M	M	companion	yes	English	yes	British	English	England	Lawton	466205 469611
5		BRANCA	MAUD	64		f	W	mother	yes	Italian	yes	Italy	American	England	Maine	112 N.I.
6		SANOBINI	ANNUNZIATA	40		f	S	dld serv.	yes	Italian	yes	Italy	Italian N.	Italy	Sagat R.	111 N.I.
7		FERMI	ENRICO	29		f	M	teacher	yes	Italian	yes	Italy	Italian S	Italy	Roma	336 N.I.
8		FERMI CAPON	LAURA	23		f	M	wife	yes	Italian	yes	Italy	Italian S.	Italy	do	337 N.I.
9	DIPLOMAT	CASARDI	Aubrey	27		m	S	Vice cons.	yes	Italian	yes	Italy	Italian S	Italy	Siena	Non imm. 327 Diplom

Figure 8-2: Detail of a passenger list showing Enrico Fermi and his wife in 1930

as "Female" on the first entry. When you examine the actual passenger list, notice that the preparer of the list made a typographical error and typed an "f" instead of an "m" under the "Sex" column. Enrico is traveling with his wife, Laura Fermi Capon. He is listed as a twenty-nine-year-old teacher from Italy who was born in Rome.

Where Ancestry.com has been able to acquire a photograph or other image of the ship, the option to "View Ship Image" is displayed on the detailed search result list. In this case, the Fermis traveled aboard the *Roma*, and an image was available (see figure 8-3). If you were related to

Figure 8-3: Image of the ship Roma

You are here: Search > Immigration > Passenger Ships and Images > R > Roma > 1926 1943

Figure 8-4: Quick Links to the image of the Roma

Enrico Fermi, the images of both the ship's manifest *and* the ship itself would be great to save to your own computer and to add to your collection of information about his life.

Note the date range in the Quick Links at the top of the page (see figure 8-4). Sometimes Ancestry.com has been able to acquire multiple images of the same ship from different time periods. If you click on the link titled "Roma," the page shown in figure 8-5 is displayed. There are two links to images: one for the years 1902 to 1929 and another for the years 1926 to 1943. These are the years for which these

Figure 8-5: Page showing multiple ship image links.

images were typically used for advertising, press releases, newspaper stories, postcards, and other print media. If you click on each link, you will see different images of the ship. Ancestry.com has matched the image from the appropriate time period, in this case 1930, with the entry on the detailed results list of my search.

Sample Immigration Databases and Titles

One of the most comprehensive immigration resources is the *Passenger and Immigration Lists Index, 1590s–1900s*. First published by P. William Filby in 1985, the index has been compiled for many published sources, manuscripts, and other resources, and a new supplement has been published annually. Gale Research has created a database of this landmark series, and Ancestry.com has made it available online. The 2005 data set contains approximately 4,461,000 individuals who arrived in United States and Canadian ports from the 1500s through the 1900s. Each entry has been indexed by name and is searchable by keyword. For each individual listed, you may find the following information:

- Name and age

- Year and place of arrival

- Naturalization or other record of immigration

- Source of record

- Names of all accompanying family members together with their ages and relationship to the primary individual

I will search for my ancestor Joseph Alexander, who was born approximately 1660 and immigrated to America. I have already proved through land records that he purchased and settled land in Virginia, so an arrival in Maryland (probably Baltimore Harbor) seems most likely. I will include this as well.

In this case, the second entry of my results (see figure 8-6)—the arrival in 1714—seems like it could be the one,

View Record	Joseph Alexander	1811	Baltimore, MD
★★★			
View Record	Joseph Alexander	1714	Maryland
★★★			

Figure 8-6: Results for Joseph Alexander

so I click it and the full record shown in figure 8-7 (on the next page) is displayed. This gives me a full bibliographic entry for a primary immigrant named James Alexander who was accompanied by his father, Joseph Alexander. This is consistent with the pedigree I have traced. I can use the "Source Bibliography" to locate the book. I can also use this information to locate and obtain copies of pertinent pages from *The Magazine of American Genealogy* mentioned in the

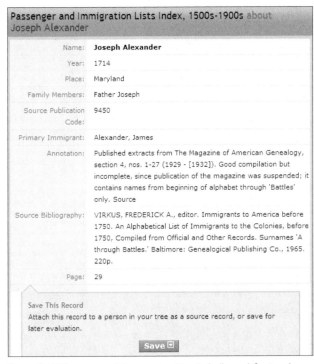

Figure 8-7: "Passenger and Immigration Lists Index" record for Joseph Alexander

"Annotation" section. Either or both of these may point me to the original records from which the information was derived.

Note that some immigration and emigration databases are record collections, while others are indexes or digitized book images. An example of the latter is the *Emigrants from Fellbach (Baden-Wuerttemberg, Germany), 1735–1930.* Books will generally be searchable using a form and browsable by table of contents, section, chapter, index, and so on.

Among the databases in this collection are some that deal with naturalization. Many of these are simple indexes to the original declarations of intention, petitions for naturalization, or naturalization certificate stub books. However, there are some digitized images of actual application files, and the overall collection continues to grow. Let's look at three examples of these naturalization-related resources.

The "Juab County, Utah Citizenship Certificate Stubs, 1908–1928" is an example of an index to actual naturalization certificates. At the time that the court grants the petition for naturalization, after having verified that all requirements have been met and that an oath of allegiance has been administered, a certificate is issued. The uniquely numbered certificate comes from a book that contains an informational stub and the certificate, perforated on one edge. The stub book acts as something like a checkbook register and lists the name of the naturalized citizen, the date, the court, and the certificate number.

Most often these stub books have remained in the courthouse in which the naturalization took place. Once you have the name of the individual and his or her certificate number, it becomes simpler to locate the person's naturalization file(s) and obtain copies of application forms and correspondence. Those documents may provide the most direct link back to the country of origin, a birthplace, a date and port of arrival, and other clues.

After searching for "Mortensen" via the "Juab County, Utah Citizenship Certificate Stubs, 1908–1928" form, I find only one match: a gentleman named Gotlieb Edward Mortensen (see figure 8-8). The information on the search results entry tells me that he was

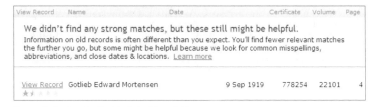

Figure 8-8: Results for Gotlieb Edward Mortensen

naturalized on 9 September 1919. He was issued naturalization certificate #778254, and the certificate was attached to the stub that resides in "Volume 22101" on "Page 4."

Normally this information would be sufficient for me to continue my research. However, if I want to save the record in one of my Family Trees or to my Shoebox, make comments, or print a copy for my files, I would click the "View Record" link and take action from there.

View Record	Name	Declaration Volume	Declaration Page	Petition Volume	Petition Page
View Record ★★★	Mary Johnson	474	381		

Figure 8-9: Results for Mary Johnson's Declaration of Intention

A second example is the "Index to Declaration of Intention for Naturalization: New York County, 1907–1924." The results page for a search for "Mary Johnson" shows one match (see figure 8-9). Mary Johnson's Declaration of Intention is recorded in "Declaration Volume 474, Page 381."

In some cases, such as that of Bernard Jones, shown in figure 8-10, when both the Declaration of Intent to become a citizen and the Petition for Naturalization are filed and processed by the same court, this database shows both index entries. Using the index entries, you

View Record	Name	Declaration Volume	Declaration Page	Petition Volume	Petition Page
View Record ★★★	Bernard Jones	1	345	12	54
View Record ★★★	Bernard Jones	224	43		

Figure 8-10: Results for Bernard Jones's Declaration of Intention and Petition for Naturalization

should be able to locate and obtain copies of the applications and any other pertinent documents. These documents are typically stored in the NARA branch that holds the records for that court district. Loretto D. Szucs's book *They Became Americans* and Christina K. Schaefer's reference *Guide to the Naturalization Records of the United States* will help you locate the correct NARA branch to contact for document copies.

The third example I want to share with you is the "New York Petitions for Naturalization" database. What differentiates this from the previous two examples is that it presents images of the actual index cards to the petitions for naturalization. Using the search form for this database, I looked for "Abraham Jones."

The results page yields seven entries for people with the name Abraham Jones. As always, you can click on the "View

Record" link and save information to one of your trees or your Shoebox, make comments, and print the record.

The index cards vary in content. The simplest list only the name of the petitioner, the date of the petition, and the petition number. However, let me show you two sample index cards with more detailed information.

The first example is located under the second entry for Abraham Jones, who was naturalized on 18 October 1879 (see figure 8-11). This card shows that he was formerly a subject of the emperor of Russia. His address and occupation are also listed. However, the entry of Superior Court, New York County, under "Title and Location of Court" is a great clue as to where to find his naturalization file. The card even tells you to seek it in Bundle 300 and record number 32.

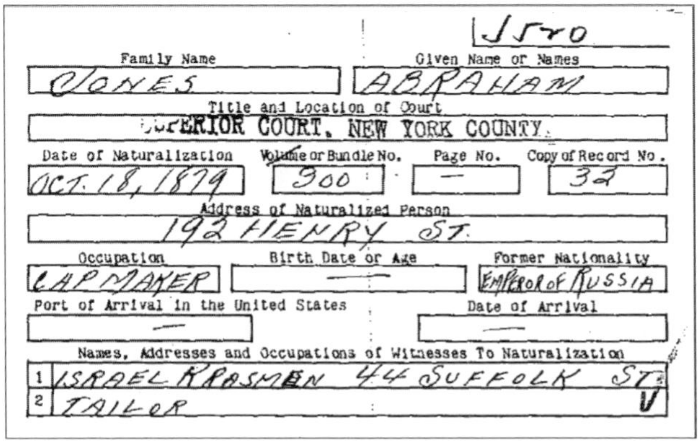

Figure 8-11: Abraham Jones's index card—18 October 1879

The second example is located under the seventh entry on the "Exact Search Results" page, this one for an Abraham Leopold Jones, who was naturalized on 18 February 1929 (see figure 8-12). This card shows his petition number, 136882, and his Declaration of Intention number, 159510. Both of these reference numbers can

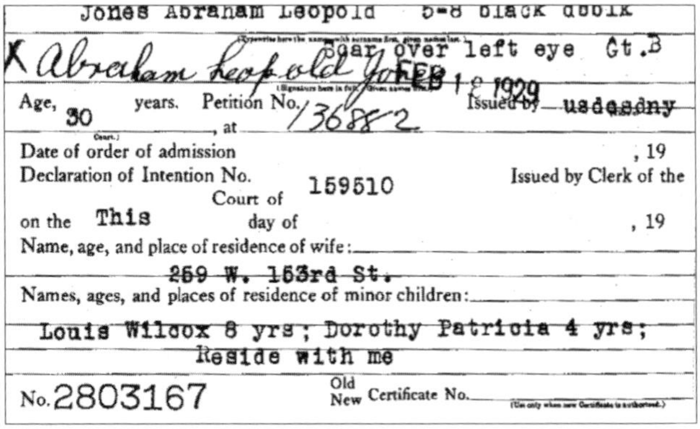

Figure 8-12: Abraham Leopold Jones's index card—18 February 1929

be used to help locate the original documents. The card also lists additional useful information, such as his address, the names of his two children, and a few physical characteristics.

The disparity of information in the formats of the index cards should make you even more curious as to what is on the actual application forms and other documents in the files.

Summary

As you can see, there are many different types of immigration-related databases in the Ancestry.com collection. You will find much to explore as you learn a great deal about immigration and naturalization across the centuries.

Chapter 9

Pictures, Newspapers, and Maps

The old adage, "A picture is worth a thousand words" is more accurate to genealogists than, perhaps, to the average person. Photographs, picture postcards, yearbooks, and newsreels are among the visual materials we use to learn more details about people and places. They help establish context and portray life at specific times.

Images of old newspapers can also add context and provide vital or interesting information, and maps, atlases, and gazetteers can help you find locations and visualize your ancestral homeland.

Ancestry.com has built an impressive library of visual materials that can contribute to your research. There are literally millions of images and names in these collections, ranging from member-contributed photographs of people and tombstones to African-American photographs, Civil War photos, panoramic shots of places, and historic postcards, as well large collections of newspapers and maps.

Searching for Pictures

The Pictures collection at Ancestry.com contains a wide variety of images. They include individuals, groups, families, buildings, cemeteries and markers, places, events, passenger ships, postcards, yearbooks, and military conflicts.

As always, you can search the entire collection or use the Card Catalog to search for specific databases. Let's start by choosing the "Library of Congress Photo Collection, 1840–2000."

The search form is just like that for any other Ancestry.com database, but because the photograph collections are indexed by caption or title and keywords, using the name fields may not be the best way to go. For example, if you enter "Judy Garland" in the name fields, you'll get no search results. Similarly, if you search for "Abraham Lincoln," the results are not photographs related to the president; they are pictures of various places.

For these collections, using keywords is the best way to find what you're looking for. Thus, if you enter "Abraham Lincoln" in the "Keyword" field (see figure 9-1), the search results will include an image of the "Gettysburg Address," photographs, portraits, statues, lithographs, stereograph cards, ships named after him, and more. If you browse through the results, you'll find an item labeled "Abraham Lincoln, bust, last photographic portrait." There are two years at the right: 1809 and 1865.

Figure 9-1: Searching "Library of Congress Photo Collection, 1840–2000" using the "Keyword" field

The first, 1809, is the year of Lincoln's birth; the second, 1865, refers to his year of death *and* to the year in which the photograph was taken. (The actual date of the photograph is 10 April 1865, four days before his assassination.) If you browse the search results, you should also see a full-length portrait of Mrs. Abraham Lincoln. There are four dates at the right: 1818, 1860, 1865, and 1882. She lived from 1818 to 1882; the photograph is undated but the photo is purported to have been taken between 1860 and 1865.

You can click on either the thumbnail image of the graphic or on the text link on the page. This will open the image record. The "Abraham Lincoln, bust, last photographic portrait" is shown in figure 9-2.

Along the same lines, if you are searching for an image of a specific place, don't enter it in the Location field; enter the name of the location in the "Keyword" field. You can use quotation marks to narrow your search. For example, I entered "hyde park, new york" in order to locate photographs of President Franklin Delano Roosevelt's. I chose to spell out the state name rather than use an abbreviation because I know the Library of Congress probably spelled it out that way. That would give me a stronger possibility for matches. However, it is never a bad idea to try searching *both* ways.

Note that when you start a new search from within an existing search, another form will be displayed. Look at the top of the form and choose whether to search all of the picture collections or just the one in which you have just been searching.

Figure 9- 2: Last photograph of Abraham Lincoln

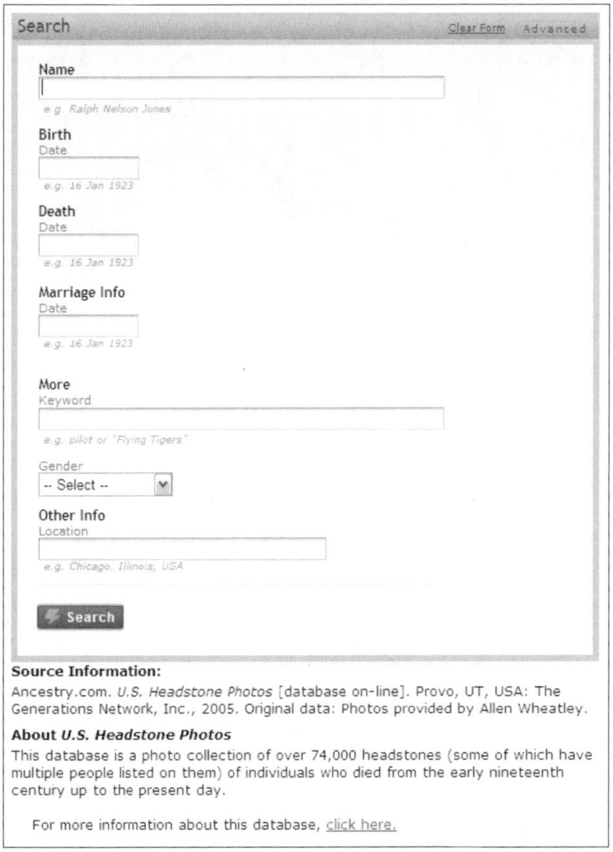

Figure 9-3: The "U.S. Headstone Photos" search form and database information

Let's look at another database, the "U.S. Headstone Photos" collection. This database is relatively small in comparison to others. However, you can contribute your headstone photographs to Ancestry.com for inclusion in the collection if you like. You'll find information about contributing to the collection under the "About U.S. Headstone Photos" descriptive section located beneath the search form (shown in figure 9-3). You will need to click "Click here" to access information on adding your own photos to the collection.

In this database, the use of the name fields is appropriate. If you know birth and/or death years, you can use those to narrow your search. The "+/-" year estimation option is available if you are unsure of the exact year. Remember, though, that not all the records include dates. The "Keyword" field can also be used to narrow your search for other information. I conducted a search for the name "Ida Wilson"; the top of the results page returned is shown in figure 9-4 on the next page.

There were 392 results, sorted by relevance. In essence, there are 392 Wilson headstones in this database. The first

three in the list have
a forename of Ida;
the fourth has an
initial "I." in the name.
These were the most
relevant possible
matches found and so
were placed at the top
of the list.

Headstone	Name	Birth Date	Death Date	Cemetery Name	Cemetery State	Relationship
	We didn't find any strong matches, but these still might be helpful. Information on old records is often different than you expect. You'll find fewer relevant matches the further you go, but some might be helpful because we look for common misspellings, abbreviations, and close dates & locations. Learn more					
	Ida Wilson	1887	1946	Peoples	Texas	Self
	Ida E Wilson	1906	1970	Oak Grove	Texas	Self

As usual, I can
click on the search
panel at the left of the

Figure 9-4: Search results for Ida Wilson

results to refine my search. If I select "Match terms exactly," for
either the whole search or specific search criteria, the search
will be performed again and only those exact matches will be
displayed. For example, if I select it for the
whole search, only results for people named
"Ida" and "Wilson" are returned.

When I click on either the graphic or the
text link for the first entry of the results page
shown in figure 9-4—the entry for Ida Wilson
who was born in 1887 and died in 1946—
you will see a record page containing an
image of the headstone (shown in figure 9-5)
and the transcription information (shown in
figure 9-6 on the next page).

Figure 9-5: Tombstone of Ida Wilson

Member Photos

One of the most interesting collections is the Member Photos
collection. Millions of photos and other images have been
digitized and added to personal Family Trees at Ancestry.com.
If the owner of the tree has designated the tree as Public, the

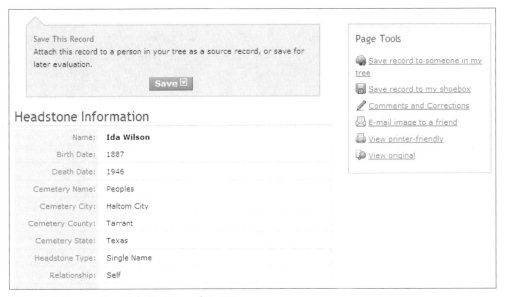

Figure 9-6: Bottom of Record for Tombstone of Ida Wilson

information becomes accessible for other members to view. If not, all the images are still listed, but you will have to contact the owner in order to get additional information and, perhaps, a copy of the image.

To view an individual record that you've found on a results page, click the photo or the name, as with other photo collections. Figure 9-7 on the next page shows the record for "Nettie Holder Sims age 85" in the Public Member Photos collection.

You have several options on this page. You can add that picture to *your* Family Tree. It will remain there until the owner chooses to delete or change the image. You will also see a link showing that this image is attached Nettie M. Holder in a tree. Click that link and the individual page for Ms. Holder from the Family Tree in which she is included will be displayed.

At the bottom of this record page is a "Comments" area where you can enter a subject and some text. Your comment

Nettie Holder Sims age 85

Added by jackinell1946 *on 14 Oct 2006*

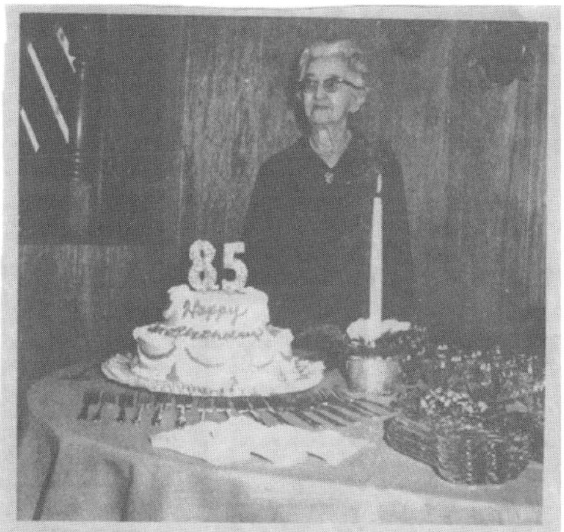

MRS. NETTIE SIMS was entertained by her children and grandchildren, with a party honoring her on her 85th birthday on Saturday afternoon, December 23, at the home of her son, Mr. and Mrs. Jack Sims and Pam. The other members of her family, all of whom were present for the occasion, were her son, Mr. and Mrs. Carl Sims of Mt. Vernon; her grandchildren and great-grandchildren, Mr. and Mrs. Donald Tinsley, Gregg, Angela and Todd of Springfield, Mo.; Mr. and Mrs. Danny Sims and Stephen, Greenville; and Mr. and Mrs. Donald Herrmann of Austin. A birthday cake, with 85 in gold on top, was served along with punch during the afternoon to about 40 other relatives and friends who called to say "Happy Birthday" to Mrs. Sims. She received many gifts. (Optic-Herald Staff Photo).

This photo was taken on the 85th birthday of "Mrs. Nettie" at the home of her son Jack M Sims.

Tools

View original
Print

Photo information

Location

Date

Attached to in this tree

Nettie M Holder
1888 - 1978

Comments

There are no comments on **Nettie Holder Sims age 85** yet. You can add a comment for others to see below.

ADD A NEW COMMENT

Add a comment below to communicate with others who may see this.

Subject:

Comment:

Add comment

Figure 9-7: Record for Nettie Holder Sims age 85

will be shown to anyone else who views this photograph. Comments are displayed just beneath the Comments header.

Private Photos

Many people designate their Family Trees as private. This means that you cannot view records or images in that tree. You can, however, still search through a database of these photos. It's called "Private Member Photos." When you've conducted a search in this database, you won't see any photo thumbnails (because they're private!). Instead, you see information about that person as well as a small icon beside the name of the Family Tree

Figure 9-8: Results in "Private Member Trees"

in which the result appears (see figure 9-8). When you hover over that icon, a popup appears, explaining why you can't view the photo and giving you the option to contact the owner of the tree for access to the photo.

On the new page, click on the orange button labeled **Make Connection** and you'll be able to try and contact the owner of the tree. Note that in some cases, the owner has opted not to be contacted. Your message will be sent anonymously through the Ancestry Connection Service. If the person responds and you have something in common to share, either or both of you can share e-mail addresses so that you can begin communicating directly.

Other Great Image Collections

There are three other very significant collections that include great images and can be found in the Pictures category. One is the U.S. School Yearbooks collection, which consists of more than a million names from middle school, junior high, and high school yearbooks from across the United States. This collection is discussed in greater detail in chapter 11.

Another collection is the Historical Postcards collection. It features more than 50,000 images of postcards (including both sides of each card) dating from about 1893 to 1963. They preserve a pictorial history of places all over the world and provide you with visual context for places where your

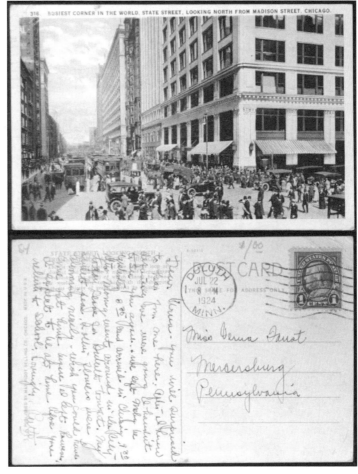

Figure 9-9: State Street in Chicago, Illinois, from the Historical Postcard collection

ancestors lived, worked, and visited. Figure 9-9 shows the intersection of State and Madison streets in Chicago, Illinois.

You can search this database, but you will probably want to browse by country, state or province, county, and location. This database provides a view into the past, and you will want to spend time looking at and saving images to your Family Tree.

Still another collection is one we discussed in chapter 8, the World War II United News Newsreels, 1942–1946. These 267 newsreel films were produced by the U.S. Office of War Information (OWI). They were shown throughout the U.S. but were targeted to overseas viewers. The reels were released in several languages, including German. However, they were primarily distributed to Allied and neutral countries. Much of the footage was taken by military combat photographers and is in excellent condition. They average ten minutes in length and contain a vivid record of the era. You will be thrilled to see these newsreels and experience the news of the era as it was presented.

Searching Newspapers and Periodicals

Newspapers and periodicals are the chronicles of everyday life. In the past, in order to locate information about our ancestors and family members, it was necessary to either wade through stacks of old and fragile newspaper copies or pore endlessly, frame by frame, through microfilmed images of newspaper pages. Unless someone had manually compiled an index to some specific type of information, such as obituaries, quick searches and rapid access were not among our options.

Ancestry.com has brought together a wealth of newspaper resources that have been OCR-scanned to produce every-word indexes to help you quickly locate all references to a name or subject. New newspapers are added frequently.

Obituaries are a good example of information found in newspapers. They vary in the amount of information they contain, but many of them are genealogical goldmines, including information such as names, dates, places of birth and death, marriage information, and family relationships. You can find many obituaries at Ancestry.com.

What is OCR?

Optical Character Recognition, also known as OCR, is a method of scanning a document and using software to interpret and convert the image of the text into actual text that can then be read, indexed, and otherwise processed by a computer.

To search the Newspapers & Periodicals collection, simply click on the **Search** tab from any Ancestry.com page. The global search form is available at the top of the "Search" page. However, scroll down to the "Go Directly to a Specific Title or Collection" section. Click on "Newspapers & Periodicals" to access the search form for this collection. You can also browse specific titles using the Card Catalog.

In addition to a general search, you can search and browse specific titles. For example, click "San Antonio Express (San Antonio, Texas)" in the "Featured" section next to the newspapers and periodicals search form. Now you have the option of searching this newspaper specifically or browsing its contents by date (see figure 9-10). When you enter a month and year into the drop-downs, the calendar below will show days for which Ancestry.com has available images. When you click on the image, you will be brought to the image directly.

Some newspapers or periodicals may have their own search forms, so feel free to fiddle with their specific features.

Figure 9-10: Search form for "San Antonio Express (San Antonio, Texas)"

The United States Obituary Collection

The United States Obituary collection contains primarily recent obituaries from hundreds of newspapers. The collection, however, is growing, and some older obituaries from as far back as the early twentieth century are being added. Ancestry.com scours the Internet daily to find new obituaries and extract the facts into this database. They also provide source information and links to the full obituary text. If you're searching for a recently deceased ancestor, a living relative who might be mentioned in an obituary, or former classmates or neighbors, this is an excellent place to start.

The wealth of genealogical and biographical information to be found in an informative obituary certainly makes the effort of searching for one worthwhile. For many of our ancestors and relatives, an obituary may be the only "biographical sketch" that was ever devoted to that individual. In addition to names, dates, and places of birth, marriage, and death, the obituary often identifies relationships of the deceased as child, sibling, parent, grandparent, and so on to numerous other individuals. Obituaries may even suggest other documentation of an individual's death: a death certificate in another county because the hospital was located there, church or cemetery records (by identifying the place of burial or the officiating minister), or records of a coroner's inquest because the death was sudden or unexpected. You may learn about immigration and naturalization, military service, employment, membership in clubs and societies, church affiliations, and much more. The wealth of details in an obituary may open up many research avenues. You just need to learn to read between the lines for potential clues.

In an obituary search, remember that it is wise to investigate the files of *all* likely newspapers. It is impossible to know beforehand which, if any, paper is going to have the best obituary. Many cities have more than one paper, and an obituary for a specific individual could appear in more than one place. Many people in their later years go to live with children and often die far from where they spent most of their adult lives. But if they still had connections with the home community, there is a good chance that an obituary will appear there, perhaps a more detailed one than will be found in the community of death, where that person was just a new or temporary resident. However, the opposite may also be true.

To search thoroughly for obituaries, the best approach is to use a variety of tools, including both the United States Obituary collection and the entire Newspapers & Periodicals collection, and to conduct traditional research through local libraries, archives, and newspapers' archives.

The obituary collection provides a number of criteria fields on the form to allow you to expand or narrow your search. For this example, I performed a search for actress Jane Wyatt, who died in October 2006. You might remember her in the role of Margaret Anderson, the wife and mother on the 1950s television program *Father Knows Best*.

Since Ms. Wyatt was such a well-known actress, there were many obituaries that appeared in newspapers around the world, so there were many results. The sixth result is the one we want to view (see figure 9-11).

View Record ★★★✦	Anita Jane Wyatt	71	8 Jun 1934	18 Mar 2006	Craig Wyatt	Athens, TX, Us
View Record ★★★✦	Anita Jane Wyatt	71	8 Jun 1934	18 Mar 2006	Craig Wyatt	Crossville, TN, Us
View Record ★★★✦	Anita Jane Wyatt	71	8 Jun 1934	18 Mar 2006	Craig Wyatt	Logansport, IN, Us
View Record ★★★✦	Anita Jane Wyatt	71	8 Jun 1934	18 Mar 2006	Craig Wyatt	Palestine, TX, Us
View Record ★★★✦	Anita Jane Wyatt	71	8 Jun 1934	18 Mar 2006	Craig Wyatt	Gainesville, TX, Us
View Record ★★★✦	Jane Wyatt	96	abt 1910	20 Oct 2006	Only Human	St. Louis, MO, Us

Figure 9-11: Search results for Actress Jane Wyatt

United States Obituary Collection about Jane Wyatt	
Name of Deceased:	**Jane Wyatt**
Age at Death:	96
Birth Date:	abt 1910
Death Date:	20 Oct 2006
Newspaper Title:	St. Louis Post-Dispatch
Newspaper Location:	St. Louis, MO, Us
Obituary Publication Date:	23 Oct 2006
Other Persons Mentioned in Obituary:	Only Human; Margaret Anderson; Meg McDonald; Christopher Ward; Frank Capra

View full obituary

Save This Record
Attach this record to a person in your tree as a source record, or save for later evaluation.

Save ▾

Figure 9-12: Record for Actress Jane Wyatt

Many of the entries include Ms. Wyatt's age, but some do not. Remember that not all obituaries include a year of birth or an age at the time of death. Therefore, this is a field you might consider omitting in your initial query.

When we look at the record for Ms. Wyatt, shown in figure 9-12, in the area about other people mentioned in the obituary, there are mentions of "Only Human," part of the name of a play in which she appeared (*We're Only Human*). It also refers to "Margaret Anderson," the character she played on *Father Knows Best*. When you click the link labeled "View full obituary," you are often rewarded with the text of the obituary itself. However, in some cases the obituary has been captured from online editions of newspapers and periodicals on the Internet. Those obituaries often do not stay online forever. It is therefore important to refer to the source citation at the bottom of the record so that you can isolate the name of the publication, its publication location, and the date of publication. Armed with this information, you can usually request a copy of the obituary from the newspaper publisher or via interlibrary loan through your local library.

As you have seen with other records at Ancestry.com, you can save this record to your Family Tree or to your Shoebox for later evaluation. You can also make comments and corrections or display a printer-friendly version of this record for printing.

Further, you can make connections with other researchers who may be researching Jane Wyatt. We will discuss more about that process in another chapter.

Maps, Atlases, and Gazetteers

Maps, atlases, and gazetteers are indispensable reference materials and finding aids. They help us understand the physical location and geographic features of the areas in which our ancestors and their families lived. They also help us study and understand the geopolitical boundaries and, therefore, the records created at the time. If we know that state, territorial, county, provincial, and other jurisdictional boundaries changed at specific times, we can then determine where, why, and by whom records were created. We can also determine where the records were kept and, by extension and research, where they are likely to be stored today.

Visualizing the places your ancestors lived and where their life events occurred in geographical relation to one another helps you better understand them and their movements. It also helps you place them into context with the historical events and social patterns of their time.

Ancestry.com has compiled a most impressive collection of cartographic resources over the years, many of which are not otherwise easily located. You will definitely want to use the gazetteers and map resources in this collection to help locate the places where your ancestors were born, lived, migrated, worked, died, and were buried.

There are three types of resources in this collection:

- **Maps**—These are graphical representations of an area.

- **Atlases**—An atlas is a compilation of multiple maps. These are logically organized and indexed to facilitate easy location of places and physical features.

- **Gazetteers**—A gazetteer is a placename dictionary that helps you detrmine the precise location of features. An older gazetteer is essential for locating places that may have changed names or no longer exist.

There are more than a hundred collections of these materials at Ancestry.com at this writing, and the collection continues to grow on a regular basis. It is important to recognize that these collections all include digitized images. Please refer to chapter 3 for details about working with the images at Ancestry.com.

An Introduction to Cartography

Cartography, the science or art of making maps, is a complex business. We have all seen the primitive-looking maps of the early explorers of the Americas and how inexact their calculations and drawings actually were. Much has changed, of course, since the thirteenth, fourteenth, and fifteenth centuries. Mapmaking became more sophisticated with the invention of astronomical and other measurement instruments, and the standardization of measurement tools made local surveying more accurate as well.

There are literally hundreds of different types of maps today, and when we as genealogists are researching our ancestors' origins, migrations, settlements, and other activities, maps are an essential tool. There are eleven types of maps in the map collection at Ancestry.com, and it is important that you know the differences between them:

- **Cadastral Map**—A cadastral map shows boundaries and ownership. Some cadastral maps also show such details as survey district names, block numbers, certificate of title numbers, positions of existing older structures, government-described runhold section and/or lot numbers and their respective areas, adjoining and adjacent street names, selected boundary dimensions, and references to prior founding maps. In the United States, the Cadastral Survey in the Bureau of Land Management is responsible for maintaining records of all public lands. These surveys often required detailed investigation of the history of land use, legal accounts, and other documents. Examples of some cadastral maps include country maps showing state boundaries, state maps showing county boundaries, and plat maps, as well as demographic maps that illustrate population growth or density, income levels, slave ownership, and other characteristics. Cadastral maps often use color, shading, or other methods to identify specific areas and/or characteristics.

- **Cartographic Map**—In the Ancestry.com collection, a cartographic map is defined as a simple map showing political boundaries.

- **Civil War Map**—This is a map specifically devoted to the United States Civil War, 1861–1865.

- **Discovery and Exploration**—This is a map that usually illustrates the discovery of an area, the shape and/or features of an area, and notations regarding flora, fauna, waterways, peoples, and other interesting discoveries.

- **Geopolitical Map**—A geopolitical map represents the boundaries of a political entity, such as a country, empire, country, province, canton, etc.

- **Land Ownership Map**—A land ownership map is typically a representation of a large tract of land and its subdivisions into townships, plats, lots, and other measurement divisions. This type of map will vary depending on the period and geographical location.

- **Panoramic Map**—Panoramic maps were very popular in the eighteenth to early twentieth centuries as a way of representing a town, city, or other area in a "bird's eye" view. They provide an interesting visualization of how a place appeared at that time. In the late nineteenth and early twentieth centuries, panoramic photography replaced the cartographic, panoramic representations of places. Photography was much less laborious, cheaper, and more accurate.

- **Park Map**—A park map is used to represent the boundaries and features, both natural and man-made, of a piece of property set aside for preservation or recreation. President Theodore Roosevelt established wildlife preservation areas in the United States, the first being Pelican Island in the Indian River Lagoon in Florida. This led to additional legislation that established wildlife and natural area preservation areas, ultimately resulting in the massive National Park Service.

- **Railroad Map**—A railroad map shows rail transportation lines in relation to the area a railroad traverses, sometimes even showing all stations, depots, freight offices, and other locations serviced for mail, freight, and passengers.

- **Relief Map**—A relief map is similar to a topographic map. However, a true relief map portrays georgraphical features three-dimensionally. Raised relief maps must be experienced in person. However, a visual representation of the physical characteristics of the geography, elevation, and features of an area can be represented on paper or digitally. A panoramic map seeks to achieve a similar visual effect.

- **Thematic Map**—A thematic map was created to represent a specific topical subject. For example, one of my favorite maps in the collection is titled "A new and accurate map of the English empire in North America; Representing their rightful claim as confirmed by charters and the formal surrender of their Indian friends; likewise the encroachments" and is dated 1755.

- **Topographical Map**—A topographical map, also referred to as a contour map or a "topo" map, shows the topography, or land contours, by means of contour lines. Contour lines are curves that connect contiguous points of the same altitude. In other words, every point on the marked line of 100 feet elevation is 100 feet above mean sea level.

- **Transportation Map**—A transportation map illustrates transportation routes, usually overland roads and trails.

As you work with maps, invest a little time in becoming familiar with the type of map you are using. Understanding the type of map is a key to managing your expectations of what information it can furnish.

Working with the Maps, Atlases & Gazetteers Collection

For this example, I am interested in browsing for maps of Pennsylvania. Once I've arrived at the "Search" page for this category, I enter "Pennsylvania" in the "Keyword" field. A portion of the results is shown in figure 9-13. The map title is shown, along with the primary area of focus and the publication year. These will help you isolate the map(s) that will be useful in

Figure 9-13: Results for "Pennsylvania"

Figure 9-14: The information record for the item in the results list

placing your ancestors into geographical and geopolitical context.

Once you find one that interests you, click the descriptive link or the thumbnail to view the record, such as the one shown in figure 9-14. There you will see the Source Information and the Description details about this database. The "Page Tools" should be familiar to you now. You can save the record for an individual in your Family Tree, save it to your Shoebox, make comments or corrections to the record listing, e-mail it to another person, and view a printer-friendly version of this record (not the map itself).

Let's now turn our attention to the "U.S. Map Collection, 1513–1990." From the Card Catalog, you can, as always, browse to find the database title or type "U.S. Map" in the "Keyword" field.

To locate a map in this collection, use the search form and fill in one or a combination of the following fields: year, state, region, country, type, or keyword. Remember that entering a location into the "Keyword" field may be more effective than entering it into the "Location" field. In this collection the latter is primarily used to represent the *publication location* and not the map reference/theme location.

Below the form is a list of links that allow you to browse the collection by location (see figure 9-15 on the next page). Once you've chosen a location, links appear showing years for which Ancestry.com has a map. Select a year to view the map or maps from that year.

Most of the gazetteers in this collection are printed, text-based books. In the previous chapter, you learned how to locate these digitized and indexed books and to either search them or browse them using the tables of contents and indexes. You will use the same method to locate and obtain information in these databases, so if you are uncomfortable working with books, refer back to that chapter.

There are thousands of images in the Maps, Atlases & Gazetteers collection. They are an indispensable resource to make your research more effective. Invest some time exploring the collection, and check back often to see what has been added.

Summary

There are so many diverse materials in both the Pictures collection and the Newspapers & Periodicals

U.S. Map Collection, 1513-1990

Search   Clear Form   Hide Advanced

☐ Match all terms exactly

Keyword
[   ] ☐ Exact
e.g. pilot or "Flying Tigers"
Publication Info
Year   Location
[   ] +/- [0 ▾]   [   ]
☐ Exact   ☐ Exact

⚡ **Search**

Source Information:
Ancestry.com. *U.S. Map Collection, 1513-1990* [database on-line]. Provo, UT, USA: The Generations Network, Inc., 2005. Original data: See source or bibliographic info attached to each map.

About *U.S. Map Collection, 1513-1990*
This database is a collection of maps detailing land areas that comprise the present United States. It contains a variety of maps created for different scopes and purposes, including political and geographical, and covers various years ranging from...

For more information about this database, click here.

Please choose a region:
To browse the images of this collection, click on a region below.

Alabama	Maryland	Oklahoma
Alaska	Massachusetts	Oregon
Arizona	Michigan	Pennsylvania
Arkansas	Mid-Atlantic States	Puerto Rico
California	Mid-Western States	Rhode Island
Colorado	Minnesota	South Carolina
Connecticut	Mississippi	South Dakota
Delaware	Missouri	South-Central States
District of Columbia	Montana	Southeastern States
Entire United States	Nebraska	Southwestern States
Florida	Nevada	Tennessee
Georgia	New England States	Texas
Hawaii	New Hampshire	Utah
Idaho	New Jersey	Vermont
Illinois	New Mexico	Virgin Islands
Indiana	New York	Virginia
Iowa	North Carolina	Washington
Kansas	North Dakota	West Virginia
Kentucky	Northampton	Wisconsin
Louisiana	Northwestern States	Wyoming
Maine	Ohio	

Figure 9-15: Search form and browse links for "U.S. Map Collection, 1513–1990"

collection that you'll feel compelled to look at everything there. From individuals' photos to headstones, yearbooks, postcards, obituaries, newspapers, and newsreels, there is a visual treasure trove at your fingertips. Please take advantage of this growing and changing panorama to explore and discover the world of the past.

Chapter 10

Stories, Memories, and Histories

Family stories provide glimpses into the personalities and activities of our ancestors and other family members. Every family has favorite stories that have been told and retold over the years, and your family is probably no different. Some of these stories may have been documented. If not, Ancestry.com allows you to write your family's stories and preserve them in your Family Tree.

Additionally, some of the most valuable resources available to you are historical books and manuscripts concerning your family history or that of the areas where your ancestors lived. The family histories may have been penned or published by other family members or by historians researching and documenting the area and/or the family. Local histories can provide geographical and historical context for the places your ancestors lived, and in some cases your ancestors will be mentioned by name. This is especially helpful in determining when and how they arrived in or departed from the area, as well as their participation in local events. These publications can, of course, contain errors and omissions and therefore should be used mainly to provide clues and leads for your own personal investigation of any original evidence.

The Stories, Memories & Histories collection includes more than twenty thousand database titles, with family and local histories, social and place histories, society and organization histories, oral histories and interviews, military histories, and reference materials covering royalty, nobility, and heraldry.

In this chapter, we will explore both the search and browse functions for this database collection. We will also examine examples of a number of the historical reference works and how they may benefit your research. These include the following:

- Public Member Stories, entered into Ancestry.com and made public with the members' Family Trees

- A representative family history

- A representative local history

- The Biography & Genealogy Master Index

- Slave Narratives

- The Dawes Commission Index (1898–1914)

These examples will only begin to scratch the surface of the wealth of information available. However, they should give you a sense of the scope of the collection and encourage you to explore it for all of your family lines.

Searching and Browsing the Collection

If you want to search in all of the more than twenty thousand databases in this category, click "Stories, Memories &

Histories" in the "Go Directly to a Database or Collection" section of the "Search" page.

I decided to perform a search on my North Carolina patriot and Revolutionary War ancestor John McKnitt Alexander, and I entered only his name (see the results in figure 10-1).

Figure 10-1: Results for John McKnitt Alexander

Let's look at examples of the different types of records found for John McKnitt Alexander in just three of the databases. The first example is a Public Member Story that has been added to a Family Tree that can be publicly viewed. Figure 10-2 (on the next page) shows this sample in which the Member entered a single comment. Of course, the story could have been substantially longer. You could add a comment to this story, print it, or save a copy of it to someone in your personal Family Tree. Note as well that you can see how many other trees this story has been added to.

The Biography & Genealogy Master Index (BGMI) is a compiled index to millions of Americans who have been profiled in collective biography volumes such as *Who's Who in America*, *Women of Science*, *Who's Who of American Women*, *National Cyclopedia of American Biography*, *Directory of American Scholars*, and *American Black Writers*. It includes information first published in the nineteenth and early twentieth centuries. In addition to providing the individual's name, birth, and death

---

⬭ Comments (1)   🖶 Print   ➕ Save story

Mecklenburg Declaration of Independance

Added by bmz29 on 22 Apr 2007

Col. Amos Alexander was a signer of the Mecklenburg Declaration of Independance, a forerunner to the one drafted by the Continental Congress.

Additional information about this story

Description	Mecklenburg Declaration of Independance
Date	May 20, 1775
Location	Mecklenburg Co, NC
Attached to	• John McKnitt Alexander (1733 - 1817) • Col. Amos Alexander (1729 - 1780)
Other trees this object is saved to	• Meyer V Family Tree • Dunlap-Holigan Family Tree • Pearce/Morris Family Tree • Linhoff Family Tree • Patricia Ann Griffin • Brown Family Tree • Brown Family Tree • Wilford-Hopper Family Tree • Sellers family tree • Steele Family Tree • Debra Jo Snyder • Williams Family of North Carolina • grandma • Long Creek NC Families • Long Creek NC Families • Morgan-Wilson/Weatherly-Holder Tree • The Sample Family Tree

Comments

⬭ **Alexander Website for Information**

Added by bmz29 on 22 Apr 2007

http://www.electricscotland.com/webclans/minibios/a/alexander_hezekiah.htm

Report Abuse

ADD A NEW COMMENT

Add a comment below to communicate with others who may see this.

Subject: [   ]

Comment:
[   ]

[Add comment]

Figure 10-2: Sample of Public Member Story

dates (where available), the reference to the source document is included. Figure 10-3 on the next page shows the record from the BGMI for Alexander and provides me with a bibliographic citation to help me search for the source information.

The next record is one of several from the multivolume set of books *North Carolina Historical Sketches, 1584–1851.* Notice the "View Image" link in the results page shown in figure 10-1. It links to the digitized image of the record, which is shown in figure 10-4. There you can see that John McKnitt Alexander was appointed secretary of the group that met in Mecklenburg County, North

Name: Alexander, John McKnitt
Birth - Death: 1733-1776?
Source Citation:
Biography Index. A cumulative index to biographical material in books and magazines. Volume 12: September, 1979-August, 1982. New York: H.W. Wilson Co., 1983. (BioIn 12)

Figure 10-3: Sample Record from the Biography & Genealogy Master Index (BGMI)

HISTORY OF NORTH CAROLINA.   69

wrong. The haughty assumption of power on the part of the Government to inflict taxation on the people without representation or their consent. Boston harbor was blockaded by British troops, and others awed by the presence of men and arms. The people of North Carolina felt deeply the crisis of our Government. None more keenly than the citizens of Mecklenburg.

On the 20th May, a convention, composed of delegates from different portions of the county, met at Charlotte. ABRAHAM ALEXANDER was called to the chair, and JOHN McKNITT ALEXANDER appointed secretary.

The Rev. Hezekiah James Balch, a Presbyterian clergyman, Dr. Ephm. Brevard, and William Kennon, Esq., an attorney-at-law, addressed the convention.

The news of the battle of Lexington arrived at this time, which had occurred just one month and a day previous; and the wanton sacrifice of American blood by English troops added fresh fuel to the flame of virtuous indignation that now swelled their patriotic bosoms.

The resolutions, from the pen of Dr. Ephraim Brevard, are as follows :—

Figure 10-4: Sample Record for the North Carolina Historical Sketches, 1584-1851, Database

Carolina, drafted, and signed the Mecklenburg Declaration of Independence on 20 May 1775.

Exploring Different Types of Books from the Collection

The Family and Local Histories collection is fully indexed, and you will find that the search tools are very helpful in locating appropriate materials. As you have just seen, some materials consist of digitized images of books or documents, while others are transcripts of the content of the resource. However, just to provide a feeling for the different types of materials, let's now look at some examples of the histories contained in this database collection.

A Family History

Published family histories can provide many insights and clues for your research. One of the family lines I am researching is the Ball family of Virginia, one of whose members, Mary Ball, married Augustine Washington and became the mother of George Washington.

I performed a search for Mary Ball in the Stories, Memories & Histories category and the Family Histories, Journals & Biographies subcategory and entered the keyword "Virginia" to narrow my search. My search results numbered in the thousands, so I filtered the list to an additional subcategory: Ball Family Records. This linked me to a specific database of a family history, *Ball family records: genealogical memoirs of some Ball families of Great Britain, Ireland, and America*, written by William Ball Wright and printed in 1986. First of all, my search results list appeared as shown in figure 10-5. The 299 matches are grouped together, in

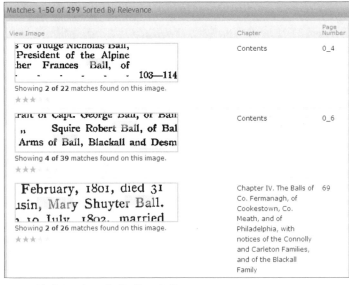

Figure 10-5: Search results for Mary Ball

sequence, by chapter and page number. A thumbnail image of the portion of the page where the specific match appears is shown, and it is a hyperlink to the actual image.

I scrolled through the results and checked many pages to locate information on the specific Mary Ball in whom I was interested. Be aware that using an exact search can backfire on you in family history books. Rather than listing "Mary Ball" as a name, the book may show only "his sister, Mary." So it may be more important to work through all the entries. One help is that the names are highlighted on the pages where matches are found.

At any time in your search, you can view your results by category rather than relevance using the drop-down at the top of the results column. This will show you the databases and records in which your search results appear, allowing you to browse your results by title. For instance, I located another family history, *Virginia, Prominent Families, Vol. 1–4*, by Louise Pecquet du Bellet and published in Lynchburgh, Virginia, by J. P. Bell Company in 1907. In the search result were 83 entries, one of which caught my attention. It started with "Augustine Washington((3)) married, second, Mary Ball, March 6, 1730. She died August 25, 1789, aged eighty-two years. Mary Ball (Joseph, William), born 'Epping Forest,' Lancaster Co., Va., 1707 or '08; d. at Mount Vernon, Va., August 25, 1789, aged eighty-two. Will dated May 20, 1787, probated Fredericksburg, Va., October 23, 1789. Married probably at 'Epping Forest,' March 6, 1730, to Augustine Washington." I clicked on the link labeled "View Full Context" and was rewarded with a detailed genealogical list of descent on the page shown in figure 10-6 (on the next page).

As you can see, there is a great deal of genealogical information here for me to review. The information shown in

Augustine Washington((3)) married, second, Mary Ball, March 6, 1730. She died August 25, 1789, aged eighty-two years. Mary Ball (Joseph, William), born "Epping Forest," Lancaster Co., Va., 1707 or '08; d. at Mount Vernon, Va., August 25, 1789, aged eighty-two. Will dated May 20, 1787, probated Fredericksburg, Va., October 23, 1789. Married probably at "Epping Forest," March 6, 1730, to Augustine Washington. They had issue:

Volume IV
Chapter III Washington.
Col. John Washington.

View Full Context

Figure 10-6: Portion of the Full Context from Some Prominent Virginia Families, *by Louise Pecquet du Bellet*

this section provides me with Mary Ball's birth, marriage, and death dates and with information about the date and filing of her will. Details about her six children are listed. All of this information is pertinent to my research on that branch of the Ball family's descendants, and the clues here point me toward original documents and other evidentiary sources.

A Local History

You can search or browse for histories of geographical areas. As an example, I began in the Card Catalog with Stories, Memories & Histories. In the "Filter by Keyword" field, I entered "rome," as I was interested in locating anything I could about Rome, Georgia, one of my maternal ancestral sites. There were nineteen search results returned. By filtering to the USA and to Georgia, I narrowed the list to eight results, a few of which are shown in figure 10-7.

I chose George Magruder Battey's *A history of Rome and Floyd County, State of Georgia, United States of America*, which was published in 1922. The record for this book is quite long. The "Source," "Notes," "Subjects," "Location," and "Table of Contents"

A history of Rome and Floyd County, State of Georgia, United States of America : including numerous incidents of more than loca	Stories, Memories & Histories	10,676
Rome and Floyd County, Georgia History, 1540-1922	Stories, Memories & Histories	10,710
Warlick family	Stories, Memories & Histories	867
Wells or Welles	Stories, Memories & Histories	1,717

Figure 10-7: Results for "Rome" and filtered by USA and Georgia

references are shown in figure 10-8.

It would be interesting to know about the earlier days, so I clicked the section "Part II. 'Ancient Rome' 1834–1861." "Chapter I. Rome's establishment and early days" would make for interesting reading. I can view the image of a page, save it to either my computer or my Shoebox, or e-mail the image. It isn't possible to perform any of these tasks for an entire chapter, section, or book. Figure 10-9 (on the next page) will give you a sense of the quality of an individual page.

Figure 10-8: Record for Rome and Floyd County history

American Genealogical-Biographical Index (AGBI)

One of the most important genealogical collections, the American Genealogical-Biographical Index, or AGBI, is the equivalent of more than 200 printed volumes. This database contains millions of records for people whose names have appeared in printed genealogical records and family histories.

CHAPTER I.

Rome's Establishment and Early Days

IN THE spring of 1834 two lawyers were traveling on horseback from Cassville, Cass County, to attend court at Livingston, the county seat of Floyd. They were Col. Daniel R. Mitchell, a lawyer of Canton, Cherokee County, and Col. Zachariah B. Hargrove, Cassville attorney, formerly of Covington, Newton County. The day was warm and the travelers hauled up at a small spring on the peninsula which separates the Etowah and the Oostanaula rivers at their junction. Here they slaked their thirst and sat down under a willow tree to rest before proceeding on their way.

Col. Hargrove gazed in admiration on the surrounding hills and remarked: "This would make a splendid site for a town."

"I was just thinking the same," returned his companion. "There seems to be plenty of water round about and extremely fertile soil and all the timber a man could want."

A stranger having come up to refresh himself at the spring, and having overheard the conversation, said: "Gentlemen, you will pardon me for intruding, but I have been convinced for some time that the location of this place offers exceptional opportunities for building a city that would become the largest and most prosperous in Cherokee Georgia. I live two miles south of here. My business takes me now and then to George M. Lavender's trading post up the Oostanaula there, and I never pass this spot but I think of what could be done."

The last speaker introduced himself as Maj. Philip Walker Hemp-

hill, planter. Learning the mission of the travelers, he added: "The court does not open until tomorrow afternoon. You gentlemen are no doubt fatigued by your journey, and it will give me great pleasure if you will accompany me home and spend the night. There we can discuss the matter of locating a town at this place."

Col. Mitchell and Col. Hargrove accepted with thanks. The three left the spring (which still runs under Broad street at the southeast corner of Third Avenue), crossed the Etowah River on John Ross' "Forks Ferry," and proceeded with Major Hemphill to his comfortable plantation home at what is now DeSoto Park. Here they went into the question more deeply. A cousin of Maj. Hemphill, Gen. James Hemphill, who lived about ten miles down Vann's Valley, had recently been elected to the Georgia legislature, and could no doubt bring about a removal of the county site from Livingston to Rome; he was also commanding officer of the Georgia Militia in the section.

After court was over, Col. Mitchell and Col. Hargrove spent another night with Maj. Hemphill, and the next morning Col. Wm. Smith was called in from Cave Spring, and became the fourth member of the company. It was there agreed that all available land would be acquired immediately, the ferry rights would be bought and the ground laid off in lots, Gen. Hemphill was requested to confer with his compatriots at Milledgeville and draw up a bill for removal. The projectors would give sufficient land for the public buildings and in time would make the ferries free and cause neces-

Figure 10-9: Page from local history book

With data from sources largely from the last century, each entry contains the person's complete name, the year of the biography's publication, the person's state of birth (if known), abbreviated biographical data, and the book and page number of the original reference. Other genealogical collections are indexed in addition to family histories. These include the "Boston Transcript" (a widely circulated genealogical column), the complete 1790 U.S. Federal Census, and published Revolutionary War records. The most recent update to this database reflects the inclusion of volumes 196–206. For people researching American ancestors, this is a valuable database.

Most of the works referenced in the AGBI are housed at the Godfrey Memorial Library in Connecticut. A photocopy service is available. Please contact Godfrey Memorial Library at 134 Newfield St., Middletown, CT 06457 or via e-mail to <referenceinfo@godfrey.org> to make use of this service.

For this example, I chose the name of John Davidson, who I know was born in Maryland and who was an officer in the

Continental Army during the American Revolution. I performed a search for him and used his birth and death years (1735 and 1832) to find information. The search results included one record (see figure 10-10).

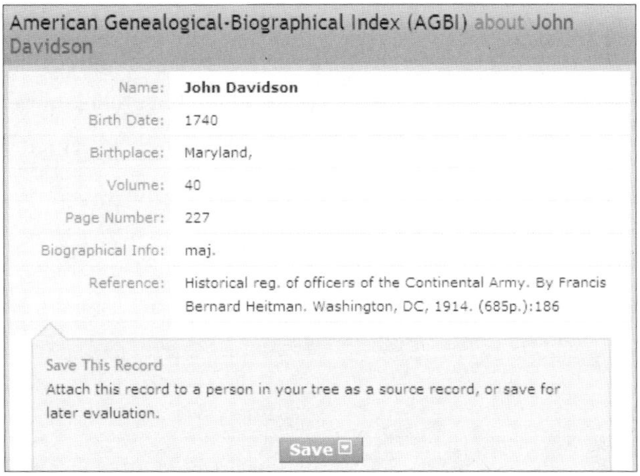
American Genealogical-Biographical Index (AGBI) about John Davidson

Name:	John Davidson
Birth Date:	1740
Birthplace:	Maryland,
Volume:	40
Page Number:	227
Biographical Info:	maj.
Reference:	Historical reg. of officers of the Continental Army. By Francis Bernard Heitman. Washington, DC, 1914. (685p.):186

Save This Record
Attach this record to a person in your tree as a source record, or save for later evaluation.
Save

Figure 10-10: AGBI record for John Davidson

Slave Narratives

During the Great Depression of the 1930s in the United States, the Works Project Administration (WPA), an agency of the federal government, commissioned a project to record the experiences of Americans from many walks of life. Perhaps no other resource approaches the range of human experience found in the Slave Narratives. The collection contains over twenty thousand pages of transcripts from interviews with more than thirty-five hundred former slaves, collected over a ten-year period.

In 1929, an effort began at Fisk University in Tennessee and Southern University in Louisiana to document the life stories of these former slaves. Kentucky State College continued the work in 1934, and from 1936 through 1939, the Federal Writer's Project (a federal work project that was a part of the New Deal) launched a coordinated national effort to collect narratives from former slaves. This database provides a poignant picture of what it was like to live as a slave in the American South. This collection is the most complete available picture of the African-American experience with slavery.

You can search the database using the search form, but

you can also browse by category within the database. You can access the categories by going to the "Slave Narratives" search page and clicking "click here" in the "About Slave Narratives" section. The categories include the following:

- Famous Personalities

- Folk Medicine, Herbs

- Ghost Stories

- Religious Experiences

- Runaway Slaves

- Songs and Hymns

- Voting

- War Stories

Figure 10-11 shows a representative sampling of extracts from the typewritten transcripts of the recorded interviews concerning voting. You can click on the "View Full Context" link to read the entire transcribed interview.

Dawes Commission Index

State: Alabama   **Interviewee:** Daniel, Matilda Pugh
"Durin' de war us warn't bothered much, but atter de surrender, some po' white trash tried to make us take some lan'. Some of 'em come to de slave quarters, an' talk to us. Dey say 'Niggers, you is jus' as good as de white folks. You is 'titled to vote in de 'lections an' to have money same as dey,' but most of us didn't pay no tention to 'em.
View Full Context

State: Alabama   **Interviewee:** Garry, Henry
"Git rid of de carpetbaggers? Oh, Yassah, dey vote 'em out. Well sah, tell you how dey done dat. De 'publicans done paid all de niggers' poll tax, an' gib 'em a receipt so dey could vote same as de whites. Dey made up to 'lect de officers at de co'te house all niggers an' den sen' yuther ones to Montgomery to make de laws. Same day de 'lection come off dar was a circus in Livingston an' de Demmycrats 'suaded de boss man of de circus to let all Sumter County niggers in de show by showin' dere poll tax receipts. Yessah, when de show was ober de 'lection was ober too, an' nobody was 'lected 'cepin' white Demmycrats.
View Full Context

Figure 10-11: Portion of the slave interview results

The Dawes Commission, commonly called the Commission to the Five Civilized Tribes, was appointed by U.S. president Grover Cleveland in 1893. It was named after its chairman, Henry L. Dawes. In return for abolishing their tribal governments and recognizing state and federal laws, tribal members of the so-called Five Civilized Tribes—the Cherokee, Creek, Choctaw, Chickasaw, and Seminole—were given a share of common property. This database indexes the original applications for tribal enrollments under the act of 28 June 1898. It also indexes documents such as birth and death affidavits, marriage licenses, and decisions and orders of the Commission.

The rolls contain more than 101,000 names recorded between 1898 and 1914 (primarily from 1899 to 1906). They can be searched to discover the enrollee's name, gender, blood degree, and census card number. The census card may provide additional genealogical information and may also contain references to earlier rolls, such as the 1880 Cherokee census. A census card was generally accompanied by a file referred to as an "application jacket." These jackets sometimes contain valuable supporting documentation, such as birth and death affidavits, marriage licenses, and correspondence. The original documents are in the possession of the National Archives and Records Administration (NARA). Today these five tribes continue to use the Dawes Rolls as the basis for determining tribal membership. Applicants are typically required to provide proof of descent from a person who is listed on these rolls.

My example is for Billy Bowlegs, a Seminole chief who also was related to Chief Micanopy. When Billy Bowlegs finally relented and moved west to the reservation in Oklahoma, he was interviewed under oath and provided information for his enrollment in the Five Civilized Tribes. A sample record for

Control Number: NRFF-75-53A-25372
Unit of Description: Item
Record Group Number: 75
Series ID: 53A
Item ID: 25372
Title: Enrollment for **Billy Bowlegs**
General Materials Designator Record Type: Textual Records
Reference Unit: National Archives--Southwest Region
Agency Name: National Archives and Records Administration
Facility Name: Building 1, Dock 1
Address: 501 West Felix Street
City: Fort Worth
State: TX
Zip Code: 76115
Telephone Number: 817-334-5525
Fax Number: 817-334-5621
Organizational Code: NRFF
Creating Organization: Commissioner to the Five Civilized Tribes, Bureau of Indian Affairs.
Scope and Content: Tribe: Seminole
Type: Parent
Sex: Male
Census Card Number: 384
City of Residence: SB
Personal Name Reference: **Billy Bowlegs**
Item Count/Item Type: item(s) |c 1
Source Project: Kiosk
View Full Context

Figure 10-12: Dawes Commission Index for Billy Bowlegs.

Billy is shown in figure 10-12.

Billy Bowlegs went on to enlist as a captain in the Union Army in 1862 and was assigned command of Company A of the First Indian Home Guards. He died in 1864 of smallpox and was buried in the Officers Circle of the Fort Gibson National Cemetery in Fort Gibson, Oklahoma, not far from Muskogee.

The index record at Ancestry.com will provide details for ordering copies of the application file, or "jacket," for the applicant from the NARA Branch in Fort Worth, Texas. The information taken on the application, narrative testimony that was recorded, and copies of documentation can be essential for your Native American research.

Summary

We have explored a number of representative samples from the Stories, Memories & Histories collection at Ancestry.com. These materials are invaluable references that you otherwise might not be able to access without visiting a library or archive some distance away from you. My own experience has shown me that there are many older books and indexes in this collection of which I was unaware, and the contents have furthered my own research beyond my wildest dreams. This is

a tremendous online resource, and I encourage you to explore
it in great depth for all your ancestral lines and locations.

Chapter 11

Directories and Member List Records

Placing your ancestors in a specific location at a specific point
in time is essential to insure that you are searching in the
right place for other records about them. Regular national
census enumerations have been taken in the United States
since 1790; in the United Kingdom, Wales, the Channel
Islands, and the Isle of Wight since 1801; and in most areas of
Canada since 1871. In addition, colonial, state, provincial, and
local censuses have been taken at other times. Genealogists
use census records more often than any others to establish
ancestors' whereabouts. But what about those intermediate
years between enumerations and those enumeration periods
for which census records have been lost?

   It is essential to recognize that there are many alternative
records that may be used to establish an ancestor's location
at a specific point in time. For Americans, this is especially
important because, with the loss of 99.99 percent of the
1890 U.S. Federal Census, substitutes must be used to locate

ancestors during the twenty-year gap between the 1880 and 1900 censuses. The types of records most frequently used in these cases include city directories, telephone directories, professional and trade directories, alumni directories and yearbooks, tax lists, religious membership rolls, and other types of annually created records. Using a sequence of local directories or other materials that are published annually may help you learn when your ancestor arrived in an area and when he or she moved away or died. Directories often include addresses, and even occupations, that can point your research in new directions and toward other sources of evidence.

Ancestry.com has long recognized the importance of directories in genealogical research and has amassed an impressive collection of various directories in their database collection. One recent addition to the collection for researchers in the British Isles is the British Telecom (BT) telephone directories archive, a growing collection of digitized telephone directories from 1880 to 1984 for BT and its predecessors. This collection debuted at Ancestry.co.uk in the fall of 2006 and will grow until the entire collection is digitized and online. What a tremendous resource this is and will continue to be for genealogists and other researchers!

While it would be impossible to compile a complete collection of city directories for every location, the existing collections at Ancestry.com can certainly be used to help you locate your ancestors and relatives, especially in between census records. And if a location where your family lived at a particular time is not included in these electronic databases, you can certainly contact the libraries and archives in that region to determine if there are printed copies of directories still in existence.

In addition to city directories, Ancestry.com has added such impressive collections as the UK and U.S. Directories, 1680–1830; the U.S. Public Records Index, 1994 to present; and U.S. School Yearbooks. The chronological span and geographic coverage of these directory and membership records bring rare and difficult-to-access materials into your research options.

In this chapter, we will look at examples of a number of different record types that fall into this category. These will give you a good idea of what to expect from the collection.

Searching a City Directory

For our example of a city directory, we'll use the "Charlotte, North Carolina Directory, 1890" database. In the Card Catalog, apply the "Directories and Member Lists" filter, as well as the USA and North Carolina filters. You may need to scroll through a few pages of results to find the database.

This database is a transcription of city directories originally published in 1890. In addition to providing the resident's name, it provides residential and occupational information. It includes over 16,000 names, mostly heads of households. For someone researching ancestors from southern North Carolina, this can be a valuable collection.

I chose as my search subject a gentleman named J. B. Alexander, a first cousin, three times removed. I entered his name into the form, and the search results list shown in figure 11-1 was displayed.

I already knew that Mr. Alexander had been a surgeon for the Confederate army during the U.S. Civil War, so the third

View Record ★ ★ ★	J BJ B Alexander	Charlotte	NC	drug clerk
View Record ★ ★ ★	J BJ B Alexander	Charlotte	NC	commission traveler
View Record ★ ★ ★	Dr J BJ B Alexander 5 w Trade	Charlotte	NC	physician

Figure 11-1: Results for J. B. Alexander in "Charlotte, North Carolina Directory, 1890"

Charlotte, North Carolina Directory, 1890 about Dr J BJ B Alexander

Name:	**Dr J BJ B Alexander**
Location 1:	5 w Trade
City:	Charlotte
State:	NC
Occupation:	physician
Year:	1891, 1892
Location 2:	410 n Tryon

Save This Record

Attach this record to a person in your tree as a source record, or save for later evaluation.

Save ☑

Figure 11-2: City directory record for Dr. J. B. Alexander

entry, for Dr. J. B. Alexander, looked right. I clicked the "View Record" link and the record shown in figure 11-2 was displayed.

Notice the *two* addresses listed. One is undoubtedly a residence and the other a business address. Using this information, there are several additional records and research directions I could pursue.

- I could contact the Charlotte-Mecklenburg County Public Library to obtain hard copies of these pages, both from the residential and business sections of the directory. I might also request that a search be conducted in other directories or using other library resources and then order photocopies of those records.

- There may be land records of interest to me at the Mecklenburg County Courthouse, including deeds and tax rolls related to Dr. Alexander.

- I could contact the probate court and request copies of the contents of his will and probate files.

- I could return to the Family and Local Histories collection at Ancestry.com and search for any matches on Dr. Alexander.

As always, I can save the record to a person in one of my Family Trees as a source or save it to my Shoebox for future reference. I can also print a copy of the record or save it to my computer. The Source Information below the record provides the basis of a source citation for my personal genealogical database and for my family tree at Ancestry.com. I also can e-mail the record to a friend or relative or anyone else who might be interested in it.

As you can see, there are many things I can do with just this one record.

U.S. School Yearbooks

We all remember having photographs taken and published in a school or college yearbook. Often a biographical profile accompanied the picture, with information about interests, school activities, aspirations, and perhaps even a nickname. The details gleaned from reading a yearbook entry can add another dimension to what you know about an individual and his or her personality.

Yearbooks are one of those home sources, usually found in an attic or basement, that many people don't think of as a family history source. While yearbooks may not provide information about the vital events that are usually associated with genealogical research, they do provide other information about individuals' lives. This information helps place people in a historical context and provides details that help turn individuals, sometimes known only by names and dates, into actual people.

The "U.S. School Yearbook" database is a collection of middle school, junior high, and high school yearbooks from across the United States. If your school's yearbook isn't included in the collection, it *can* be added. If you would like to contribute yearbooks to this collection, you may send a CD with digital scans of the entire book to:

MyFamily Yearbook Submissions
4800 North 360 West
Provo, UT 84604

Top row: Chester Alderman, Ramo Amicarella, Paul Anderson, Terry Anderson
Middle row: Tom Anderson, Frank Aragone, Don Bach, Jean Bachaud
Bottom row: Joe Bauer, Ed Beck, Jack Besse, Gail Billesbach

CHESTER ALDERMAN, JR.—"Scoop"; "Oky Poky"; St. Francis of Assisi; Latin-English; Honor Roll 1; "G" Club 3, 4; Glee Club 3; Track 2, 3, 4.
RAMO AMICARELLA—"Colonel"; "I hope you win, Banjo"; St. Aloysius; Latin-English; Honor Roll 4; Sodality 1, 2, 3, 4.
PAUL A. ANDERSON—"Swede"; "Salutations"; St. Patrick; General; Debating 4; "G" Club 4.
PAUL TERRY ANDERSON—"Andy"; "Here I am, you lucky people"; Orient High School 3; General; Honor Roll 3, 4; Dramatics 4; Glee Club 3; Campus Kids 3, 4.
THOMAS C. ANDERSON—"Cuff"; "Let's go down to Jacoy's"; St. Anthony; General; Class Officer 3, 4; Sodality 1, 2; "G" Club 3, 4; Football 4; Baseball 3; Rifle 2.
FRANK ARAGONE—"Dom"; "Hi, want a ride"? Garden Springs; Latin-English.
JAMES DONALD BACH—"Jock"; "Look out or I'll drop you"; North Central 3; General.
JEAN D. BACHAUD—"Bushy"; "I can't help it"; St. Maries High 4; General; Debating 4; Gold Medal Debate 4; Band 4.
JOSEPH BAUER—"Joe"; "That's me, a boarder"; St. Martin's 4; General; Campus Kids 4; Sodality 4.
EDWARD BECK—"Ed"; "Give me a lift"; St. Ann; Latin-English; Class Officer 1, 2; Sodality 1, 2, 3, 4; "G" Club 4; Football 3, 4.
LORNE J. BESSE—"Jack"; "Want a bottle of beer"? Hollywood Military Academy 3; Scientific; Honor Roll 4; Leash 4.
GAIL BILLESBACH—"Handsome"; "I'm working now, Mister"; Sacred Heart; General; Sodality 1, 2, 3, 4; Class Officer 3; Baseball 3.

14   THE LUIGIAN—1939

Figure 11-3: Page from The Luigian, *1939, yearbook from Gonzaga High School in Spokane, Washington*

You can certainly search by name in this database, using its regular search form, but you can also browse the collection using links beneath the search form. Narrow your search by state, city, and school. You can then browse through images of the yearbook itself.

I selected the state of Washington, the city of Spokane, Gonzaga High School, and had a choice of 1938 or 1939. I chose 1939 and was rewarded with images of all 199 pages of *The Luigian*. Figure 11-3 shows a page from the yearbook.

U.S. Public Records Index

The U.S. Public Records Index is a compilation of various public records spanning all fifty states in the United States from 1984 to the present. These records are accessible to the general public by contacting the appropriate agency. Ancestry.com has made the process of finding certain public records easier by making them available in a searchable, online database. Each entry in this index may contain any or all of the following information:

- A person's first name, middle name or initial, and last name

- A street or mailing address

- A telephone number

- A birth date or birth year

The U.S. Public Records Index also can be a key resource to help do the following:

- Trace living relatives

- Find old friends and classmates

- Locate a long-lost love

- Track down military buddies

- Conduct an adoption search

- Trace the descendants of someone who has died since 1984

This database is accessible only by searching it; there is no browse function. You access this database as you do any other in the collection. Fill in the information that you know and press the **Search** button. Figure 11-4 shows an example of a record.

U.S. Public Records Index about Elizabeth L Summer	
Name:	Elizabeth L Summer
Birth Date:	Jan 1919
Street address:	601 E 5th Ave
City:	Gastonia
County:	Gaston
State:	North Carolina
Zip Code:	28054
Phone Number:	704-864-1681
Record Number:	460572605

Save This Record
Attach this record to a person in your tree as a source record, or save for later evaluation.

Save ⏷

Figure 11-4: Individual record from the "U.S. Public Records" database

UK and U.S. Directories, 1680–1830

Let's look at another database, one of great international genealogical research significance. The "UK and U.S. Directories, 1680–1830" were originally published under the name *Biography Database, 1680–1830*, by Avero Publications, but Ancestry.com has renamed it online to help researchers better understand what it contains. The database is actually a massive collection of UK and U.S. biographical records, directories, and lists from the following sources:

- National, town, and trade directories of the UK and the U.S.

- All known book subscription lists

- All birth, marriage, death, promotions, and bankruptcies from a number of regular journals, including the *Gentleman's Magazine* from its inception in 1731 to 1870

- All extant society membership lists from the period

- A number of miscellaneous additional biographical sources contributed by individual academics who consulted for the project

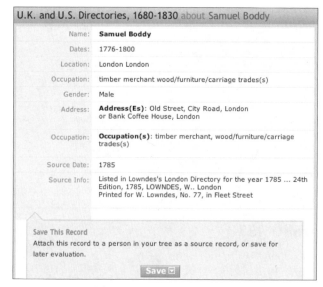

Figure 11-5: Record for Samuel Boddy from Lownde's London Directory

You will find a complete description of the content sources for this database on the "UK and U.S. Directories, 1680–1830" page.

I performed an exact search for Samuel Boddy, who I believe may have lived in the vicinity of London in the late 1700s.

Viewing the first record in the list, which is in *Lownde's London Directories in the 1780s* (see figure 11-5), I see that Samuel Boddy was, indeed, living in London and was involved in selling timber and was in the wood, furniture, and carriage trades. Between the years of 1776 and 1800, he apparently resided or did business at Old Street, City Road, or at the Bank Coffee House in London. All of these are clues to his personal location and business records. The Guildhall Library in London may be a repository I could contact for trade union records for the carriage trade and furniture makers. I may also want to try to trace property and tax records at The National Archives in Kew or at the London Metropolitan Archive.

U.K. and U.S. Directories, 1680-1830 about Samuel Boddy	
Name:	**Samuel Boddy**
Dates:	1776-1800
Location:	London
Occupation:	timber merchant wood/furniture/carriage trades(s)
Gender:	Male
Address:	**Address(Es)**: City Road, Old Street, London
Occupation:	**Occupation(s)**: timber merchant, wood/furniture/carriage trades(s)
Source Date:	1784
Source Info:	Listed in Bailey's British Directory [for 1784]; or, Merchant's and Trader's Useful Companion for the year 1784 ... in 4 Volumes ... Volume 1. London; Volume 2 The Western Directory; Volume 3 The Northern Directory; Volume 4 The Eastern Directory. The First Edition, 1784, BAILEY. London Printed by J. Andrews, Little Eastcheap, and to be had of the Author, No. 53, Basinghall-street; No. 4, Queen-street, Cheapside; Mr. Long, Optician, Royal Exchange, and of every Bookseller in Town and Country

Save This Record
Attach this record to a person in your tree as a source record, or save for later evaluation.

Save ☑

Figure 11-6: Record for Samuel Boddy in Bailey's British Directory

Now go back to the results page and take a look at the record from *Bailey's British Directory* (see figure 11-6). The information is very similar to that of *Lownde's London Directories*.

British Phone Books 1880–1984

This image database is the last example to explore. You must have a World Deluxe subscription or be a UK Deluxe subscriber to use this resource.

There are three required data elements that must be completed on the search form for this database:

• First Name

• Last Name

• County

This requires that you know something of the geography of the area you are searching. The "County" drop-down list includes the counties for which directories are available. "London," in this case, refers to the one-mile-square area known as The City of London. The remainder of the metropolitan city spans the counties of Middlesex and, to the west, part of Surrey.

In this search, I want to perform an exact search for a specific person, Michael Sissons, who lived in London. The person I am seeking is the Michael Sissons on the search results page associated with the Tate Gallery, and you will see that there are directory listings for him in the 1978, 1980, 1982, and 1983 phone books. If I had specified a year in my search, I may have isolated the results to a single year. However, if I had specified the year 1981, I would have received no matches for the Michael Sissons I was seeking.

Clicking the "View Record" link for 1983 (see figure 11-7) yields the address, telephone exchange, directory title and year, county, year, and the page number in the directory where Michael's listing will be found. All of this, along with the "Source Information" below the box, can be used to produce a high-quality source citation.

British Phone Books, 1880-1984 Releases 1-4 about Michael Sissons

Name:	**Michael Sissons**
Address:	1024 Kings Ho,St. James CT Sw1.
Exchange:	01-828
City/Town:	Tate Gallery, Victoria
Directory Title:	London Surnames S - Z
Publication Year:	1983
Directory County:	London
Page Number:	140

View original image

Save This Record
Attach this record to a person in your tree as a source record, or save for later evaluation.

Save ☑

Figure 11-7: Record for Michael Sissons

I have all of the usual "View Records" options here, and when I click the graphic or the link labeled "View Original Image," the digitized image of the directory page is presented.

Figure 11-8 shows
a magnified image
taken from the actual
page in the directory.

Sissons J.W, 15 Lessing St SE23	01-291	3269
Sissons Michael, 1024 Kings Ho,St. James Ct SW1	01-828	3693
Sissons M.G, 19 Waterbank Rd SE6	01-697	8509

Figure 11-8: Michael Sissons in "British Phone Books 1850–1984"

Michael Sissons's name, address, and telephone number are
listed for my reference. By comparing his multiple listings
throughout the years, I might determine that he did or did not
relocate to a new address or change his telephone number.
Verifying his presence at a specific address for any years helps
me trace him, especially between censuses. It also allows me
to investigate the possibility that additional record types might
exist in that area, such as parish records, land and property
records, voter records, and others.

Summary

Directories and member lists provide you with access to a
wide range of materials that ordinarily would be difficult if
not impossible to track down yourself. These records, most
of which are secondary sources derived from transcriptions,
provide you with excellent evidence of an ancestor's location
at a place and point in time. As an alternative source to
census records and other nonannual records, the information
found in this collection can point you to other primary and
secondary records and evidence to establish your ancestor's
arrival or departure dates at a location or help narrow the
time of his or her death.

Ancestry.com continues to add resources to this collection,
so it is prudent to check it through both searches and browsing
on a regular basis. You may be surprised at what treasures you
find here!

Chapter 12

Court and Land Records

The Ancestry.com collection of court, land, and probate records is an extensive compilation of reference materials that can further your genealogical research and expand your knowledge of your ancestors' lives and deaths. You will find many different types of records in this collection that perhaps you have not considered before. Some examples include the following databases:

- "Bute County, North Carolina: Minutes of the Court of Pleas and Quarter Sessions, 1767–1779"

- "Caswell County, NC Will Books, 1777–1843; 1784 Tax List; and Guardians' Accounts, 1794–1819"

- "Darke County, Ohio Common Pleas Court Records, 1817–1860"

- "Davis County, Utah Divorce Case Files, 1875–1886"

- "Denver Land Office Records, 1862–1908"

- "Florida Land Records"

- "Frederick County, Virginia, Wills & Administrations, 1795–1816"

- "French and British Land Grants in the Post Vincennes (Indiana) District, 1750–1784"

- "Georgia Cherokee Land Lottery, 1832"

- "Hartford, Connecticut Probate Records, 1635–50; 1700–29; 1729–50"

- "Henry Mining District, Sevier County, Utah, 1883–1896"

- "Kansas Settlers, 1854–1879"

- "Kentucky Land Grants"

- "Leavenworth, Kansas Voter Registration, 1859"

- "Massachusetts Applications of Freemen, 1630–91"

- "Nevada Car Registration Records, 1913–18"

- "Nevada Orphan's Home Records, 1870–1920"

- "New York City Wills, 1665–1782" (multiple databases)

- "Providence Early Town Records"

- "Salem Witches"

- "Salt Lake County, Utah Civil and Criminal Case Files, 1852–1887"

You will probably find the sheer diversity of record types referenced in the list above intriguing. Many of the databases consist of transcriptions of indexes, which can provide the necessary information for you to request original copies of the records from the source repository. Remember that the source is listed under the search form for the specific database.

Other databases consist of digitized books from the Family and Local Histories collection. As an example, a book by Katharine Kerr Kendall, *Person County, North Carolina Compilations: Land Grants; 1794, 1805 & 1823 Tax Lists; Record Books Abstracts, 1792–1820; Letters of Attorney*, is an assemblage of indexes and abstracts to some unique period documents for Person County, North Carolina. I have used the database and have requested copies of the original records for several of my ancestors from the courthouse in Roxboro, North Carolina.

Searching the Databases

As I mentioned earlier, this collection of databases is very diverse indeed. However, let's examine a few of them by performing searches. This will allow you, as you follow along and input these searches on your own computer, to see and work with the search results. If you see additional areas or links that interest you as you work through the examples, I urge you to explore further.

Let's perform a search from the general search form for the category that includes these databases, "Court, Land, Wills, & Financial." I want to locate my great-great-grandfather William Whitefield, who was born and died in North Carolina. In the first search, I have entered his name and have specified "North Carolina, USA" exactly (see figure 12-1).

Figure 12-1: Court, Land, Wills, & Financial search form

For results, I get a list of different databases that contain matches (see a in figure 12-2 on the next page). Notice in figure 12-2 the preview of the

Figure 12-2: Results for William Whitefield

record on the results page, which allows you to determine more accurately which results are useful to you. For me, the one that shows a reference in "Person County, North Carolina Deed Books: 1792–1825" looks promising.

I want to see the full image from this book, so I click the preview. The image displayed contains a page of typed deed abstracts (see figure 12-3). In the entry labeled 410-1, Lumpkin Winstead has conducted a business transaction and there are two witnesses to it with the surname of Williams. You will note that their surnames are highlighted. These appeared as part of the general search. However, in the next entry, James Whitefield, Senior, sold a

410-1 Lumpkin Winstead (in debt to Cary Williams for $100 & as security on bond of $70 for hire of negro payable to Alexr Winstead, plus other debts) to William Williams, for $1, in trust, negro man Dick alias Richard age 20 yrs. 12 May 1821. Wit: Haywood Williams, Alexr Williams.

412 James Whitefield Sen. to William Whitefield of CC, for $100, 80.5 A on Double Cr of S Hico & was purchased of Wm. McKissack Jun. adj Wm. McKissack Sen., Robt Stanfield. 9 June 1821. Wit: Minchew Whitefield, Mary Whitefield.

Figure 12-3: Results for William Whitefield in "Person County, North Carolina Deed Books: 1792–1825"

parcel of 80.5 acres to William Whitefield. This was my great-great-grandfather's land, on which he built a new home. The witnesses are Minchew Whitefield and Mary Whitefield, a brother and sister.

Let's look at another type of record. Use the Card Catalog to find "Alabama Land Records." I entered the surname of "Swords" into the "Last Name" field, clicked "Match all terms exactly," and then clicked **Search**.

Each of the individuals shown on the results page is related to my family: John N. Swords is another of my great-great-grandfathers. If you click on the "View Record" link for John N. Swords's purchase of 80.11 acres from the Lebanon Land Office on 1 August 1849, the record shown in figure 12-4 is displayed.

Figure 12-4: Alabama land record for John N. Swords

Here you see even more information, including the land description. This can be used to locate the exact piece of property he purchased. In addition, you can also visit the NARA website at <www.archives.gov> and their Order Online facility at <https://eservices.archives.gov/orderonline>. You will be asked to register and establish a user ID and password, and then you can order many record types, including land record case files.

Summary

It would be impossible to demonstrate all the different types of records in the court, land, and probate records in this chapter. There simply are too many. By now, however, you should feel comfortable using the different search forms, the results pages, and the records that are displayed. You can explore any of the other databases here to discover what clues they may hold for your research.

Chapter 13

Reference and Finding Aids

Reference materials are a hallmark of genealogical research. Ancestry.com has the largest collection of searchable databases, many of which, as you already know, consist of indexed, digitized document images. It should therefore be no surprise that Ancestry.com would also provide the largest collection of online reference works and finding aids.

We explored the impressive Stories, Memories & Histories collection in chapter 10, and that collection continues to grow to support your research. In addition, the Reference and Finding Aids collection contains a diverse amount of printed resources, including dictionaries, maps, and gazetteers, that will help family historians find and understand genealogical records. Among the resources here are *The Source: A Guidebook to American Genealogy*, the *Genealogical Library Master Catalog*, *PERSI*, *Genealogical Publications: A List of 50,000 Sources from the Library of Congress*, the *U.S. Cemetery Address Book*, and other core reference works, all in full text and every-word searchable.

In addition to general family history resources, the collection includes country studies for numerous countries outside of the United States and the United Kingdom. These studies can provide invaluable information about the native lands of your non-Anglican ancestors. Some of the more unique countries included in these studies are Egypt, Belarus, Cyprus, Hungary, Italy, Japan, Mongolia, Poland, and Russia, as well as many others. The *World Fact Book* is an excellent supplement to the country studies.

You will find that the Reference and Finding Aids collection, along with materials in the Learning Center, will provide you with an excellent online genealogical reference library at your fingertips twenty-four hours a day, seven days a week. (We will explore and discuss the Learning Center in chapter 17.)

For the examples in this chapter, go to the search form for this collection by clicking "Reference & Finding Aids" in the "Go Directly to a Specific Title or Collection" section of the "Search" page. For more information about searching, see chapter 2.

Searching the Reference and Finding Aids Records

The databases that comprise the Reference and Finding Aids collection are many and diverse. It is important for you to realize that some deal with geographical locations and some with "how-to" topics. Some contain individuals' names—maybe including one of your ancestors—and others are strictly indexes that can direct you to other materials.

Look at the main search form for this collection. You will be using this and other search forms in the Reference and Finding Aids collection differently than you have used them before. Let me explain.

Since the databases here are so diverse, you may or may not be searching for a name, and you probably won't be using dates to narrow your searches. Instead, you may find yourself wanting to locate information on a geographical location, in which case you may use only the exact search facility and then only a country or the "Keyword" field. Let me show you some examples.

Let's say that I want to search for the name "Stephen Danko." In this example, I am going to search for him specifically in the "Biography & Genealogy Master Index (BGMI)," one of the databases in this collection.

The search results consist of a several records, but the one I am interested in is from *Who's Who of Emerging Leaders in America. Third edition, 1991–1992* (see figure 13-1). With this

Figure 13-1: Search form for the "BGMI"

information, I can check to see if my local public or academic library has a copy of this book. If not, they should be able to help me initiate an interlibrary loan, which will make it possible for me to obtain a photocopy of the entry for this individual.

In this case, if I had checked "Match all terms exactly" on the search form, I would have had a similar, though

```
Name: Danko, Kevin Stephen

Birth - Death: 1959-

Source Citation:
         Who's Who of Emerging Leaders in
         America. Third edition, 1991-1992.
         Wilmette, IL: Marquis Who's Who,
         1991. (WhoEmL 3)


Name: Danko, Stephen Gaspar

Birth - Death: 1942-

Source Citation:
         Who's Who in American Law. Fourth
         edition, 1985-1986. Wilmette, IL:
         Marquis Who's Who, 1985. (WhoAmL 4)

         Who's Who in American Law. Fifth
         edition, 1987-1988. Wilmette, IL:
         Marquis Who's Who, 1987. (WhoAmL 5)

         Who's Who of Emerging Leaders in
         America. First edition, 1987-1988.
         Wilmette, IL: Marquis Who's Who,
         1987. (WhoEmL 1)
```

Figure 13-2: Results for Stephen Danko in the "BGMI"

significantly narrowed, result. Figure 13-2 does, indeed, show several Stephen Dankos.

Searching Books

Many reference books have been made into every-word searchable databases and are included in the Reference and Finding Aids collection. Two of the most important are published by Ancestry Publishing: *The Source: A Guidebook to American Genealogy*, rev. ed., and *Ancestry's Red Book: American State, County, and Town Sources,* rev. ed. *The Source* covers all the important aspects of genealogical research, including censuses, land records, military records, church records, and many more. It describes the records in detail, what they contain, where they can be located, and how they can be used in your research. *Ancestry's Red Book* is the definitive work about United States research. Organized by state, this reference easily directs you to information-rich resources for vital, census, land, probate, church, and military records and much more.

I want to search *The Source* for references to the word "obituaries" and read more about them (see figure 13-3 on the next page).

The results page indicates there are seventy-three matches for the word "obituaries." Figure 13-4 shows the first two matches. The records are displayed in the search results list in the order that they appear in the reference work. In this case, the first record is taken from the "Introduction" (page 3); the second record is from "Chapter 1" (page 11). In this

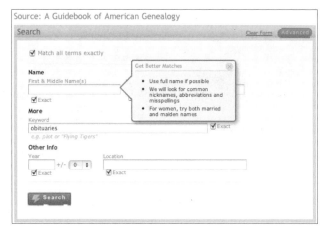

Figure 13-3: The search form for The Source.

way, you can easily progress through the book's contents on the subject. If one of these text records seems to contain the

information most pertinent to what you want to know, you can click on the "View Full Context" link and see the record in its place in the book. You can then read text before or after that text, or even read the entire chapter or the whole book. If you want to revise your search or enter a new search, simply go to the

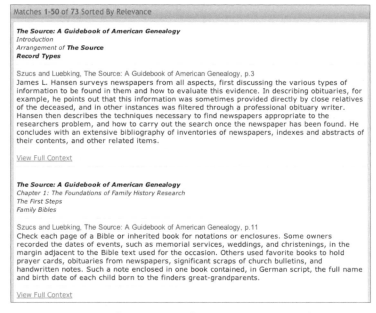

Figure 13-4: A portion of the results page for the word "obituaries" in The Source.

"Refine your search of the Source: A Guidebook of American Genealogy" search form at the bottom of the page and enter the new search word(s).

The *Periodical Source Index* (*PERSI*)

The *Periodical Source Index* (*PERSI*) is the largest and most widely used subject index covering genealogy and local history periodicals written in English and French (Canada). The collection dates from approximately 1800. There are currently over 1.7 million searchable records and nearly 6,000 different periodicals, which library staff at the Allen County Public Library (ACPL) in Ft. Wayne, Indiana, have been compiling for a number of years. *PERSI* is widely recognized as essential for high-quality indexing to genealogical and historical periodical publications.

PERSI provides you access to materials you would otherwise not have available. *PERSI* is not a full-text database. Rather, it is an index to names, locations, and subjects published in the periodicals of genealogical and historical societies in the United States, Canada, and some other areas of the world. *PERSI* also organizes articles into locality, but only those where the geographic categorization is clearly valuable, e.g., cemetery transcriptions or newspaper extracts. Locality entries are classified by the type of record the article includes, such as biography, cemetery, census, and so forth, to indicate the content of the article to researchers.

Societies submit their newsletters, magazines, and journals to ACPL, where they are indexed and filed. Obviously, with the volume of incoming publications, it takes a library some time to accomplish all of this work. However, as updates to the *PERSI* are provided to Ancestry.com, they are then applied to the online database.

In this example, I chose to look for a cemetery of which I was aware. It is the Cooper Cemetery, and I was only certain that it might be in Person or Caswell County, North Carolina. The new search allows me to enter multiple words enclosed in quotation marks in order to force the search engine to seek to match exact phrases (see figure 13-5). There were many search results, the first three of which are shown in figure 13-6. It is important to note the title of the publication, the title of the article, the volume, and the number, season, and year information.

Click on the hyperlink for the publication title—*Piedmont Lineages*—and another, more detailed screen appears, as shown in figure 13-7 (on the next page). This screen shows bibliographic details about this publication, including

Figure 13-5: PERSI search form with exact phrases in quotes

Matches 1-5 of 5 Sorted By Relevance

Article Title: Cooper cemetery burials, Fu-Ru

Locality: United States, North Carolina , Caswell

Record Type: Cemeteries

Volume: 19

Number, Season, Year: 3 (August 1997)

Periodical Title: Piedmont Lineages

Article Title: Cooper cemetery burials, Ru-Ya

Locality: United States, North Carolina , Caswell

Record Type: Cemeteries

Volume: 20

Number, Season, Year: 1 (February 1998)

Periodical Title: Piedmont Lineages

Article Title: Cooper cemetery

Locality: United States, North Carolina , Sampson

Record Type: Cemeteries

Volume: 11

Number, Season, Year: 4 (December 1989)

Periodical Title: Huckleberry Historian

Figure 13-6: Results in PERSI

the publisher's address, the ISSN, and ACPL's holdings. Other major genealogical repositories are listed that may have complete or partial holdings. All of these locations are hyperlinks, and a click on each link brings up a window with the repository's address. Of especial interest is the *PERSI* Code for the publication. In this case, the *Piedmont Lineage PERSI* Code is VANC. This code, coupled with the information you copied about the specific article, is essential in ordering a copy of the article itself.

Following the information shown in figure 13-7 is a list of all of the issues of *Piedmont Lineages*, their publication dates, volumes and serial numbers, and the titles of all of the articles in each issue.

Matches 1-50 of 10,328 Sorted By Relevance
Periodical Title: PIEDMONT LINEAGES
Persi Code: VANC
Topics: VA,NC
Issues Per Year: 4x
ACPLHoldings: v.13- 1991-
ACPLCall Number: OPEN
Other Titles: old title: VA-NC PIEDMONT GENEALOGICAL SOCIETY BULLETIN
Repositories: Allen County Public Library
Publisher: Virginia-North Carolina...Gen Soc
Address: POB 2272 : Danville , VA 24541-0272

Figure 13-7: PERSI *bibliographic record for* Piedmont Lineages

You now have several options available for obtaining a copy of the publication or article for your reference.

If you live close to one of the repositories listed, you can go online to the library's website, access their online catalog, and determine if they have the publication, volume, and issue in question. You may consider visiting the library.

If you you don't live near the library, consider ordering a copy of the article. This can be done in several ways.

- Provide the information you copied (or printed) from *PERSI* to your local public library and ask that they process an interlibrary loan request to obtain a photocopy of the article.

- At the bottom of the Refine Search filters on the left side of the new "Search" page is a link labeled "Learn more about this database." Click here and you'll be taken back to the *PERSI* search form. Scroll down to the section titled "Where to go from here," which informs you that the Historical Genealogy Department at ACPL has each issue of the periodicals indexed in *PERSI*.

- A link near the bottom of the search form page provides you with the *PERSI* Order Form, shown in figure 13-8. Using the information you obtained about each article in each periodical you may want to obtain, and the *PERSI* Order Code, you can complete the form and mail it to ACPL. You must pay $7.50 per letter in advance and may submit a form with up to six articles at a time. ACPL will make copies of the articles you request and bill you at the current rate of $.20 per page copied.

Periodical Source Index (PERSI) Order Form

Name:_____
Address:_____

To obtain copies of articles in the PERSI index, contact the Allen County Public Library Foundation, P.O.Box 2270, Fort Wayne, IN 46801-2270. Send this form describing the articles to be copied, provide the full entry from PERSI and the name of the journal. Request only six articles at a time. The charge is $7.50 for each letter, pre-paid, plus $0.20 per page copied to be billed to you. Requests not acceptable by phone, fax, or e-mail. Please allow 6-8 weeks.

Title of article:_____
Title of journal:_____
Code: Vol: No: Mon: Yr:

Title of article:_____
Title of journal:_____
Code: Vol: No: Mon: Yr:

Title of article:_____
Title of journal:_____
Code: Vol: No: Mon: Yr:

Title of article:_____
Title of journal:_____
Code: Vol: No: Mon: Yr:

Title of article:_____
Title of journal:_____
Code: Vol: No: Mon: Yr:

Title of article:_____
Title of journal:_____
Code: Vol: No: Mon: Yr:

Figure 13-8: The PERSI *Order Form*

You may also choose to directly contact the organization that published the journal, magazine, or newsletter. You can inquire about the availability and cost of purchasing the back issue of the publication in which the article was published. You may want to consider joining the society.

Summary

The Reference and Finding Aids collection is filled with information to help you learn and improve your skills and work with all types of genealogically important records and materials. New materials are added often, so you should make this area a regular stop in your online research visits.

Chapter 17 will discuss the Learning Center, another collection of important reference materials that can help you with your research. Let's proceed there and explore the wealth of that collection too.

Chapter 14

Printing and Sharing

By now, you've likely gathered a fair amount of information and built a Family Tree that includes records you've found, pictures you've uploaded, and more. If you have, you may be wondering if Ancestry.com offers any features that allow you to print or share what you've found.

Using a service called MyCanvas (previously Ancestry Press), which is available on Ancestry.com, you can print records, gather your Family Tree and present it in a beautifully made book, and share what you've found. The great thing about the printing and sharing features on Ancestry.com is that they make it easy for you to get exactly the results you want.

MyCanvas is a full-featured, simple-to-use publishing tool that lets you create handsome, custom books. You can create a book about your family history, a photo album, a cookbook of family recipes, or use your imagination to create another type of book. The books are professionally printed and bound and make wonderful keepsakes and gifts. Like a traditional book, MyCanvas books are printed on both sides of the page.

You don't have to be an Ancestry.com subscriber to use MyCanvas; it is available to any registered user as well as subscribers. You also don't have to be a graphic designer or a computer guru to use MyCanvas. It allows you to select from page templates and backgrounds, add and manipulate text, upload photos, add embellishment artwork, print proof pages, and use your creativity and imagination to create professional-quality results with ease.

In this chapter, we'll cover the three basic printing features available:

- Creating a family history book or poster using MyCanvas

- Sharing your book or poster

- Printing high-quality versions of records using MyCanvas

One important thing to keep in mind in this chapter is that MyCanvas is still being actively developed, so the images in this chapter may not always accurately reflect what you see in your own browser. The principles, however, should remain the same.

To access MyCanvas, click the **Print and Share** tab. (This used to be called the **Publish** tab, and as with every area on Ancestry.com, its name is subject to change.)

Getting Started

To start making a book or poster, click "Get Started " (see figure 14-1 on the next page).

You can get more information about the products offered by clicking them. In general, MyCanvas offers two types of products: books and posters. The type of product you create has a lot to do with the content you have. For instance, if you just returned from a family reunion and have lots of great photos, you might want to make a photo book or a photo collage. If you have a lot of content on your Family Tree, you might want to make a family history book or poster instead.

Figure 14-1: "Get Started" on the MyCanvas homepage

I will not go over the details of the various product types here because your options are constantly growing, but I suggest you browse through the product offerings and read the descriptions so you know what's available.

If you've come to MyCanvas through Ancestry.com (which, if you're reading this book, you likely have), you are probably most interested in the family history offerings, so in this chapter we'll focus on using your Family Tree at Ancestry.com to create a family history book.

For family history books and posters, MyCanvas imports information, photos, and records from one of your Family Trees and organizes them in an attractive way within a book or poster layout. From there, you can add content, embellishments, photos, and more.

Keep in mind that if you don't have your Family Tree completely filled out, it's okay. You can still use MyCanvas. The project creation tool makes it easy for you to start from scratch and add information manually, if you want.

Making a Family History Book

While you are signed into Ancestry.com, click **Print and Share** to get to MyCanvas. Follow the steps to start your

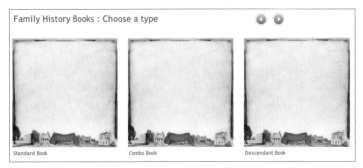

Figure 14-2: Three family history book types

project by clicking "Get Started," then selecting "Family History Books." Note that at this time, you can also choose other project options, such as photo books, posters, and so on.

Next, you need to choose the type of book you want to create (see figure 14-2):

- Standard books start with a person from your Family Tree and create a traditional pedigree chart. Each subsequent page in the book displays family group sheets and individual pages for each individual in your tree, including any photos, stories, and records you have attached to that person.

- Combination books start with a couple from your Family Tree and create a pedigree chart for both people. As with the standard book, each subsequent page in the book displays family group sheets and individual pages for each individual in your tree, including any photos, stories, and records you have attached to that person.

- Descendant books start with a person from your Family Tree and then present a chart of all of that person's descendants. Each subsequent page in the book displays family group sheets and pages for each individual in your tree, including any photos, stories, and records you have attached to that person.

Once you've selected the type of book you want, select a book size and the number of generations you want included (each book type allows for different generation limits). Next, choose which of your Family Trees you want to import from, select a starting person from within that tree, give your project a name, and click **Continue**.

Note that once you've started a project, it is possible to import information from other Family Trees, but in the initial creation process, you can pull from only one tree.

Now, MyCanvas will build your project. If you have your popup blocker turned on, you may need to click a second link to open the project building tool and your project.

Working with Your Project

With the project building tool open, you're now ready to view and work with your project. Let's take a look at the different sections on the page.

Workspace

The main part of the page is your workspace (see figure 14-3). This is where you view the pages of your project and work with elements on the page. We'll talk about working with page elements in greater detail later, but the most important thing to remember about the workspace is that

Flash

The project building tool was built using Flash, a technology used on much of the Internet today. In order for you to use features built in Flash, you will need to have the *Flash Player* installed on your computer. To get the *Flash Player*, go to www.adobe.com and click the link there.

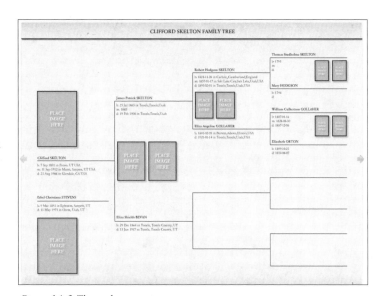

Figure 14-3: The workspace

you have control over everything. Every element on the page can be edited, moved, or deleted.

Thumbnails and Main Toolbar

Below the workspace, you'll find thumbnails of each page in your project (see figure 14-4). You can click each one to view and edit that page.

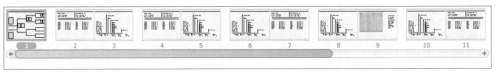

Figure 14-4: Page thumbnails

Above the workspace is the main toolbar (see figure 14-5). The main toolbar includes options that help you work with entire pages or your whole project. For example, you can zoom in and out on a page, add new pages, open the Page Manager, synchronize your project with your Family Tree (using the **Update** button), and more.

Figure 14-5: Main toolbar

Add Pages

One feature that you'll want to get used to is the "Add Pages" drop-down. This gives you options to add blank pages to your project (perhaps for photos or a story) or to add a template page. If you select the "Add pages" option from the drop-down, you'll have the option of choosing a page type to add (see figure 14-6 on the next page).

If you select a page that pulls information from your Family Tree (such as a pedigree page), you'll be prompted to select a Family Tree to pull from and a starting person, just as when you began the project.

Page Manager

Another important feature of the main toolbar is the Page Manager (shown in figure 14-7 on the next page), which you

access by clicking
Manage Pages.
Here you can view
your entire project,
arranged in two-
page spreads. You can
zoom in and out to
get better detail or
see more pages using
the slider. The page
manager is a great way
to move pages, delete
groups of changes, and
more. If you want to
affect multiple pages,
hold down the Ctrl.
key while clicking the
pages you want.

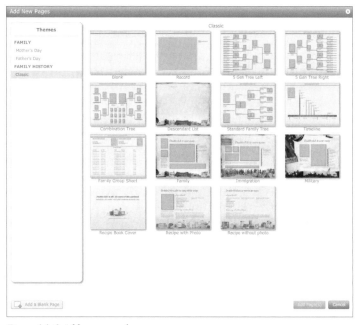

Figure 14-6: Add page templates

Content Panel

To the left of the
workspace, you'll
find the content panel
(see figure 14-8 on
the next page). The
content panel consists
of various drop-downs,
each dedicated to one
kind of content, such as

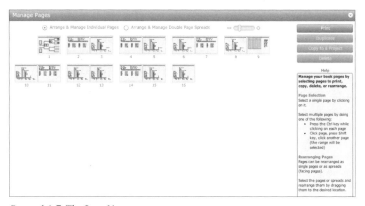

Figure 14-7: The Page Manager

photos, or your Family Trees. The drop-downs are where you
find content to add to your project. In general, you add content
to your page from the content panel in one of two ways:

Figure 14-8: The content panel

- **Dragging**—Most content (such as photos or records from your Family Tree) can simply be dragged from the content panel onto the page, where you can then edit as you deem necessary.

- **Previewing**—Other kinds of content (namely backgrounds and frames) work a little differently. With this content, you simply hover over the content you're interested in (a background, for example). As you do, that content will appear on your page as a preview. If you like it, click the content; otherwise, try another selection. In the case of frames, you need to have a picture selected in order to preview a frame around it.

The "Ancestry Records" drop-down also works a little differently. It provides options for you to select which of your Family Trees you'd like to pull content from and then a person from within that tree. Once you have chosen these, you will be able to access whatever content (such as records or photos) is attached to that person. (You can also access content in a tree that is not attached to anyone.)

Editing Page Elements

As I mentioned, you can edit or modify virtually every element on a page (even elements that were part of a page template you selected). This includes lines from timelines. To modify a page element, simply click it to select it.

Once selected, you'll notice the editing toolbar above it (see figures 14-9 and 14-10). Using this toolbar, you can edit an element in a variety of ways. Note that the toolbar is a little

Figure 14-9: The image editing toolbar

Figure 14-10: The text editing toolbar

different depending on what you're editing (the image editing bar is shown in figure 14-9 and the text editing bar in figure 14-10). The editing toolbar for an element will include some of the following features:

- **Spell Check**—Using the "ABC" icon, you can spell check a selected textbox.

- **Size**—Using the size drop-down, you can change text size.

- **Font**—Using the font drop-down, you can change the text font.

- **Text Color**—Using the text color drop-down, you can change text color.

- **Alignment**—Using the four alignment options (left-aligned, centered, justified, and right-aligned), you can change text alignment.

- **Style**—Using the style options (bold, italic, and underlined), you can apply different font styles to text.

- **Zoom**—Using the slider, you can make your image larger or smaller (images only).

- **Drag**—Using the crosshairs, you can reposition your picture within the frame (images only). If your photo is not within a frame, this feature is disabled.

- **Color Effects**—Using the color effects drop-down, you can keep the full color of the image, apply a sepia filter to it, or make it black and white (image only). You can change back to the original color whenever you want.

- **Border**—Using the border drop-down, you can apply a border to an image (not text). You can also alter existing borders this way.

- **Border Color**—Using the border color option, you can change the color of a border.

- **Flip**—Using the "Flip" icon, you can flip an image horizontally.

- **Transparency**—Using the "Transparency" icon, you can adjust how transparent an image is. Clicking the icon opens a slider.

- **Drop Shadow**—Using the drop shadow option, you can give your image or text a sense of depth by applying a drop shadow to it.

- **Position**—Using the forward and behind options, you can move an image or text in front of or behind other elements.

- **Copy**—Using the "Duplicate" icon, you can copy an image or text.

- **Remove**—Using the "Remove" icon, you can remove an image or text from the page.

You can also crop, resize, and rotate an image or textbox using the tools attached to the image or textbox itself:

- The squares on each edge of the box let you crop the image or textbox. Click the edge you want to move, hold down the left mouse button, and move the edge however you like.

- The "Rotate" icon in the top left corner allows you to rotate your image or text. Simply click it and, while holding the left mouse button, move your mouse in the direction you want the box to rotate.

- The "Resize" icon on the bottom right allows you to resize the entire image. Simply click it and, while holding down the left mouse button, move your mouse until the image is the desired size. You cannot resize a textbox.

You can also move your image or text by grabbing it and dragging it to a new location. Note that you can always undo changes using the "Undo" icon on the main toolbar.

Previewing and Ordering

When you're happy with your project, click the "Preview / Print" drop-down on the main toolbar. Selecting "Preview" brings you to an interactive preview of your entire book where you can see it as it will be printed (see figure 14-11). Be sure to page through your book carefully to make sure everything is as you want.

When you are satisfied with your project, you can do one of two things: print it from home or order a professionally printed copy.

You can always choose to print your project from home for free by simply clicking **Print**. This is a great option if you are on a budget, or if you simply want to print out some proof pages to see how your project is looking on paper. It

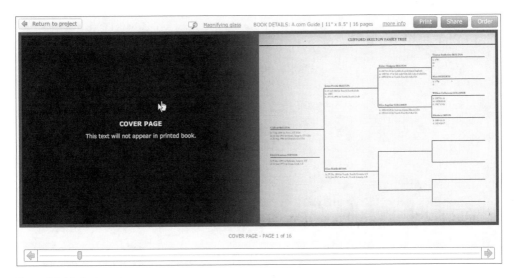

Figure 14-11: Book preview

Low-Res Images

Print publishing requires images of higher resolution than the Internet. In general, photos should be higher than 200 pixels per inch (PPI). If a photo in your project is of low enough resolution that it will print poorly, you will see a yellow triangle on that image. You should swap it out for a better image. Note that in the preview mode, low-res images will look just fine, but they will still print poorly.

is unlikely, however, that you will be able to recreate the professional quality of a MyCanvas book from home without a significant investment in paper and ink.

To order a copy or copies of your project, click **Order**. Simply follow the ordering procedure, and you should receive your book or poster within a few weeks. Prices vary depending on which project you choose and how many pages it has, so be sure to consult the MyCanvas pricing guide.

Sharing Projects

Once you've finished a project (or maybe while you're still working on it), you might want to show it to someone else without printing or ordering it. You can do this at any time. From within the project building tool, click "Share" (one of the links along the top). This opens a page where you can add e-mail addresses for people you'd like to share your project with. Once you've sent it, those people will receive a link to view your project in a way similar to when you preview it.

One consideration when sharing a project is whether or not to allow your invitees to copy your project. If you do, those you invite will be able to add a copy of your project to their own list of projects and modify it as they choose. This is a great way to give your friends and family a leg up on starting projects of their own, but it also introduces a potential security risk, as it moves control of the information in your project out of your hands. You will have to decide for yourself how you want to proceed.

Printing Records

Ancestry.com now allows you to use the functionality of MyCanvas to print high-quality versions of records you view on Ancestry.com. While you are viewing a record in the Image Viewer, click the print option.

In the new window (shown in figure 14-12), you're given the option of printing the record from your printer (as you have always been able to) or using the customized printing option.

If you select the customized printing option, the project building tool will open,

Figure 14-12: Printing options

displaying a page that includes an image of the record you want to print, as well as information on the person highlighted in that record (see figure 14-13). Note that there is no content panel here. Also, keep in mind that, just as with any MyCanvas project, you can edit anything on this page to your liking. For instance, you could change the text or enlarge the image.

When you are ready to print, you do so in the same way as any project.

This option works well when you want to print an image to put in your personal archive or to display, rather than to simply analyze it or read it more carefully. For that, you will likely want to use the standard printing option.

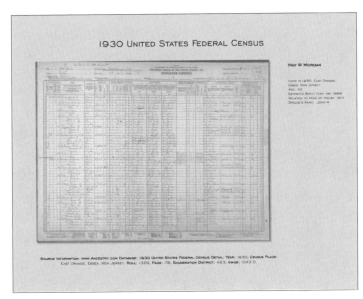

Figure 14-13: Customized record printing

Summary

As you have seen, the interconnections between your Family Tree and the Ancestry.com databases and community intertwine great information into a consolidated whole that you can use to publish stunning family history books. MyCanvas is a robust and easy-to-use online tool, and as you work more with it, you will find that it is very intuitive and that your speed will improve. There are as many possibilities for using MyCanvas as you can imagine. But the best part is that you really can produce professional-looking results in a short time.

Chapter 15

Ancestry Community

We have focused in this book so far on the essential concepts of genealogy, how to navigate the Ancestry.com site, and how to search, access, and use the databases at Ancestry.com. We have also discussed Family Trees, including searching existing trees and building and growing your own Family Trees. This is all very exciting for the modern genealogical researcher. However, it can be truly exhilarating to make connections with other researchers who are researching the same people or lines that you are studying.

Ancestry.com makes this process easier than any other online service through the Ancestry Community. Here you can post queries to message boards and share information with other researchers. You can also make connections with people who share common interests in a particular surname, location, or other criteria.

It has not been too many years since the only way to make these connections was through submitting queries to printed publications. That method of networking with other people was slow, tedious, and haphazard at best. With the explosive growth and proliferation of the Internet in the past twenty years, more people have become interested in genealogy and family history and are actively searching every resource they can find on the Web. It truly *is* a wonderful time to be a genealogical researcher!

The Components of the Ancestry Community

The primary component of the Ancestry Community is people like you—researchers seeking information, clues, leads, and connections with other researchers. It is important to remember, as we've discussed before, that not every person is as conscientious in his or her research work, source citations, and attention to accuracy as perhaps you want to be. I always urge researchers to treat their genealogical research work as a scholarly pursuit and to assess the evidence and document the findings in a way that other researchers will find to be as reliable and accurate as possible.

The Ancestry Community is primarily accessible by clicking the **Community** tab (see figure 15-1 on the next page). Of course, as you read this chapter and as you return to other areas of Ancestry.com, you'll notice many other references to connecting with people researching the same names. Once you've read this chapter, you'll have a better understanding about making contacts from other areas.

We will discuss each of the following areas in this chapter:

- **My Public Profile**—This feature allows you to share information about yourself and your research interests. This helps other people seeking to connect with you to know that you share interests with them.

Figure 15-1: The "Ancestry Community" page

- **My Site Preferences**—This link is also located in the upper right-hand corner of the page. Here, you can specify an e-mail address and your preferences for messages and alerts from Ancestry.com, as well as other members who may be trying to contact you.

- **Message Boards**—The Message Boards at Ancestry.com are the largest collection of their type anywhere on the Internet. A message board is devoted to a topic, such as a surname, geographical location, record type, ethnic group, religious group, research methodology, event, genealogy software, heraldry, and an abundance of other subjects. You can read messages there and respond. You can post messages there and read other researchers' responses. You can also make contacts from the message boards to discuss common research and perhaps begin collaborating on your research.

- **Member Directory**—The Member Directory utilizes information that members enter in their public profile and allows you to search for others who

  - share your research interests;

  - are located in the area you are researching, are the same gender, or who are of a particular age;

  - have certain experience, longevity, and frequency in genealogical research;

  - are of a specific nationality, ethnic group, or geographical heritage or lineage;

  - speak or read specific a language; or

  - share a common faith.

- **Member Connections**—The Member Connections section is an important tool that allows you to search for other Ancestry members who are researching the same ancestors as you.

These component areas all work together to help form a solid networking facility at Ancestry.com. In addition, RootsWeb.com hosts e-mail mailing lists on topics similar to the Message Boards at Ancestry.com. You can learn more about them and subscribe to one or more at <http://lists.rootsweb.com>.

Let's now explore the Ancestry Community so you understand how to use its features to your best research advantage.

My Public Profile

Your public profile can contain as much or as little information as you would like to share with other Ancestry.com members.

Figure 15-2 shows the "My Public Profile" page that I set up when writing this book. It shows my username which, in this case, is AncestryUserID. It also displays where I am from, the date I became a member (with this username), and the last time I updated the profile.

Figure 15-2: My Public Profile

You can access your profile to edit it by clicking **Edit your profile** in the profile section of the "Community" page. You can also access it from anywhere on the site by clicking "My Account" in the top right corner of most pages.

Let's take a look at what you can do:

- **Edit personal information**—By clicking **Edit name, location & intro** in the main section at the top of the page, you can change your username (which would also change your log in information), choose whether your profile displays your username or your real name, edit your location, and add some descriptive text about yourself. In the same main section of your profile, you can also add a photo of yourself. You can also flesh out your profile by clicking the pencil icon in the "About [username]" section in the right column. Here you can specify more personal information (like gender, age, lineage, and so on),

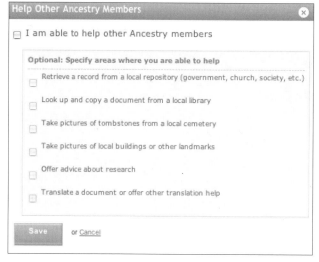

Figure 15-3: Options for helping others

define your family history experience, and specify your own personal website or sites you like.

• **Offer help to others**—Click the pencil icon in the "Can you help other members?" section. Here you can specify if you are able to perform services for other researchers (like looking up a record in a library, taking pictures of sites, and so on; see figure 15-3). One the real strengths of the community comes in researchers helping each other.

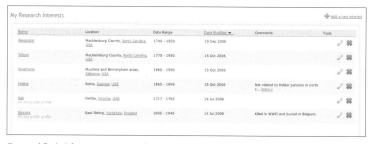

Figure 15-4: Editing your research interests

• **Define research interests**—Click the pencil icon to specify your research interests, which help Ancestry.com suggest possible research routes and help you connect with other researchers (see figure 15-4). You can add new research interests or remove ones that you no longer need.

On your profile page, you can also view your Family Trees and message boards you've posted to. You can access the Member Directory as well.

Message Boards

The Message Boards at Ancestry.com are among the most powerful tools for communicating, sharing, and collaborating with other researchers. A message board is defined as a place on the Internet where people visit and exchange information. They do so by either posting a message and waiting for replies or by reading messages and sending replies. It's as simple as that.

Format

A message posted on a message board may be similar to an e-mail message. It consists of two important parts: the subject line and the body of the message.

Subject Line

A subject line should be meaningful and informative. It should communicate to the reader what is inside the message. If you use a subject line like "HELP!!!!!" don't expect a lot responses. Likewise, if you are posting a message to the Wilson surname message board with a subject line that reads "Looking for Wilsons," don't expect many responses there.

A good subject line will include a name, a location, a time period, and then perhaps what you are seeking. For example, if I were looking for information about my grandmother, I might write a subject line as follows:

Laura A. "Minnie" Wilson (1873–1966)—Mecklenburg Co., NC

This tells the reader who I am looking for and where. By including that much information in the subject line, it may be enough to attract the attention of a reader to open the message and read it—and then to respond if he or she has information to share.

Message board users sometimes use a form of shorthand to indicate certain information, particularly migration movement. The use of the ">" character indicates that someone moved from one place to another. Therefore, another good subject line for a message board posting might look like this.

> Brisco Holder (1877–?)—GA>IA>?—Seeking Death Location

In this case, I am indicating that I am seeking information about a man named Brisco Holder who was born in 1877 in Georgia. I know that he migrated to Iowa and then somewhere else. I do not know where he went from Iowa or when he died. The subject line of this message would indicate the who, when, where, and what is being sought inside the text of the message.

Body of the Message

Just as the subject line of a message should be informative, the body of the message should also contain enough detail to help the reader determine if he or she knows anything about the subject of your inquiry that could be helpful. There are a number of important points to keep in mind when writing the body of the message:

- Provide enough information to let the reader know what you are seeking.

- Do not go into excessive detail that may only confuse the reader.

- If seeking information about an individual, include the person's full name and any nickname(s) by which he or she may have been known. Be sure to provide a woman's maiden and married names.

- Include the dates and locations where you know the person to have been at key periods in his or her life.

- Include names of parents, siblings, spouse(s), and children.

- Describe *exactly* what you are seeking.

- Tell the reader what you already know *and* where you have already researched. Don't make the reader respond with information you already have or check sources you have already exhausted.

- Indicate if you want the reader to respond to you on the message board or privately by e-mail.

- Offer to share information you have about a person or family line if you have such information.

- Thank the readers for taking the time to read and respond to you.

An example of a well-written message posted at Ancestry.com is shown in figure 15-5. It has an informative subject line regarding surnames and a location, and the body of the message is informative but concise.

As a result of this good posting, four strong responses were posted to it, as shown in figure 15-6 (on the next page).

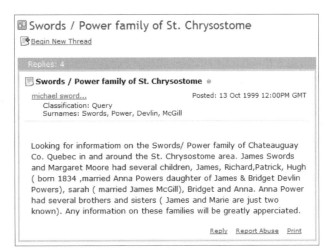

Figure 15-5: Example of a well-written message board posting

You can read any message in the list shown in figure 15-6 by clicking the subject line. The orange dot to the left of a message indicates that you have not read it. Likewise, you can click on the name of the author of the e-mail. As a result, you might see a summary of that member's profile, from which you

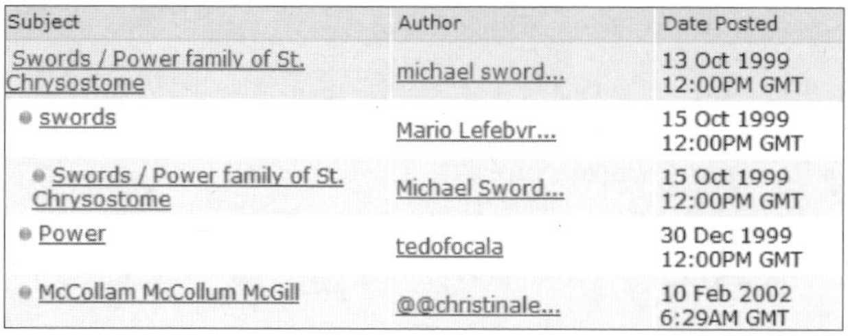

Subject	Author	Date Posted
Swords / Power family of St. Chrysostome	michael sword...	13 Oct 1999 12:00PM GMT
● swords	Mario Lefebvr...	15 Oct 1999 12:00PM GMT
● Swords / Power family of St. Chrysostome	Michael Sword...	15 Oct 1999 12:00PM GMT
● Power	tedofocala	30 Dec 1999 12:00PM GMT
● McCollam McCollum McGill	@@christinale...	10 Feb 2002 6:29AM GMT

Figure 15-6: List of original message board posting and responses to it

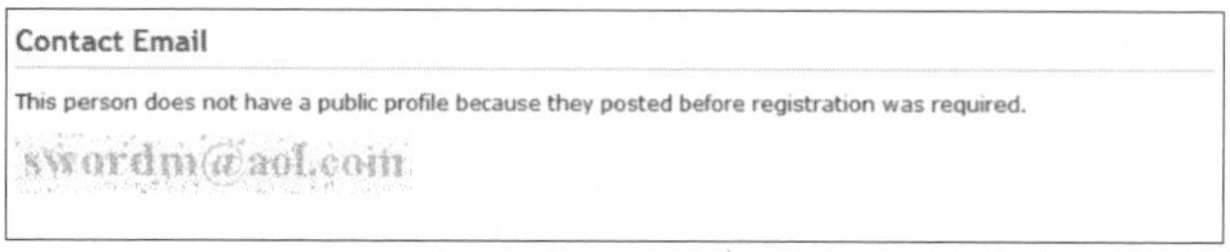

Contact Email

This person does not have a public profile because they posted before registration was required.

swordm@aol.com

Figure 15-7: Contact e-mail for a member without a public profile

can contact him or her. Also, because the message board postings go back a number of years before Ancestry.com made a number of Ancestry Community enhancements, you might see a page with an image (see figure 15-7).

Before Ancestry.com required someone wishing to use the Message Boards complete a registration, only e-mail addresses were required to make a posting. The person who in 1999 posted the message I used in the figure 15-5 is now identified simply by his e-mail address.

Searching the Message Boards

With the concepts of good subject line and message body content in mind, let's return to the "Message Boards" section of the "Ancestry Community" page and begin discussing how to browse and search the Message Boards effectively.

You'll see links to message boards related to surnames that you may be researching, based on your Family Trees. From here, you can also search all the board.

In the "Search the message boards" field on the "Message Boards" section, you can enter anything: surname, location, topic, and so on. Note, however, that the Ancestry.com Message Boards search tool does not function like an Internet search engine. It does not use an exact phrase search, for example. If I enter "madison, nc" into the field, I will receive matches for postings in which both terms appear, such as

"Madison County,"
"James Madison, NC,"
and on and on.

You can perform a
more finite search by
clicking the "Advanced
Search" link and using
the page shown in
figure 15-8.

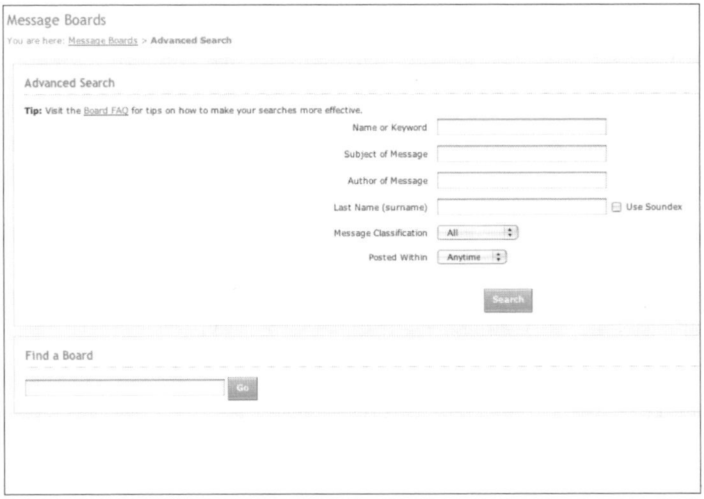

The first thing I
would recommend
you do is click the
link labeled "Board
FAQ." The page
displayed contains all

Figure 15-8: Advanced search form for the Message Boards

the information you will need to successfully understand and
work with the Ancestry.com Message Boards.

As shown in figure 15-8, there are two forms on this page:
the Advanced Search form and the Find a Board search form.
The Advanced Search form can be used to search for one or
multiple things about a posting using the different search fields.

The Find a Board form allows you to search directly for
a message board. Simply enter a surname, location, or other
topic and click the **Go** button. Sometimes your search will
come up empty. When that happens, it makes sense to return
to the Advanced Search form shown in figure 15-8.

You can expand your searching and browsing options by
clicking "Go to the boards" on the "Ancestry Community"
page. This brings you to the main page for the Message Boards.

Here you can search, just as you did from the "Ancestry
Community" page and the "Advanced Search" page. You can
also browse by surname or category.

Browse by Surname

To browse by surname, refer to the "Surnames" section, where letters A through Z are shown (see figure 15-9). If I click the letter "P," I see another line with two-letter abbreviations.

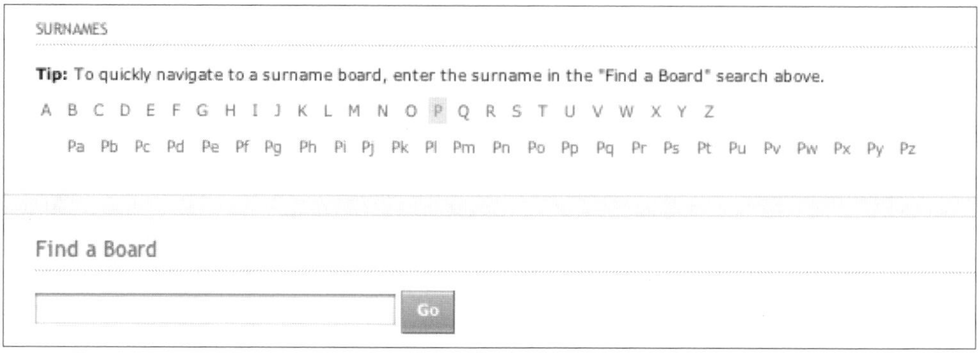

SURNAMES

Tip: To quickly navigate to a surname board, enter the surname in the "Find a Board" search above.

A B C D E F G H I J K L M N O P Q R S T U V W X Y Z

Pa Pb Pc Pd Pe Pf Pg Ph Pi Pj Pk Pl Pm Pn Po Pp Pq Pr Ps Pt Pu Pv Pw Px Py Pz

Find a Board

[   ] [Go]

Figure 15-9: Browsing surnames

Perhaps I am searching for the Patterson surname. I will then click the "Pa" combination and am given a new list of three-letter options.

Next I click on the three-letter abbreviation for "Pat" and am rewarded with a list of the first ten surname listings within that group, shown in figure 15-10. Because there are 181 matches, I will need to scroll through the list until I locate the Patterson message board.

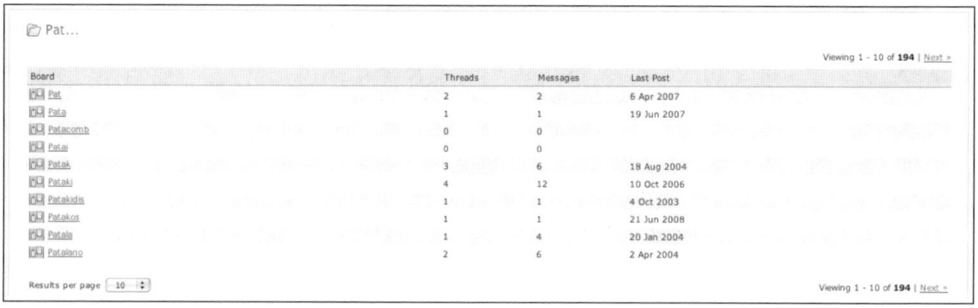

📁 Pat...

Viewing 1 - 10 of **194** | Next »

Board	Threads	Messages	Last Post
Pat	2	2	6 Apr 2007
Pata	1	1	19 Jun 2007
Patacomb	0	0	
Patai	0	0	
Patak	3	6	18 Aug 2004
Pataki	4	12	10 Oct 2006
Patakidis	1	1	4 Oct 2003
Patakos	1	1	21 Jun 2008
Patala	1	4	20 Jan 2004
Patalano	2	6	2 Apr 2004

Results per page [10 ◆]

Viewing 1 - 10 of **194** | Next »

Figure 15-10: First ten search results for "Pat"

The other information displayed on the match shown in figure 15-10 bears a little explanation. Look at the Patane surname and you will see that there are fourteen threads and thirty-seven messages, and the last post was made on 4 December 2006. You may very well ask, "What is a thread?"

A thread is a series of messages posted on a specific subject. It consists of the original message and all responses to it. And so, in this case, the Patane surname has had fourteen original subjects posted to the message board, and to those fourteen messages, there have been a total of thirty-seven various responses posted there, the last one made on 4 December 2006. We will look at threads and how they are displayed a little later in this chapter.

When I reached the Patterson surname in the list, there were thousands of messages—a whole lot of messages to work my way through! However, I clicked on the Patterson surname (see figure 15-11).

The "Names or Keywords" search field at the top of the page can come in very handy on a message board. If, as in the case of the Patterson board, there are thousands of messages, you certainly may want to narrow the scope of what you have to search. I am looking for my great-grandmother,

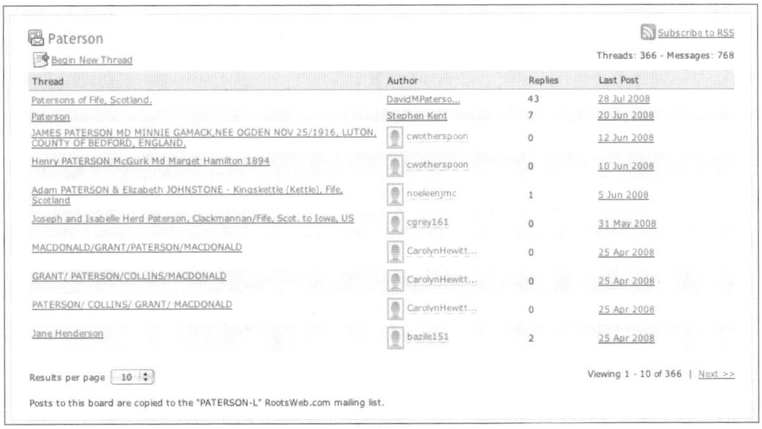

Figure 15-11: The Patterson message board

Lydia Lenora Patterson from North Carolina. I therefore enter "lydia" and "nc" in the "Names or Keywords" field and then click the "Patterson Board" option. In this case, doing so narrows thousands of messages to three. Now, be careful not to make any assumptions about what another researcher might enter in a message board posting. He or she may have entered "North Carolina" rather than "nc." You should therefore try "carolina" as another search keyword option rather than "nc."

Let's return to figure 15-11. Look at the message with the thread (subject) titled "Rachel Patterson b: August 29, 1746." The author posted this new subject on 2 December 2006 and had received one reply by the time of this writing. (You will notice that other postings include both a date *and* a time; they were written on the current day's date and are time stamped to assist you in following the thread of postings. Let's proceed to click the thread name/subject of this posting and examine the result in detail. The resulting page is shown, in part, in figure 15-12.

The author wrote a good subject line and has indicated in his message body what he was seeking. You will note that the message was originally posted on 10 April 1999 but that a response was not received until 2 December 2006. The answer he received

Figure 15-12: Posting about Rachel Patterson

looks like a great match too! (See figure 15-13.)

There are two different ways to view message board postings. Look at figure 15-12 again. What you see is the "Thread View." In this view, the initial message in the thread is displayed in its entirety. It is then followed by each of the responses,

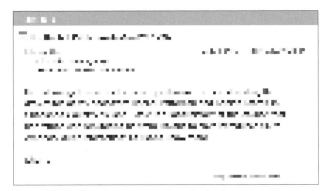

Figure 15-13: Response to posting about Rachel Patterson

displayed only with its subject line. You must click on each response to read it, which is great when you may want to read only certain replies.

Beneath the initial message is a link titled "Change to Flat View." If you click that link, the display changes so that the initial message in the thread and all responses, in chronological sequence, are displayed in full. This is an easy way to read *all* of the responses and print them. When you are in "Flat View," a "Change to Thread View" link is present.

Ancestry.com remembers from session to session which view you last selected and will use that for all message board displays until you change the view again.

You will note that at the bottom of every message are three links. The first is "Reply." This allows you to respond to the message board posting with another posting. A new page is displayed into which I can type a reply to the message, shown at the bottom of the page.

The second of the three links at the bottom of each message is labeled "Report Abuse." If you read the Community Guidelines, you will clearly understand what is and is not acceptable behavior at Ancestry.com. The "Report Abuse"

Figure 15-14: The "Report abuse" page

page, shown in figure 15-14, is displayed with an area for you to type a description of an infraction you believe has occurred. See, also, that there is a drop-down list of different categories of objections from which you can choose.

The third link at the bottom of each message is a "Print" link. This allows you to get a clean print image, without the boxes and shading. Simply display this page and press the "CTRL" and "P" keys simultaneously. This will send the page to your printer. Click "Return to Message" to return to where you were.

At the top of the Patterson message board and on every thread's page is a link that allows you to "Begin New Thread." Click that link to begin a new thread on your own, and a new page, like the one shown in figure 15-15, will appear.

Note a check box labeled, "Send me an alert when anyone replies to this thread." By checking this box, Ancestry.com will send me an e-mail whenever anyone responds to this message or any reply posted to it. Use the "Surname" field to list any surnames mentioned in the post. This helps when someone is searching for

Figure 15-15: "Post new thread" page

those surnames to find my new thread. Since I am seeking information about a marriage record, I have used the "Classification" drop-down list to select an appropriate subject. Finally, if I wanted to attach a file, such as a GEDCOM or a photograph, I could do so.

Once you have finished writing your new message, you can click the **Preview** button to see what it looks like. It's always good to proofread your messages for accuracy. You can also click on the **Post** button to place your new message on the message board. However, if you change your mind about posting it, you can always do so by clicking "Cancel."

Using the links on any page of the Ancestry Community, you can also determine how you want to keep track of boards you'd like to follow:

- **Board Information**—The administrator of the message board will post guidelines for getting the most out of the message board. There will be a link to allow you to contact him or her as well. There may also be Web links to other sites of interest.

- **Add Thread to Favorites**—Rather than have to re-search for a message board, thread, topic, or location of interest to you each time you want to check it, simply click on "Add Thread to Favorites" and it is automatically added to your list. (When looking at boards, you can also add them to your favorites.) You can manage your favorites from within the Community page by clicking "My Favorites" at the top of the page (see figure 15-16 on the next page).

- **Add Board to Alerts**—This third link allows you to add this message board to a list of your personal alerts. Whenever a new thread or reply is posted, Ancestry.com will send you an e-mail with a link to the message board.

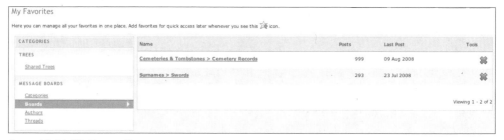

Figure 15-16: "My Favorites" page

Figure 15-17: "My Alerts" page

You can manage your favorites at any time from within the Ancestry Community pages by clicking "My Alerts" in the top right of the page (see figure 15-17).

Note that you can also subscribe to a board using the RSS feed provided on the board page.

The Ancestry.com Message Boards may seem complicated, but once you begin working with them, you will wonder what you ever did without them. Message boards really can extend your research reach exponentially. They can also introduce you to many wonderful people who are part of the Ancestry Community and happy to help you with your research.

Browse by Location and Other Topics

So far, we have concentrated on surnames. However, the "Message Boards" page also includes a link to search by locations, and the world is grouped into geographical areas and then by localities within each area. You will want to explore by country or other locale for yourself. Remember, too, that you may post a message to a surname list *and* to a geographical location in order to maximize your exposure and opportunity to make connections with others. You can also explore message boards for every conceivable genealogical topic by clicking the "other topics." Topics range from "Adoption" to "Volunteer Projects." There is a wealth of information to be gleaned from other members of the Ancestry Community on the Ancestry.com Message Boards.

Member Connections

Beneath the Message Boards on the "Ancestry Community" page is the section labeled "Member Connections." Here Ancestry.com provides you with names of others who are searching for names found in your trees or who have similar research interests, and they allow you to annonymously contact those people for help, if you choose.

You can also input an ancestor's name into the search fields at the bottom of the secion to find other members searching for that person.

The Member Directory

Another component on the Ancestry Community is the Member Directory (see figure 15-18).

The first tab of the "Member Directory" section is **Interests**. I performed a simple search and selected England from the drop-down

Figure 15-18: "Member Directory" section

list of countries, and then chose the county of Essex. I clicked the **Find** button and the page shown in figure 15-19 was displayed. I might now make contact with any of the 441 users in this search results list. I could also revise my search or choose to search in another way.

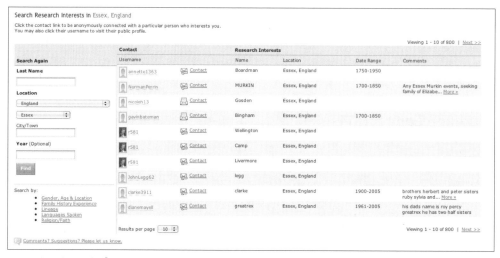

Figure 15-19: Results for "Interests"

The second tab of the Member Directory is **Location/ Age**. I can choose to find other members who completed their profile for the fields of gender, age group, and location.

The third category is **Experience**. The drop-down lists indicate experience in terms of "Beginner," "Intermediate," "Advanced," or "Professional." You specify the length of time the members you are seeking have been involved with their research and how frequently they currently engage in research.

The **Lineage** tab is used to search for persons of specific geographical or ethnic heritage.

The **Language Spoken** tab has a drop-down list of languages, and you can search for persons who speak or are studying ancestry based on language.

Finally, the sixth tab, **Faith**, is used to locate other members who indicated their faith in their profile.

Summary

The Ancestry Community is a vast group of highly active genealogical researchers. They are a friendly and helpful group overall who want to share and collaborate on their genealogical research.

The Ancestry.com Message Boards are a tremendous tool for expanding your research possibilities and making new contacts. It is not unusual to make a "cousin connection" on a rather frequent basis.

The Member Directory can bring you together with other people with interests similar to your own. And the Member Connections facility can definitely help you find others conducting research on your lines and other collateral lines.

When you combine the content of the Ancestry.com databases, the search facilities, the indexes, the images, the message boards, and the communications facilities, you can certainly understand why this really *is* the right online genealogy service to be using.

DNA

Genetics has become an important genealogical tool for confirming relationships and descent from common ancestors. As more and more people participate in DNA testing, the possibility of identifying matches with other researchers will keep going up. By comparing your DNA test results with others, you can determine to what extent you are related. For example, the more closely your result set matches another's, the narrower the range of generations between the two of you and a common ancestor.

Genetics is the science of heredity and variation in living organisms. The study of the inheritance of characteristics began in the mid-1800s with Gregor Johann Mendel, a German-Czech Augustinian monk and scientist who made detailed studies of the nature of inheritance in plants. He observed and developed an understanding of the inheritance of specific traits; the basic units of inheritance are now called genes.

Genes are arranged along a long cellular structure called a chromosome. The core of a chromosome is a long molecule called deoxyribonucleic acid, or DNA for short. In the 1950s, James D. Watson, Francis Crick, and Maurice Hugh Frederick Wilkins solved the question surrounding DNA's structure, determining that it is composed of four types of nucleotides. DNA is a three-dimensional, double-stranded helix, with the opposing nucleotides on each strand physically paired to each other. Each strand acts as a template for synthesis of a new partner strand, providing the physical mechanism for the inheritance of information.

In modern times, the study of genetics has led to an understanding of the components of living organisms. DNA is present in cells, including skin, hair follicles, and bodily fluids, and the genetic code of each individual is mathematically unique, with the exception of most twins.

There are two types of DNA testing. The first type tests the Y chromosome, which is used to trace the paternal lineage of an individual to determine the Most Recent Common Ancestor (MRCA). The second tests the mitochondrial DNA (also represented as mtDNA), which can predict your ancient maternal ancestry and confirm whether two people are *not* genetically related.

Don't let the technical jargon and genetic chemistry confuse you or put you off. The concepts of genetic genealogy are explained in an excellent book written by experts Megan Smolenyak Smolenyak and Ann Turner titled *Trace Your Roots with DNA: Using Genetic Tests to Explore Your Family Tree* (Rodale Books, 2004). It is a must-read for understanding genetic testing's role in genealogical research. In addition, you should read the "DNA Basics" article in the Learning Center at Ancestry.com.

Testing at Ancestry.com

At the time of this writing, you can order DNA test kits through Ancestry.com. The testing will be performed by an accredited DNA testing laboratory, and your test results will be posted to your area of Ancestry.com, accessible whenever you log in. You can manually enter mitochondrial DNA (mtDNA) test results you have obtained through another testing laboratory, and you can input your Y-DNA test results from other labs who also do DNA testing, such as the Family Tree DNA and the National Geographic Genographic Project. With the strength of more than 15 million Ancestry members worldwide, more and more people are having their DNA tested, and the numbers of potential matches will be growing rapidly. What's more, when the Ancestry DNA database detects that a new match has been added, an e-mail will automatically be sent to you. This will alert you that there is someone else in the Ancestry Community to whom you may be related. You can then use the Ancestry Community services to contact matching participants without revealing your personal e-mail address.

Now that you have all this background information, let's explore the **DNA** tab at Ancestry.com and learn what you can find there.

The DNA Homepage

When you click on the **DNA** tab, you will be taken to the page shown in figure 16-1 (on the next page). Here you will find a great deal of information to help you get started on your odyssey of DNA discovery.

From here, you can join or search DNA groups, look for people with certain surnames who have taken DNA tests, and learn more about the DNA process. Because much of this is

Figure 16-1: The "DNA" page

irrelevant unless you have a test of your own, we'll discuss the process of getting and reading your test first and then discuss some of the these other features.

Your DNA Test

Ordering your DNA test is simple. From the "DNA" page, click on the orange **Order Now** button. The next page, shown in figure 16-2, first asks for the gender of the person being tested. A male may have any or all of the three tests—paternal, advanced paternal, and maternal—performed. A female, on the other hand, may

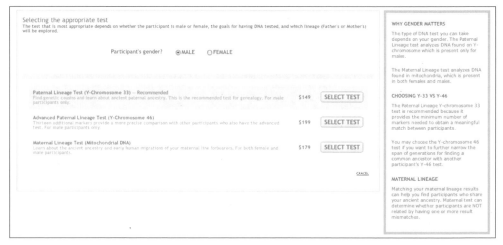

Figure 16-2: Ordering DNA tests

have only a maternal mtDNA test performed. If a female is interested in exploring her paternal lineage, a DNA sample must be provided by her father, brother, or a male cousin on her father's side. For a Y-DNA test, choose "Male" for the participant's gender and select a Paternal Lineage Test.

Once you have received your test in the mail, taken the sample, and submitted it, it takes up to four weeks for the testing to be completed. Throughout the process, you will receive e-mails reporting on the status of your test. When the testing is complete, the results will be posted for you on Ancestry.com. When you log in, you can access your test results report by clicking on the "View Console" link in the upper right-hand corner of the DNA homepage or by clicking on the link labeled "Go to Your Test Results" that appears below the orange **Order Now** button.

By the way, you can manually enter DNA test results from Family Tree DNA, the National Geographic Genographic Project, and other testing laboratories using the links on the "DNA" page beneath the **Order Now** button.

Looking at Your Test Results

The results of your test will appear on their own set of pages. In this chapter, we'll look at samples of both paternal DNA and mtDNA test results.

The top half of the page showing my paternal lineage test results is shown in figure 16-3. I have had both paternal and maternal testing

Figure 16-3: My paternal lineage test results

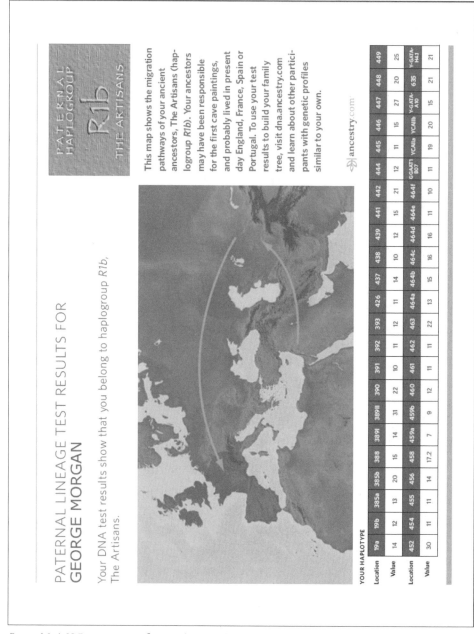

Figure 16-4: PDF print version of paternal test results

done, so there are several tabs at the top of the page: **My Results**, **Paternal Matches**, **Maternal Matches,** and a link back to the DNA homepage.

A link above the results grid is labeled "Understanding your results," and the information shown there can help you learn more about the fields and their contents. To the right side of the page is a link that allows you to download and/or print a copy of your test results as a PDF file, a sample of which is shown in figure 16-4.

This page includes a map indicating the probable migration path taken by my ancient ancestors. It also shows my haplo-group—R1b—and a description of my ancient ancestors. A haplogroup, and subgroups called subclades, can be used to define genetic populations and track their migration patterns.

You can view the default map, or you can click on the hybrid or satellite versions of the map.

When I click on the **Paternal Matches** tab on the test results page, the page shown in figure 16-5 is displayed.

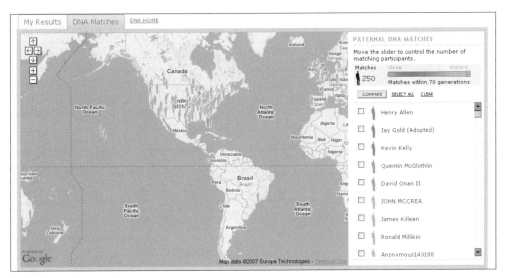

Figure 16-5: Paternal DNA matches page

As you can see, a map is displayed that uses small green icons to represent where a potential match is located. In my case, there are 250 potential matches, and their usernames are included in the scroll box below. Those 250 matches, however, represent matches within seventy generations. That is a very, very long time—actually more than 1,750 years ago. I probably want to make contact with people whose matches are close to mine within many fewer generations. The button on the slider bar on the right side of the screen can be clicked and dragged to the left to move closer to the current generation. In my case, I moved the slider to the most recent matches and found there are three matches within fifteen generations. While that is still almost 400 years, connections could conceivably be made.

You can click one or more boxes beside the individuals' username(s), or you can click the link to select all of the matches. Then, when you click on the **Compare** button, a page similar to that shown in figure 16-6 will be displayed.

The table displayed will compare the genetic markers of each of the participants you selected. Your closest matches

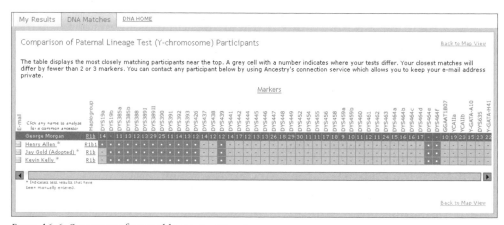

Figure 16-6: Comparison of parental lineage participants

will differ by fewer than two or three markers. You can contact any participant shown by using the Ancestry Connection Service, which allows you to communicate while keeping your e-mail address private.

The "Common Ancestors" graph shows the results of a statistical analysis comparing your results with those of

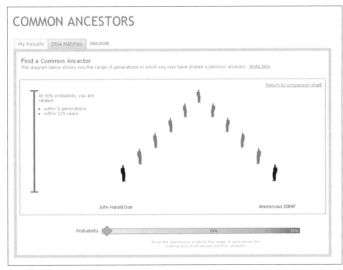

Figure 16-7: Maternal DNA test results page

other participants (see figure 16-7). This analysis calculates a range of generations in which you might have shared a common ancestor. This Most Recent Common Ancestor analysis provides a great starting point for comparing your family trees. The range of generations increases with the greater number of mismatches between your Y-chromosome profiles. In addition, this graph identifies the most likely generation in which you share a common ancestor.

If you order an mtDNA test, the results displayed for the test will differ from the paternal results in terms of coding. The map and description of ancient migrations is still used.

You can click on the **Maternal Matches** tab to display the "Comparison of Maternal Test (mitochondrial DNA) Participants" page. Figure 16-8 (on the next page) shows an example of part of this page from my mtDNA test matches. As you can see, this page differs from its corresponding paternal test matches page as well.

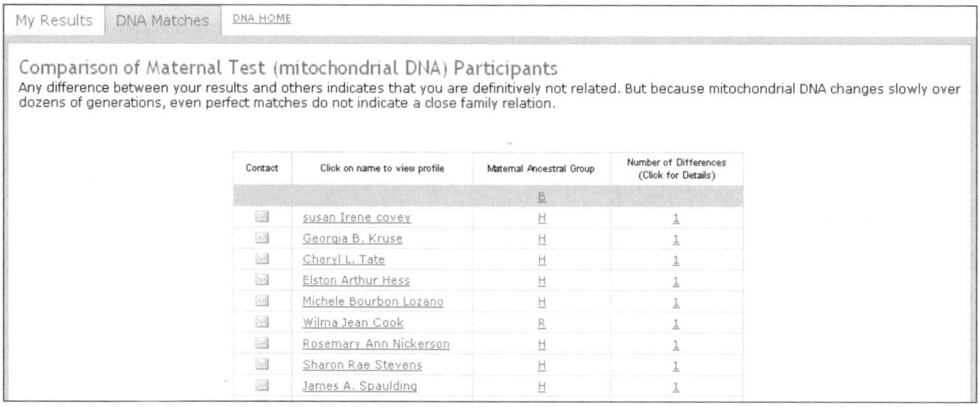

Contact	Click on name to view profile	Maternal Ancestral Group	Number of Differences (Click for Details)
		B	
	susan Irene covey	H	1
	Georgia B. Kruse	H	1
	Cheryl L. Tate	H	1
	Elston Arthur Hess	H	1
	Michele Bourbon Lozano	H	1
	Wilma Jean Cook	R	1
	Rosemary Ann Nickerson	H	1
	Sharon Rae Stevens	H	1
	James A. Spaulding	H	1

Figure 16-8: "Comparison of Maternal Test Participants" Page

In both the Paternal and Maternal test results areas, you will see links labeled "Understanding your results, click here." These lead to additional descriptive information. And you can always return to the DNA homepage for information about the testing and results, FAQs, and more.

Again, *Trace Your Roots with DNA: Using Genetic Tests to Explore Your Family Tree* is a great manual for in-depth study and understanding of genetic genealogical testing.

DNA Groups

DNA groups are a kind of social networking feature that allow you to connect with others who have similar DNA results and research interests.

Each group is created and administered by a member (as opposed to someone in the company) who regulates who joins the group and so on. Groups are by invitation only (though you can request admission), protecting the privacy of members.

Once formed, the groups are places where members can share their research, photos, stories, and more. You do not have to have taken a DNA test, but it usually helps you to get the most out of the group.

To see if a group surrounding your surname exists, go to the "Ancestry DNA" page and type a name into the search form under "Search DNA Groups." This will present you with a list of results from which you can choose (see figure 16-9).

From the DNA homepage you can also browse all existing groups by clicking **Browse All**. You can then narrow your search by letter and find a group that you're interested in.

SEARCH DNA GROUPS
Find groups that may share in your family history.
Or Create your own group.
[ ] Submit → -OR- Browse All

Figure 16-9: "Search DNA Groups" field of the Ancestry DNA homepage

Once you've found a group that looks interesting to you, click "View & Join" from the results page. This takes you to a summary page for that group and shows you details about it. Click **Request Membership** to ask the administrator to consider your admittance into the group.

If you don't find a group that matches your needs, you can always start your own group. On the main DNA page, click "Create a New Group," follow the prompts, and you're on your way. Once you have joined or created a group, you will have access to all the group features, including the ability to add photos and videos, set up various discussions, and a variety of others. Note that DNA groups are built on the framework of MyFamily.com, so they function similarly.

Summary

The future of genealogical research is finally here with the addition of DNA to our toolkits. You can expect to see additional enhancements to the DNA area of Ancestry.com over the coming years. There is no time like the present to get involved with DNA testing so you can begin exploring matches as other people are tested and their results are added to Ancestry.com.

Chapter 17

The Learning Center

The Learning Center at Ancestry.com has been completely redesigned and was launched in mid-December 2007. Like a modern library, it is also an exciting multimedia experience that provides you access to more genealogical guidance and online information resources than anywhere else on the Web.

The intent of this chapter is to help you understand how the Learning Center is organized and to provide examples of how you can use it to both expand your knowledge *and* improve your research successes. And while you may be an experienced Ancestry.com user, the reorganized Learning Center has regrouped some of your favorite resources. This chapter will help you find your way around the new Learning Center, and I think you will find yourself agreeing with me that the new Learning Center is an invaluable, well-organized improvement for Ancestry.com users of all skill levels. So let me give you a guided tour!

Welcome to the Learning Center

Today's Ancestry.com Learning Center is quite different from its predecessor. The previous version was essentially a single page, while the new version consists of seven main topic pages and a variety of resources.

When you click on the **Learning Center** tab, you will arrive at the Learning Center "Welcome" page (shown in figures 17-1 and 17-2). When you arrive at the "Welcome" page, a video by Megan Smolenyak—a noted genealogist and expert in the field—introduces you to the Learning Center. Megan has made numerous helpful videos for the Learning Center. The six videos under the "More Videos" heading are excellent starting points. The "View All Videos" link will display the entire list of Megan's videos—twenty of them at this writing. Each is a mini lesson in itself and enough to get you started on your own research in many areas.

You will notice that there are six links that run across the top of the page. They are repeated in a list to the right of the video field. They are

Figure 17-1: Top of the "Welcome" page in the Learning Center

Figure 17-2: Bottom of the "Welcome" page in the Learning Center

- **Getting Started**—This area will introduce you to lots of "how-to" guidance, including how to start your research, a methodology for collecting information and evidence from others in your family, an overview of how Ancestry.com works, access to free charts and forms, and lots more.

- **Find Answers**—Learn about many of the records used most by genealogy researchers, how to find your ancestors and family members in them, how to analyze them, and how to organize what you find.

- **Build a Tree**—Discover how simple it is to use the Ancestry.com online Family Tree facility to create your personal family tree and how you can grow it with the databases and other resources at Ancestry.com.

- **Join the Community**—Communication and collaboration with others is a great way to learn more about your family, get questions answered, and build your knowledge. Here you'll learn about building your Public Profile, using the Ancestry.com Message Boards, and locating other members with similar research interests. You'll also discover the blogs and other electronic communication facilities offered at Ancestry.com.

- **Discover More**—This area is your gateway to a variety of projects you can undertake. Some of these will help you organize and preserve your research and evidence. Others will take you into more detailed research with many record types and evidence resources.

- **Keep Learning**—This area provides you access to a virtual library of magazine and online articles, reference materials, and more. You can search by author, keyword, or record type, and you can browse by year and month the full complement of Ancestry publications. You can find articles by many experts on the full range of genealogical research—an online library at your fingertips!

The complete set of links at the top of this page appears on every other Learning Center page, allowing you to quickly navigate from one area of learning and reference resources to another.

At the upper right-hand of the "Welcome" page is a small scroll box labeled "The Community." Here you can read comments by other users and even click to go to the "Message Boards" page to begin reading, posting, and responding to other people's queries.

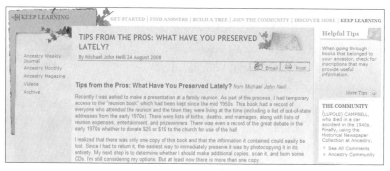

Figure 17-3: Example of online articles

The lower half of the "Welcome" page contains three important areas. The first, labeled "What's New," shows the most recent articles from the online *Ancestry Weekly Journal*. If you click on any of the title links, you'll be taken to the item, as shown in figure 17-3. There you can explore more links; browse the contents of the *Ancestry Weekly Journal*, the *Ancestry Monthly*, *Ancestry* Magazine, or the complete list of videos that we've discussed earlier; or search the archive of hundreds of articles from all the Ancestry periodicals and online newsletters. You can search for topics, authors, and/or keywords.

The second area is labeled "Tutorials" and contains multimedia overviews of four key items:

- **How does Ancestry.com work?**—A video presents information to help you learn how to find your ancestors and begin building your family tree.

- **See a sample tree**—This example of a family tree allows you to browse through each of the tabs of a My Ancestry Family Tree to see the variety of data, images, audio, and video that can be added. In this case, other people have been invited to participate or collaborate, and their comments are also shown.

- **AncestryPress**—AncestryPress (now MyCanvas), covered in detail in chapter 14 in the book, is illustrated in this rich video presentation. Examples of projects that you can do and publish in handsome keepsake albums are shown.

- **Family Tree Maker**—The #1-selling genealogy database software is introduced, and you can explore text, page shots, and a video, as well as download the latest updates to the software.

The third area is titled "Facts About Your Surname" and provides various information about the surname you designate. Simply enter the surname in the field below the chart and click on the button labeled **Get Facts**. A new page, shown in figure 17-4 (on the next page), will be displayed. Information is derived or calculated from the Ancestry.com databases.

This page allows you to select any of the ten fact types in the left column. You can e-mail the displayed results to yourself or to another person by clicking the link in the upper right of the page. The e-mail will contain a link which, when clicked, displays the page exactly as it appears on the Ancestry.com site.

The ten fact types include the following:

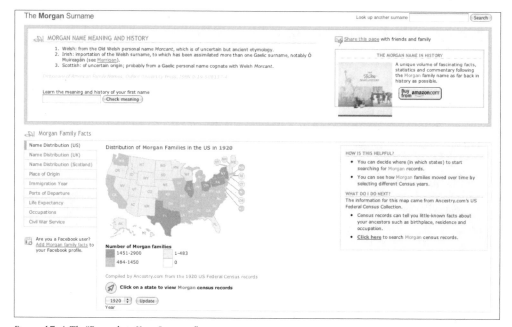

Figure 17-4: The "Facts about Your Surname" page

- **Civil War Service**—You can click on links associated with Confederate, Union, and Combined records to view a search results list of all veterans' Civil War records at Ancestry.com that match your surname.

- **Immigration Year**—A graph shows 1851 to 1891 immigration patterns based on New York passenger lists.

- **Life Expectancy**—This area displays a graph based on data from the Social Security Death Index from 1940 to 2001. Results for both the general public and the surname are plotted. You can click the circles on the surname graph line to see the results from the SSDI for all people whose deaths were recorded for the year represented by the circle.

- **Name Distribution (UK)**—A color-coded map of England and Wales indicates numerical ranges of people with your surname living there in 1891. By clicking on a county, the search results for all persons of the surname you input will be displayed, and you can then search for your ancestors or family members.

- **Name Distribution (U.S.)**—This works similarly to the UK version of the name distribution map. Clicking on a state displays the search results for all people with the surname you input. A drop-down list at the bottom of the page allows you to select from several census years.

- **Name Meanings**—This selection provides interesting historical background information about the surname, its meaning, and its usage.

- **Newspaper Headlines**—This section provides the top headlines from the decades of 1850 to 1990 that would have been of interest to your family members. You can select a year from the drop-down list at the bottom of the page. Click on the **Update** button, click on the key headline at the right of the image, and the newspaper image from the Historical Newspaper collection at Ancestry.com will be displayed for you to read.

- **Occupations**—Ancestry.com has produced a bar graph derived from the occupations of heads of households from 1880 U.S. federal census records. The occupations of the general population and people with the surname you selected are represented separately. Click on the surname bar, and all people of your surname who declared that occupation will be presented in the census search results list. You can go to the bottom of the search results page to narrow your search by forename, state, or other criteria.

- **Place of Origin**—Based on information compiled by Ancestry.com from the New York passenger lists, this graph gives you an idea of the numbers of people with the surname you chose who came to America and the countries from which they departed. Click on the country name, and you'll be presented with search results from the New York passenger lists based on country of origin.

- **Ports of Departure**—Ancestry.com has produced a pie chart compiled from information from the New York passenger lists to indicate the ports of departure for immigrants with the surname you chose. This may be used in conjunction with the **Place of Origin** facts to perhaps improve your chances of locating the immigration path for those people.

Taken altogether, you can see how the Learning Center's "Welcome" page provides access to a tremendous amount of foundation information for your research. However, this is just the beginning of what is available in the Learning Center. There are five more areas jam-packed with excellent, reliable information that can help you extend your knowledge and your research range. Think of the Learning Center as a virtual online library available 24/7 to help you.

Find Answers

The link to the "Find Answers" page opens another excellent source of information. Once again, we'll split the page into two figure images and describe what you'll find in each group of data. This page offers informative instruction, regardless of your research experience, so I strongly recommend taking the full tour and then coming back periodically for a refresher course, especially when you start working with a new record type or one you haven't worked with for a while.

Let's begin our tour at the top of the "Find Answers" page, which is shown in figure 17-5 on the next page. Megan Smolenyak presents six great videos that are listed beneath the

video window, and
you will also find
links to all the videos
in the sequence.
These are filled with
excellent guidance.

To the left of the
video field is a group
of topics relating
to specific record
types. Whatever you
do, don't ignore
these links. Each one

Figure 17-5: Top of the "Find Answers" page

is a well-written primer. Let's click on the link to "Census
Records." You will be taken to the page shown in figure 17-6.

The primary text in this portion of the Learning Center
provides information about what census records are, the years
for which U.S. and UK census schedules are available, facts
about census content, Frequently Asked Questions (FAQs)
and answers about census research at Ancestry.com, and links
to online articles specifically concerning the subject in the
Ancestry.com library.

Now look at the
left-hand column of
links, highlighted in
figure 17-7 on the
next page. Notice
additional subtopics
beneath the "Census
Records" title. You
will find helpful
content in this area.

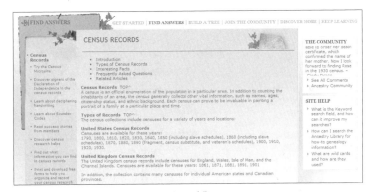

Figure 17-6: "Find Answers in Census Records" page

Figure 17-7: Additional topics under "Census Records"

- **Discover signers of the Declaration of Independence in the census records**—This link provides access to a fascinating article discussing each of the signers of the Declaration of Independence and the censuses in which you can find them.

- **Learn about deciphering handwriting**—This is an excellent starting point to help you understand how to work with older documents and interpret their sometimes confusing handwriting styles.

- **Learn about Soundex Codes**—Soundex is a method of coding surnames that sound alike but are spelled differently. Using Soundex, and the similar Miracode system, can be an excellent way to locate misspelled or misindexed surnames. This page explains Soundex coding and is sure to be a reference tool you will use again and again.

- **Read success stories from members**—Enjoy some great stories and tips on census research.

- **Discover census research helps**—Here are some of the most common pitfalls encountered when researching U.S. census records.

- **Find out what information you can find in census records**—This page explains what information is found in each U.S. federal census.

- **Print and download free forms to help you organize and record your census research**—Ancestry.com has prepared a number of free forms in PDF file format that you can either print or download to your computer for future reference and use.

You will find similar supplemental materials beneath most of the topics listed here. There are two exceptions. The "Military

Records" link connects you to the extensive collection of
military records, including indexes, digital images of military
records, and video newsreels. The "African-American Records"
link takes you to a comprehensive collection of "how-to"
instructions and discussions of specific Ancestry.com databases
that relate specifically to African-American research. These
include resources such as Slave Narratives, U.S. Colored
Troops Records, Freedmen's Bureau Records, Freedman's Bank
Records, African-American books online, WWI Draft Cards,
and the African-American Photographic Collection. Additional
records scheduled for addition at this writing include the
Southern Claims Commission Records and the Freedmen's
Bureau Marriage Records.

The bottom part of the "Find Answers" page consists of
two additional sections, shown in figure 17-8. The first is titled
"Choosing Historical Records" and contains links to articles

about census records and
military records that have
been discussed earlier.
The article concerning
vital records contains
interesting hints for
finding birth, marriage,
death, adoption, and other
records.

The other section
shown is titled "Piecing
Together Your Family
History" and is a succinct
recap of great starting
strategies for your family
history research.

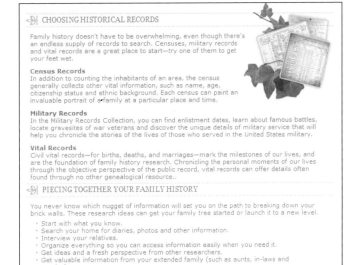

CHOOSING HISTORICAL RECORDS

Family history doesn't have to be overwhelming, even though there's
an endless supply of records to search. Censuses, military records
and vital records are a great place to start—try one of them to get
your feet wet.

Census Records
In addition to counting the inhabitants of an area, the census
generally collects other vital information, such as name, age,
citizenship status and ethnic background. Each census can paint an
invaluable portrait of a family at a particular place and time.

Military Records
In the Military Records Collection, you can find enlistment dates, learn about famous battles,
locate gravesites of war veterans and discover the unique details of military service that will
help you chronicle the stories of the lives of those who served in the United States military.

Vital Records
Civil vital records—for births, deaths, and marriages—mark the milestones of our lives, and
are the foundation of family history research. Chronicling the personal moments of our lives
through the objective perspective of the public record, vital records can offer details often
found through no other genealogical resource..

PIECING TOGETHER YOUR FAMILY HISTORY

You never know which nugget of information will set you on the path to breaking down your
brick walls. These research ideas can get your family tree started or launch it to a new level.

· Start with what you know.
· Search your home for diaries, photos and other information.
· Interview your relatives.
· Organize everything so you can access information easily when you need it.
· Get ideas and a fresh perspective from other researchers.
· Get valuable information from your extended family (such as aunts, in-laws and
  cousins).

Figure 17-8: Bottom portion of the "Find Answers in Census Records" page

Be sure to look for and read the content of the sidebars on the right side of the various pages for excellent hints on improving your searches. For example, the "Census Records" link brings up a page with a sidebar containing links to three important topics:

- What is the Keyword search field, and how can it improve my searches?

- How can I search the Ancestry library for how-to genealogy information?

- What are wildcards, and how are they used?

As you can see, the "Find Answers" area of the Learning Center has a tremendous amount of great reference material logically organized for easy access.

Build a Tree

This section of the Learning Center allows you to explore the elements of the Family Trees you can build in the "My Ancestry" area of Ancestry.com. Your personal Family Tree can combine all the elements of a traditional tree created in a commercial genealogical software program and more. When you build a tree at Ancestry.com, you can not only add names, dates, places, and notes, but you can also add an unlimited number of photographs, written stories, audio recordings, and video recordings. Furthermore, as you discover records in the Ancestry.com databases, you can link them to individuals for immediate access in the future *and* for inclusion in heirloom family books you can create with MyCanvas.

The Learning Center includes a complete section on how to build a Family Tree at Ancestry.com, including how to incorporate all the different elements that can make your tree uniquely yours. Look at figure 17-9 to see how this page provides step-by-step instructions for creating a dynamic, multimedia Family Tree.

There are six tutorial steps for building a Family Tree, each numbered and with a sample you can explore. For each step, simply click on the orange **See a Sample** button. Explore all the tabs on the sample tree to

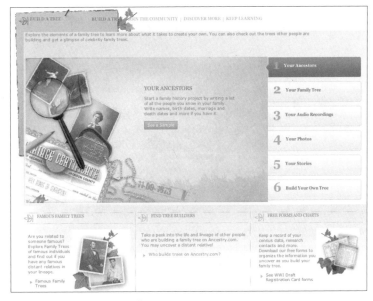

Figure 17-9: The "Build a Tree" page

get a better idea of the possibilities for your own project.

1. **Your Ancestors**—Start a family history project by making a list of all the people you know in your family. Write names, birth dates, marriage and death dates, and more if you have it.

2. **Your Family Tree**—The information you start to record will eventually take the shape of a family tree, an ever-growing link to your ancestors.

3. **Your Audio Recordings**—When you talk to your family members, try recording them. Audio clips add authenticity and interest to your family tree.

4. **Your Photos**—Collect photographs of family members, scan them, and upload them to your family tree. You will soon have an online family photo album.

5. **Your Stories**—Write down the stories you remember or have heard from your relatives. You can associate each story with specific family members in your tree.

6. **Build Your Own Tree**—Now that you know all the elements that make up a family tree, it's time to get started building a tree of your own. Click on the orange **Get Started** button, and you'll be taken to the **My Ancestry** tab, where you can begin working on *your* family tree!

There are three additional sections located on the lower portion of the page. The first is labeled "Famous Family Trees." You can click on a link to access and view a collection of celebrity family trees, from Abraham Lincoln to Brad Pitt and many others. The "Find Tree Builders" area allows you a look at other people who are building Family Trees at Ancestry.com. Click on the link "Who builds trees on Ancestry.com?" and you'll be taken to the **Ancestry Community** tab. Here you will find a multitude of connection options, all of which you can learn about in the "Ancestry Community" chapter. Finally, the "Free Forms and Charts" collection will provide you with preformatted forms as PDF files. These can help you organize your research or transcribe information for documents and other resources when you are out researching your ancestry.

Be sure to check out all the Helpful Tips, starting with the one posted in the upper-right corner of this page. You'll find access to hints on a number of Learning Center pages. These have been prepared by professional genealogists and by Ancestry.com product program developers, and they are designed to steer you toward research success.

Join the Community

The next section of the Learning Center is titled "Join the Community" and will introduce you to opportunities to communicate and collaborate with other researchers. The page for this section is shown in figure 17-10.

It begins with a photographic panel of three researchers: Joanna, Jerry, and Jim. By clicking on each person in turn, you can learn how each is each using the Ancestry.com community to further his or her research. When you click on Joanna, for example, her picture moves to the right side of the page, as shown in figure 17-11.

Figure 17-10: The "Join the Community" page

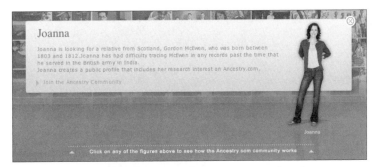

Figure 17-11: Joanna's use of the Ancestry.com Community explained

Joanna's research focus is explained, and you learn why she decided to use a public profile in the Ancestry.com community to gain more exposure to other researchers who may share her interests. To close Joanna's story, click on the X in the circle in the upper-right corner of the text box behind her. You can then learn how Jerry and Jim are using the community. In addition, to the right of the photo panel is a scroll box labeled "The Community," which contains a link to comments by other users just like you who have achieved more research success using the Ancestry.com facilities. These can give you new ideas for your own research.

The bottom portion of the "Join the Community" page contains three important areas that you are sure to want to check out. The first is titled "Family History Blog." A blog is essentially a diary or newsletter that is simple to access and read. Veteran genealogical editor Juliana Smith hosts the *24/7 Family History Circle*, an excellent blog that is a source of news; interesting, informative, and fun articles; tips from the pros and from users like you; research suggestions; and contributed photographs. Click on the link labeled "Family Circle Blog" to access the current edition of this great newsletter.

The second area is titled "Join the Conversation" and provides a link to the Ancestry.com Message Boards. The third area is titled "Make Yourself Known." Here you can click the link to create a Public Profile so that others with your same or similar research interests can locate you. You can add as much or as little information about yourself as you like, but the more you add, the better your chances for making connections with collaborative researchers.

Discover More

There are many ways to learn about genealogical research and share the information you've already gathered with other family members. The "Discover More" section provides several interesting venues for you to do just that. The "Discover More" page is shown in figure 17-12 (on the next page).

The photographic panel features projects you can create using content you've added to Ancestry.com or additional information. Notice the green arrows at the left and right ends of the panel. These allow you to scroll left and right to see other projects. Like the photographic panel in the "Join the

Community" section, click on each of the projects to learn more, and then click on the X in the upper-right corner of the text box holding the project description to close the screen. See figure 17-13 for an example.

Figure 17-12: Top of the "Discover More" page in the Learning Center

• **Family Cookbook**— You can access MyCanvas under **Print and Share** at the top of the Ancestry. com homepage (formerly the

Figure 17-13: Project Description Sample from the "Discover More" page in the Learning Center

Publish tab). You'll find professionally designed book page templates that are perfect for your favorite family recipes.

• **Family History Portrait**—Using MyCanvas, your personal Family Tree, photographs you have uploaded, and historical documents you have located and linked to your ancestor, you can generate a professional-looking family book up to one hundred pages long. Professionally designed template pages, embellishment clip art, and colorful backgrounds will make your book a unique family treasure.

• **Greeting Cards**—Create a keepsake family photo card using current or old photographs. These send a wonderful message on multiple levels.

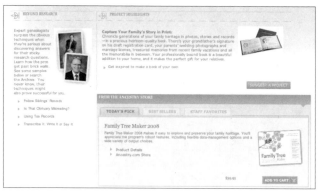

Figure 17-14: Bottom of the "Discover More" page in the Learning Center

Notice, too, that there are "Helpful Tips" and links to "The Community" on the right side of the page.

The bottom of the "Discover More" page, shown in figure 17-14, is comprised of three important areas. The most important area for you is the one titled "Beyond Research." This column of materials includes articles by expert genealogists from past issues of Ancestry publications of all sorts. Along with the *Ancestry Weekly Journal* and the *24/7 Family History Circle* blog, these articles will provide a quick way to expand your genealogical education.

"Project Highlights" showcases the instructions for one of the projects listed in the photo panel above. If you would like to suggest another type of project, you can click the orange **Suggest a Project** button. Ancestry.com staff will evaluate your suggestion's feasibility and respond.

The final section is "From the Ancestry Store," which highlights items from best sellers to staff favorites.

All of the resources in the "Discover More" section are sure to pique your interest. However, you'll find that you will never want to stop learning about genealogy in order to help you find more and more information. With that in mind, let's move to the last and largest area of the Learning Center.

Keep Learning

The final section in the Learning Center is one of the richest of all—"Keep Learning." This collection of information provides

you with access to
the massive library
at Ancestry.com.
There are literally
thousands of articles
that Ancestry has
published in *Ancestry*
Magazine, the
Genealogical Computing
quarterly, the online
Ancestry Daily News, the
Ancestry Weekly Journal,
the *Ancestry Monthly*,
the *Ancestry 24/7
Family Circle* blog, plus
selections from some

Figure 17-15: The "Keep Learning" page in the Learning Center

reference books by Ancestry Publishing. This growing body of
information won't replace your public library's genealogical
reference collection, but it *will* provide you with around-the-
clock access to reference materials written by the very best
genealogy experts.

There is a lot in the "Keep Learning" section, so let's begin
the tour with the page shown here in figure 17-15. We will
again explore by area, starting in the center of the page.

The "Featured Article" changes to provide you access
to an important article written by one of the many expert
genealogists in the world today. A brief description of the
article appears here, followed by a link you can click to read
the entire piece. Don't miss the opportunity to learn about
different subjects from the perspectives of the experts.

The next area is titled "Family History Articles" and consists
of organized collections addressing a number of topical areas.

These, too, will be changed so that you gain access to great resources. In figure 17-15, these subject areas include the following:

- **Using Ancestry.com**—You can always learn more about searching, saving records, and developing research strategies for making the most of the thousands of databases at Ancestry.com by checking out these topical articles.

- **Getting Organized**—One of the most difficult challenges for any genealogist is deciding how to arrange, organize, and file evidence. Most of us have tried multiple organizational schemes, and often one system does not fit all cases and needs. The articles you see here will give you new ideas and perspectives from the experts.

- **Sharing Your Family History**—It is important to preserve and communicate your family history to your relatives and others researching the same family lines. The articles found here will help you do just that.

- **Beginning Family History**—We were all beginning family researchers at one time, and no Learning Center area would be complete without articles for beginners. The *Beginner's Guide to Online Family History* is a series of tutorial articles to help you get started with research in general or record types you may not have encountered or used before.

- **Developing Research Skills**—These articles will help you learn how to locate and obtain training in research methodologies and procedures. These are some of the very best ways to keep on learning.

A portion of one of the articles is shown in figure 17-16 (on the next page). Other informational links are available to the left and right of the article to provide more places to explore.

The "Thought for the Day" and "Tip for Today" change each day and provide inspiration and guidance.

Let's now explore the left side of the "Keep Learning" page shown in figure 17-15. Here you will find a number of links as well as a search form.

The first link is to the *Ancestry Weekly Journal*, often referred to as the *AWJ*. The

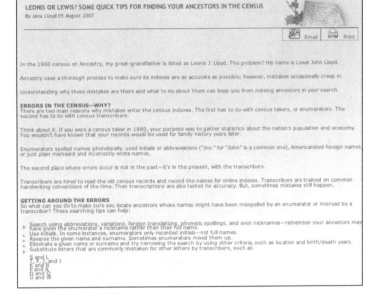

LEONIS OR LEWIS? SOME QUICK TIPS FOR FINDING YOUR ANCESTORS IN THE CENSUS
By Jana Lloyd 05 August 2007

Email   Print

In the 1900 census on Ancestry, my great-grandfather is listed as Leonis J. Lloyd. The problem? His name is Lewis John Lloyd.

Ancestry uses a thorough process to make sure its indexes are as accurate as possible; however, mistakes occasionally creep in.

Understanding why these mistakes are there and what to do about them can keep you from missing ancestors in your search.

ERRORS IN THE CENSUS—WHY?
There are two main reasons why mistakes enter the census indexes. The first has to do with census takers, or enumerators. The second has to do with census transcribers.

Think about it. If you were a census taker in 1880, your purpose was to gather statistics about the nation's population and economy. You wouldn't have known that your records would be used for family history years later.

Enumerators spelled names phonetically, used initials or abbreviations ("Jno." for "John" is a common one), Americanized foreign names, or just plain misheard and incorrectly wrote names.

The second place where errors occur is not in the past—it's in the present, with the transcribers.

Transcribers are hired to read the old census records and record the names for online indexes. Transcribers are trained on common handwriting conventions of the time. Their transcriptions are also tested for accuracy. But, sometimes mistakes still happen.

GETTING AROUND THE ERRORS
So what can you do to make sure you locate ancestors whose names might have been misspelled by an enumerator or misread by a transcriber? These searching tips can help:

▸ Search using abbreviations, variations, foreign translations, phonetic spellings, and even nicknames—remember your ancestors may have given the enumerator a nickname rather than their full name.
▸ Use initials. In some instances, enumerators only recorded initials—not full names.
▸ Reverse the given name and surname. Sometimes enumerators mixed them up.
▸ Eliminate a given name or surname and try narrowing the search by using other criteria, such as location and birth/death years.
▸ Substitute letters that are commonly mistaken for other letters by transcribers, such as:

S and L
T, I, J, and I
V and R
B and K
O and Q
U and W

Figure 17-16: Sample featured article from the Learning Center

Ancestry Weekly Journal brings a weekly boost to your research with helpful articles, tips, and information on the latest tools to help you discover your family's history. It's also a gateway to the *24/7 Family History Circle* blog, where you can interact with columnists and other readers and share your own tips and comments on newsletter posts. A sample from the *Ancestry Weekly Journal* page is shown in figure 17-17 (on the next page).

You can click on either the image of the diary *or* the title in bold to visit another page with the full content of the article. On each of the article pages are little links at the top labeled "Email" and "Print." These allow you to share the article with other people via e-mail (or send a copy to yourself), or you can send a printer-friendly document. At the bottom of these *AWJ* articles, you may also submit a comment for others to read—and you can read the comments others have already

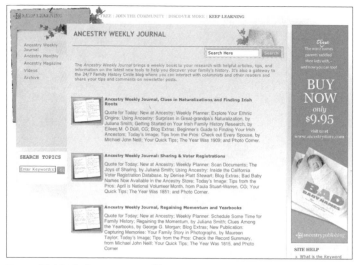

Figure 17-17: The "Ancestry Weekly Journal" page

posted. You can sign up to receive the *AWJ* each week via e-mail by clicking the orange button at the bottom of the right-hand column. It will be e-mailed to the e-mail address you included in your personal profile on Ancestry. com.

The next link in the list on the left side of the page is labeled "Ancestry Monthly"; it takes you to the page shown in figure 17-18. The *Ancestry Monthly* is an e-mail newsletter created specifically for Ancestry.com subscribers and registered users. Each issue contains great articles that tell you what's new on the site and explain how to get the most out of your subscription.

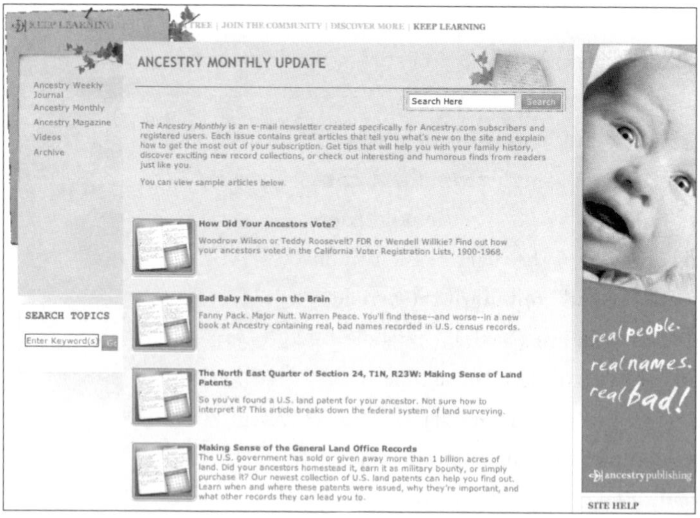

Like the *AWJ* page, you can click on the diary graphic or the article title beside it to access the article on

Figure 17-18: The "Ancestry Monthly" page

another page. You can also e-mail or print the article. In addition, you will see a Search box and button at the top of the center section. Click in the box and type a term or phrase that describes a feature or database at Ancestry.com, and then click the orange **Search** button. Any available articles will be displayed for your review.

The next link is labeled "Ancestry Magazine," and it will take you to a page that looks like the one in figure 17-19. *Ancestry* Magazine is one of the

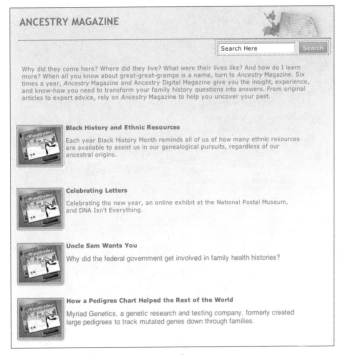

Figure 17-19: The "Ancestry *Magazine*" page

most respected genealogical publications in the United States. Six times a year, *Ancestry* Magazine will give you the insight, experience, and know-how you need to transform your family history questions into answers. From original articles to expert advice, you can rely on *Ancestry* Magazine to help you uncover your past.

The "Ancestry Magazine" link allows you to click on the graphic image of the magazine *or* on the title to the right to access another page (just like the "Ancestry Weekly Journal" and "Ancestry Monthly" links) where you can read, e-mail, or print an entire article. In addition, you can enter a term or an entire article's title in the Search box and then click the orange **Search** button. An updated page, like the one in figure 17-19,

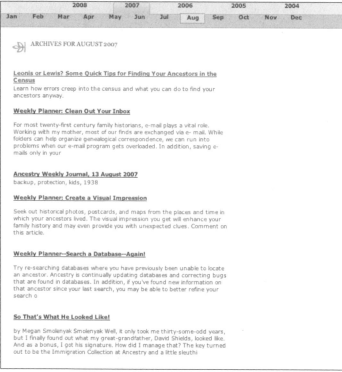

Figure 17-20: The "Browse Archives" page

will be presented with a search results list with the article(s) that were found matching your input.

The next item on the list is "Videos." This is the same list of short videos by Megan Smolenyak that you saw when we explored the "Find Answers" area and clicked on the link labeled "View All Videos." Please don't overlook this collection of video training materials.

The last of the links is "Archive." Here you can browse by year and month, going back a number of years. Browsing the archive can be fun and addictive, with so many excellent articles and tips and so much interesting news. A sample of the browse page is shown in figure 17-20.

Click on a year and a month and begin exploring. You can click on the page number links at the bottom of the "Archives" section to move from page to page.

Searching the Archive

Beneath the list we have just explored is a search form labeled "Search Topics." This is a powerful tool that can help you locate

specific materials
within the massive
online Ancestry.com
archive. All you have
to do is enter one or
more keywords and
then click the orange
Go button. A new
search results list will
be presented on a
new page. There will

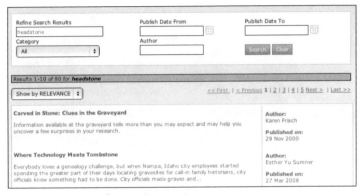

Figure 17-21: Results for an archive search

be two graphic icons used to indicate the source of the article,
but you've already seen them: the diary icon indicates that
the entry is an article from an online publication, such as the
Ancestry Weekly Journal; the magazine graphic signifies that the
article appeared in *Ancestry* Magazine. See figure 17-21 for an
example of this type of combined search results list that came
from entering "military" in the Keyword[s] box.

Summary

The Ancestry.com Learning Center is filled with great
materials suitable for every level of researcher. The
reorganization of the area in December 2007, the addition
of video tutorials, and the installation of an improved
search engine throughout this area have all made significant
improvements to an already content-rich library.

Invest some time becoming familiar with the Learning
Center and you will soon be using it all the time to help
you continue expanding your knowledge *and* improve your
research successes!

Chapter 18

The Ancestry Store

Just as Ancestry.com provides access to the world's largest online repository of genealogical records, the Ancestry Store offers the most extensive collection of retail products relating to genealogy and family history. The store, located at <www.theancestrystore.com>, was relaunched in November 2006 with a new design and a selection of more than 10,000 products. New products and features are constantly being added, so be sure to check back often to see what's new.

You can access the Ancestry Store from the **Store** tab at the top of Ancestry.com pages. The main landing page changes frequently to showcase featured offers but will look similar to figure 18-1 (on next page). Notice the search template in the upper right-hand corner of the page, which allows you to search the entire store or use the pull-down list to search within a specific category.

In the six categories of merchandise available, you will find a wide variety of products that are appropriate for the casual

Figure 18-1: The Ancestry Store homepage

family historian as well as the experienced genealogist. Let's briefly discuss each category.

Books

In the "Books" section, you can purchase Ancestry publications—which include many of the best-selling titles in the genealogy field—as well as thousands of other books on genealogy, family history, and related topics.

The "Books" category includes titles in the following areas: "Staff Favorites"; "Ancestry Magazine"; "Ancestry Publishing";

"Biography and Memoir"; "Custom Products"; "Family";
"Genealogy" books organized by geographic areas, ethnic
groups, and specific reference topics, including a large selection
of how-to books for beginners; "Heritage Cookbooks";
"History" organized by geographic areas and special interests,
including a large collection of military history books; and
"Reference and Pictorial." Ancestry.com has taken extraordinary
pains in evaluating and selecting books that address the interests
of novice and advanced family historians and history buffs.

Records

Ancestry.com is not only the industry's leading provider of
online content, but the company also provides many records
on CD-ROMs and in other formats. The "Records" section
provides access to a wide variety of products and services:

- **Census Records**—These CDs include indexes to records
  from colonial America, the United States, Great Britain,
  and other areas.

- **Church and Parish Records**—These CDs contain English
  county parish records of births, christenings, baptisms,
  burials, tombstone inscriptions, and more.

- **Immigration**—This group contains CDs and books of
  passenger lists, atlases, emigrant lists, and more.

- **Location**—This group consists of vital records, parish
  records, local and family histories, and other records
  organized by geographic areas.

- **Military**—You will find CDs with muster rolls from the
  American Revolutionary War, the War of 1812, the Civil
  War, World War II, and the Korean Conflict. In addition,
  there are military books dealing with American, British,
  and Canadian military history and regiments.

- **Other**—This group includes reference library CDs and miscellaneous record types, including a Slave Narratives CD and the Biography and Genealogy Master Index (BGMI) on CD.

- **Trees**—These CD bundles include the family trees submitted for inclusion in the Ancestry World Family Tree.

- **Vital Records**—This group includes parish registers, primarily in book form, for many areas of England, along with Irish marriage registers and a selection of CDs containing U.S. states' vital records indexes.

- **Certificate Service**—VitalChek Express Certificate Service is a government-authorized service offering expedited delivery of certified copies of birth, death, marriage, and divorce certificates for you and your ancestors.

Software

The past decade has seen an explosion in genealogical database software products and in the development of utility software to complement your family history research. Ancestry.com has compiled an impressive collection of genealogy-related software for this category. Its own *Family Tree Maker* software and bundles, *Legacy*, *Roots Magic*, *The Master Genealogist*, *Clooz*, *Personal Historian*, and *Family Atlas* are among the software titles. In addition, there are DVD training products in this collection to help you learn how to use the leading genealogy database software packages.

Photos

The past lives again in this magnificent collection of photographs. There are three groups of photos included in this category: "People, Places and Things"; "War and Conflict," which includes military photos from the U.S. Civil War forward; and "Staff Favorites" that you will recognize as classics, such as the image shown on the ordering page in figure 18-2.

Available in a number of sizes, each photograph is a silver-halide photo print using high-quality, archival-safe paper, suitable for gallery framing and display. These photos make a lovely gift or a treasured addition to your own collection.

Figure 18-2: One of the "Staff Favorites" shown on the ordering page

Maps

Maps are essential for effective genealogical research, and Ancestry.com has compiled a collection of more than two thousand historical U.S. and international maps, including a large selection of railroad maps. All maps are available as high-quality silver-halide photo prints in a variety of sizes, ranging from ten to forty inches.

Gifts

The "Gifts" section presents suggestions to help you find the perfect gift for almost anyone: a custom book filled with fascinating facts about your friend's surname, a framed historic print or photograph from your relative's hometown, a puzzle featuring the *New York Times* front page from your family member's birth date, a military history book for a veteran or war buff, an introductory genealogy book for a novice family historian, or a more advanced genealogy product for an experienced researcher. The "Gifts" section is refreshed often

Figure 18-3: Expanded product information

with products from the store's large collection.

Ordering

When you click on a product, you will see a page with a larger product image, more descriptive text, and a price. Other related products are sometimes displayed for your consideration. See figure 18-3 for an example for the book *They Became Americans*.

You may also see another small button labeled **More Information**. Click it and you will see the full product description and product specifications, as shown in figure 18-4.

Anytime you see the orange button labeled **Add to Cart**, you can click to add this item to your order. When you do, your "Shopping Cart" page, shown in figure 18-5 (on the next page), will be displayed. You can change the quantity of any item you have added to the cart, or you can click the check box in the "Remove" column to delete an item. When you are finished making changes, click the **Update** button to display a refreshed, revised "Shopping Cart" page.

You can now click either "Return to shopping" or the orange **Checkout** button to complete your purchase. If you do the latter, you will be prompted to enter your shipping information and

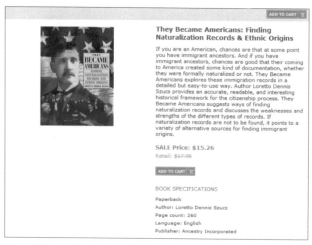

Figure 18-4: Full product description and specifications

then your billing and payment information.

You will then be taken to the "Review and Confirm" page, where, if necessary, you can change the quantities of your orders (or delete them by changing the quantity to "0"). If you make any changes, click the **Update** button. Otherwise, if everything looks good, click the orange **Complete Your Order** button.

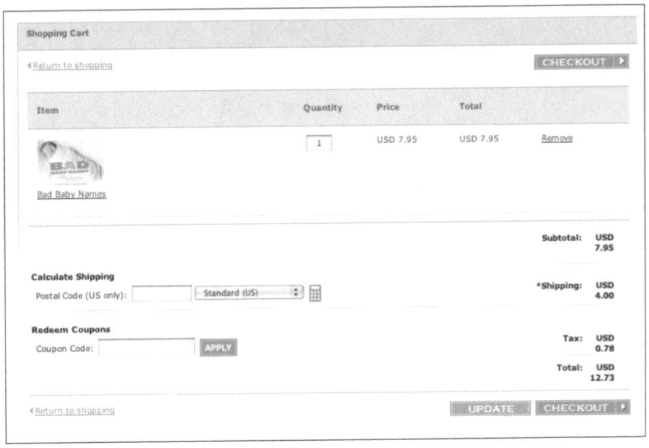

Figure 18-5: The "Shopping Cart" page

A confirmation page will appear that you can print for your reference.

You will also note that there is a "Customer Service" link at the top of the "Ancestry Store" pages. Here you will find contact information, policies, shipping options, and FAQs (Frequently Asked Questions).

Another link at the top of the page is labeled "My Account." This is the account information that you entered as you placed your order. You can also update your username and password, e-mail address, and mailing address and telephone number here.

Summary

As you have seen, the Ancestry Store has thousands of products that appeal to customers with varied interests and backgrounds. Regardless of your level of family history experience, you are sure to find products that will help you better understand and appreciate your heritage. The store's navigation makes it easy to browse or search for specific products or services, and the ordering process could not be simpler. Take a tour to see what the store offers, and check back frequently for new products and features, promotions, and sales.

Chapter 19

Putting It All Together

We have covered a *lot* of material in this book. But then again, Ancestry.com is the largest genealogy site on the Web. You should now have a strong understanding of what kinds of information can be found at Ancestry.com, how to navigate the site, how to effectively search the site, how to create and expand your Family Trees, and how to use the Ancestry Community facilities to extend your research and make contact with other members. The skills you have learned by reading this book, studying the examples, and practicing searching and should have prepared you to be a much more effective user of Ancestry.com.

Remember, however, that Ancestry.com is only part of The Generations Network, Inc. Currently, there are Ancestry sites in the UK and Ireland. Canada, Australia, Germany, Sweden, Italy, and China, with more to come. In addition, the other sites in The Generations Network, Inc., family also provide exceptional content.

The understanding you have gained by working with Ancestry.com is important because it has prepared you to succeed in working with the other sites, as well as helping you develop the research thought processes you will use to search the Internet and work with other databases.

Traditional versus Electronic Evidence

Contrary to some people's perceptions, the electronic content found on the Internet has not replaced traditional documents and other genealogical evidence in our research. Likewise, not everything on the Internet is correct.

It is imperative that you *personally* verify the information you find on Ancestry.com for yourself. Remember, your detailed knowledge of your ancestors and their family members gives you the advantage of applying that knowledge when assessing and interpreting details from an original evidential document. Likewise, you cannot be sure that the quality and accuracy of another researcher's work is as accurate and reliable as what you would produce.

Ancestry.com has amassed more than 23,000 databases and titles containing more than 5 billion names. The company continues to acquire and add new content on a regular basis. There is a massive quantity of digitized original material available to help further your research. You will, of course, evaluate that material, develop hypotheses, and reach conclusions based on that original content weighed against other evidence you uncover.

Other resources at Ancestry.com include indexes and transcribed records. You know that these materials are secondary evidentiary sources. They may contain inaccurate or incomplete information. Ancestry.com knows, too, that its indexes are not infallible. It is difficult to read old handwriting and dim original documents and microfilmed document images. Human indexers, despite the best intentions, may make typographical errors. You will undoubtedly find indexing and transcription errors at Ancestry.com and in original documents as well. Remember that you can always report errors and omissions to Ancestry.com for correction, and doing so benefits everyone.

Using the Help Tool at Ancestry.com

Ancestry.com is committed to providing solid help to its users. In the upper right-hand corner of almost every page we've examined is a link labeled "Help." A click on that link takes you to the page shown in figure 19-1.

The Help tool actually includes several services. The core piece is the Knowledge Base. A knowledge base is a special kind of database for knowledge management. It is the base for the collection of information and often FAQs. A good knowledge base has a carefully designed classification structure, content format, and search engine, and the Knowledge Base at Ancestry.com is no exception.

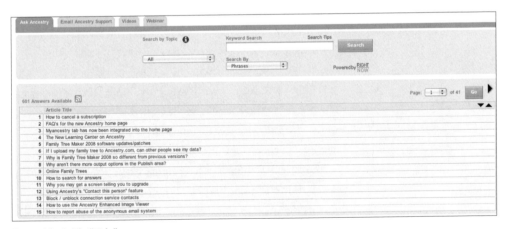

Figure 19- 1: The "Help" page

In figure 19-1, you will notice that there are four tabs at the top of the "Help" page:

- **Ask Ancestry**—This is the core of the Knowledge Base, where questions and answers are stored and which you can search by topic.

- **Email Ancestry Support**—This tab provides a formatted template that you can use to send a message or inquiry to the Ancestry.com customer support group.

- **Videos**—Here you can watch a number of tutorial videos on a variety of topics.

- **Webinar**—This tab offers information about a variety of webinars available through Ancestry.com. A webinar is basically a short class offered over the Internet. From this tab, you can enroll in upcoming webinars and watch older ones.

Ask Ancestry

Figure 19-1 shows the Ancestry.com Help tool, displaying, as it always does, the default **Ask Ancestry** tab. You certainly could browse through all the pages of the Knowledge Base, but it would be much easier to search for what you want to know.

On the page, there are a variety of ways to search the Knowledge Base. Let's discuss how these work.

The first is a drop-down, "Search by Topic," listing major subject areas in the Knowledge Base. If you click on a topic, another drop-down list will appear with subtopics. You can select one of these subtopics and then click the **Search** button.

Your search will yield a list of possible articles that might answer your question. If I click on one, a page loads that contains the question, answer, and links to other areas where information may be found.

There is another way to get to the topic and subtopic areas in the Knowledge Base. Beside the "Select a Topic" drop-down list is a dark blue circle with an "i" in it. This is an informational link, and when you click on it, another page will pop up. It allows you to view the entire hierarchical list of topics and subtopics. Click on one of the links and you will immediately be presented with the same list as if you had used the topic and subtopics from the drop-down lists.

The "Keyword Search" field allows you to enter one or more terms and have the search engine locate responses for you. Here are some tips for using this search field. You can use the "Search by" drop-down options to help you focus your search.

Email Ancestry Support

When you click on the **Email Ancestry Support** tab, the page shown in figure 19-2 is displayed. It is a formatted template you can use to send a message to the Ancestry.com customer

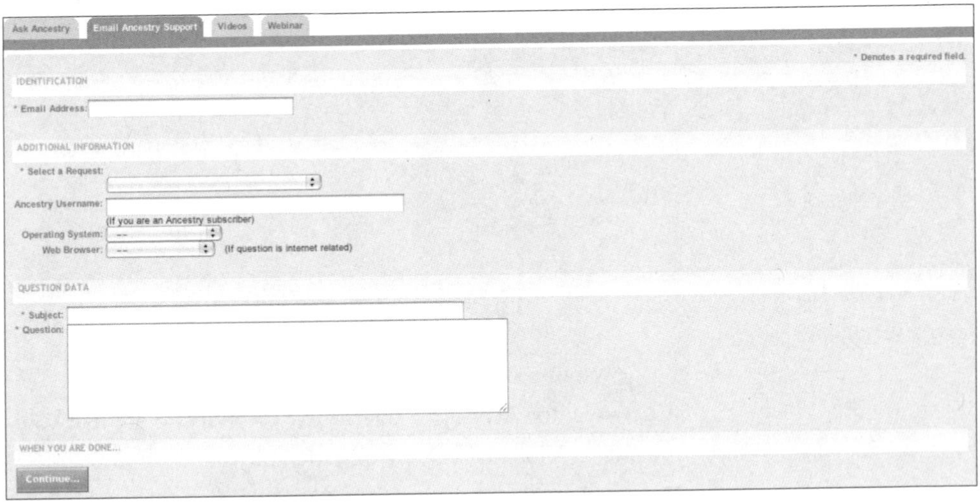

*Figure 19-2: The **Email Ancestry Support** tab*

support group. Use it only if you were unsuccessful in finding an answer to your question using the **Ask Ancestry** tab. All fields marked with a small red asterisk must be completed. You will note there are drop-down lists again on this page for "Select a Topic" and "Select a Product."

When you have completed the information in the fields, click **Submit Question**. Your message will be sent to the customer support group. You will receive an e-mail response, answering your question.

Videos

Sometimes, everybody can use a little demonstration. On the **Videos** tab (see figure 19-3), you will find tutorial videos for a variety of tasks at Ancestry.com, from how to print your Family Tree to how to cancel your subscription.

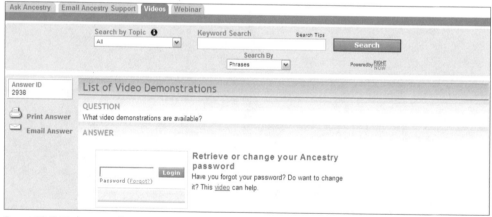

*Figure 19-3: The **Videos** tab*

To watch a video, click the image or the "video" link. A new window will open and display the video. Note that you must have Adobe *Flash Player* installed on your computer for these videos to play. If you do not have it, click the Adobe link beneath the video player to install it.

Webinar

A webinar is a class offered over the Internet. Occasionally, Ancestry.com offers webinars about family history and their site. For instance, when Ancestry unveiled their new search features, they hosted a webinar with Kendall Hulet, the product manager in charge of the search function.

On the "Webinar" page shown in figure 19-4, you can learn about upcoming webinars or view older ones. To watch an archived webinar, simply click **Watch Video** next to the one in which you are interested. On the subsequent page, fill out the registration information (or if you have already registered for it, simply enter your e-mail address) and click **View Archive**.

Next, select the media type you want to use and click **Launch Presentation**.

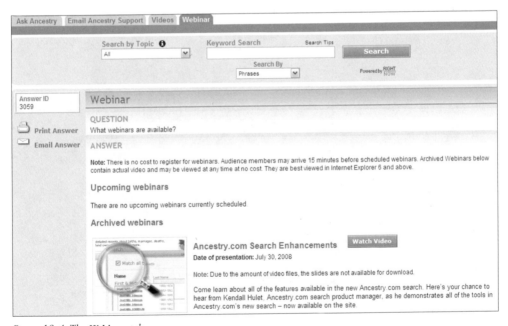

*Figure 19-4: The **Webinar** tab*

Happy Hunting

As you can see, the Ancestry.com Help tool and its Knowledge Base are easy to use and will provide you with a great deal of help information. In the meantime, you will want to keep this book handy too. Use the table of contents and the index to locate just what you need to know.

Now, get started on your genealogical odyssey and discover the wealth of great information available at Ancestry.com.

Index

24/7 Family History Circle blog, 13, 264, 266, 267, 269

A

Add a Comment, 39
Add a Correction, 75
Add a new audio story, 66
Add an Alternate Name, 39, 75
advanced searching, 24–25
African-American records, 259
   African-American Photographic Collection, 259
   slave narratives, 167–69, 259
alerts for message boards, 231
alumni directories, 174
American Genealogical-Biographical Index (AGBI), 165–66
Ancestry archive searching, 272–273
Ancestry.com homepage, 1–2

Ancestry Community, 11–12, 62, 239, 262–63
Ancestry Daily News, 13, 267
Ancestry Magazine, 13, 252, 267, 271–72
Ancestry Monthly newsletter, 252, 267, 270–71
AncestryPress (replaced by My Canvas), 9–10, 201, 253, 260, 265–66
Ancestry Product Watch, 4
Ancestry Store, 14–15, 266, 275–82
   ordering from, 280–81
Ancestry Weekly Journal (AWJ), 13, 252, 266, 267, 269–70
Ancestry World Tree, 54
Ask Ancestry tab, 286–87
atlases, 149–50
   searching, 153–55

B

Beginner's Guide to Online Family History, 268
biographies, 165–66, 276–77
slave narratives, 167–68
Biography Database, 1680–1830, 180–81
Biography & Genealogy Master Index (BGMI), 159, 193
Birth, Marriage, and Death Records Collection, 94–96
blogs, 251, 264
24/7 Family History Circle, 13, 264, 266, 267
DNA, 12
bookmarking favorite message boards, 231
books
buying in Ancestry Store, 276
searchable online, 194–195
British Phone Books 1880–1984 database, 181–83
buying Ancestry products, 14, 275–82

C

cadastral map, 150
Canada/Canadian
census records, 87–91
immigration records, 129
military records, 119, 277
PERSI, 196
searching Canadian records, 31
canceling Ancestry subscription, 4, 191
Card Catalog, 9, 30–32, 36
cartographic map, 151
cartography, 150–53
CDs (historical records), buying in Ancestry Store, 277–78

census records, 123–24
alternatives to, 173–74
Canada, 87–90
blank forms, 88
overview, 69–71
printing, 75
searching, 71–77
state and county, 77–80
United Kingdom, 80–87
overview, 80–81
Scotland 1841 Census, 86–87
searching, 82–85
United States
overview, 70–80
searching, 71–77
church records, 95, 101
city directories, 174
searching, 175–77
civil records
defined, 93
civil registration records
defined, 93
Civil War
maps, 151
muster rolls, 277
photos, 279
records, 109, 111–13, 254
Clooz, 278
comments, 75–77
adding to records, 39
Common Ancestors graph, 245–46
communities for Ancestry members, 11–12, 62, 216–19, 239, 262–63
Community tab, 11–12, 216–19, 262
Comparison of Maternal Test (mitochondrial DNA) Participants page, 245
corrections, 75–77

Court, Land & Probate Records
        Collection, 185–94
Court, Land, Wills, & Financial
        Collection, 187–89
court records, 185–89, 185–94

D

databases
    DNA, 12
    finding through Card Catalog, 9,
        30–32
    new, 7–8
    searching, 7, 18–22
    searching for, 29–30, 36
Dawes Commission Index, 169–71
directories
    city, 174
    overview, 173–75
    phone books, British, 181–83
    searching, 175–77
    U.S. and UK, 1680–1830, 179–81
Directories & Member Lists
        Collection, 173–85
discovery and exploration (map), 151
DNA, 12–13, 237–48
    groups on Ancestry.com, 239,
        246–47
        browsing, 247
        creating, 247
        joining, 247
        searching, 247
    haplogroup, 243
    homepage on Ancestry.com, 239–40
    tab, 12
    testing
        through Ancestry.com, 239
        "Common Ancestors" graph,
            245–46
        matches, 243
        maternal, 241

DNA, testing (*continued*)
    Maternal Matches tab, 245
    mitochondrial DNA (mtDNA),
        238, 241
    ordering on Ancestry.com, 240
    paternal, 240
    Paternal Matches tab, 243–45
    results, 241–46
        downloading, 243
        printing, 243
    types of, 240–41
    Understanding your results link,
        243
    Y DNA, 238, 241
draft registration cards, WWI,
        113–15

E

e-mail address, changing, 4
e-mail
    alerts for message boards, 231
    sending images to others, 49–50
    updating preferences, 4
E-mail the image to a friend link, 40
enlistment records, WWII Army,
        115–16
errors
    reporting, 75–77
exact matches searching, 24–26, 28

F

Facts About Your Surname, 253–56
Family and Local Histories
        Collection, 161–66
Family Atlas, 278
family cookbook
    creating, 265–66
family histories, 157–58
    *American Genealogical-Biographical
        Index* (AGBI), 165–66

family history book
    creating, 203–11
family history portrait
    creating, 265
Family Records Centre, London, 103
Family Tree DNA, 241
Family Tree Maker, 253, 278
Family Tree tab, 63, 64
Family Trees, 6–7, 51, 251, 260–63
    accessing, 51
    adding audio to, 66–67, 261
    adding comments to, 61
    adding photos to, 60, 261
    adding stories to, 66–67, 262
    adding video to, 58–59
    building, 260–61
    changing home person, 59
    creating, 52–56
    famous, 262
    from a GEDCOM, 55–57
    history of, on Ancestry.com, 54
    home person, 59
    Home tab, 57–60
    living relatives in, 53
    Manage my tree, 58
    navigating, 63–65
    People page, 59–62
    Photos tab, 65–66
    privacy for, 52, 58
    public, 54–55
    searching from, 60–61
    sharing, 201
    source records attached to, 62
    timelines, 61–62
    viewing, 63–65
Famous Family Trees, 262
Favorites, 11
federal census reords. *See* census
        records; records, census
Filter by Collection, 72
Find Famous Relatives, 62

finding aids
    searching, 192–96
forms
    blank, 37, 37–38
    genealogical, 258
FreeBMD Indexes for Births,
        Marriages, and Deaths,
        104–07
Freedman's Bank Records, 259
Freedmen's Bureau Marriage
        Records, 259
Freedmen's Bureau Records, 259

G

gazetteers, 149–50
    searching, 153–55
GEDCOM
    uploading to Family Tree, 55–56
Genealogical Computing, 13, 267
*Genealogical Publications: A List of
        50,000 Sources from the Library
        of Congress*, searchable online,
        191
genealogy software, buying in Ances-
        try Store, 278–79
General Register Office (GRO), 104
genetics, 237–39
geopolitical maps, 151
greeting cards
    creating, 265

H

handwriting
    deciphering, 258
haplogroup, 243
Having trouble viewing the image?,
        40–41
Help tool, 285–88
    Ask Ancestry, 286–87
    Email Ancestry Support, 287–88

Historical Newspaper Collection, 255

Historical Postcards Collection, 143–44

home person for family tree, 59

I

images
  accessing, 35–36, 35–37
  displaying in full page mode, 42–43
  dragging, 42
  enhanced and original, 45–46
  magnifying specific areas, 44–45
  moving between multiple, 47
  printing, 47–48
  reporting problems with, 39, 40
  resizing, 43
  resolution, 45
  saving, 48–49
  sharing with others, 49–50
  thumbnails of, 45–46
  viewing, 40–41
  zooming in and out of, 42–43
Image Viewer
  help for, 50
  overview, 46
  toolbar, 41
immigration records
  at Ancestry.com, 121–23
  overview, 121–23
  Passenger and Immigration Lists
    Index, 1590s–1900s, 128–30
  searching, 123–36
    entire collection, 123–29
  stub books, 131
Immigration Records Collection, 121–23

K

Knowledge Base, 4

L

land ownership maps, 151
land records, 185–90
Learning Center, 13–15, 249–76
  Build a Tree, 251, 260–63
  Community, 252
  Discover More, 251, 264–65
    Beyond Research, 266
    Project Highlights, 266
  Facts About Your Surname, 253–256
  Find Answers, 251, 256–60
    Census Records, 257–60
    Choosing Historical Records, 259
    Piecing Together Your Family
      History, 259
  Getting Started, 251
  Join the Community, 251, 262–63
    Join the Conversation, 264
  Keep Learning, 251, 266–72
  Learning More
    Family History Articles, 267–68
  Tutorials, 252
    AncestryPress, 253
    Family Tree Maker, 253
    How does Ancestry.com work?, 253
    See a sample tree, 253
  videos available, 250–51, 256
  Welcome page, 250–56
  What's New, 252
Learning Center tab, 13, 250
Legacy, 278
life expectancy by surname, 254
living relatives, in family trees, 53
local histories, 125, 157–58
  Family and Local Histories
    Collection, 161–66
  searching, 164–65
logging in, 1–3

M

mailing address, updating, 4
Make a Connection, 40
managing your account, 3–5
maps, 149–56
   buying in Ancestry Store, 279
   searching, 153–55
Master Genealogist, The, 278
Member Connections, 11, 40, 233
Member Directory, 12, 218, 233–35
member login, 1–2
Member Photos collection, 139–41
message boards, 11–12, 251, 252,
     264
   bookmarking favorites, 231
   browsing, 226–33
   creating posts, 221–25
   e-mail alerts for, 231
   searching, 224–26
military records, 259
   accessing on Ancestry.com,
     108–09
   Civil War (American), 109, 111–14,
     254
   early American databases, 109
   housed at, 107–08
   non-American databases, 118
   Revolutionary War, 109–12
   types of, 108
   U.S. World War II Army Enlistment
     Records, 1938–1946, 115–16
   World War I Draft Registration
     Cards, 1917–1918, 113–15
   World War II United News
     Newsreels, 1942–1946,
     116–18
Military Records Collection, 107–19
Miracode, 258
mitochondrial DNA (mtDNA), 238,
     245

Most Recent Common Ancestor
     (MRCA), 238, 245–46
My Account, 3–5
MyCanvas, 260
   combination book, 204
   descendant book, 204
   editing in, 208–11
   ordering projects, 212
   printing projects, 211–12
   sharing projects, 212
   standard book, 204
   toolbar, 206–08
   workspace, 205
My DNA link, 241
My Public Profile, 216–17, 218–25
My Site Preferences, 217

N

National Geographic Genographic
     Project, 239, 241
naturalization records, 121, 125–26,
     130–34. *See also* immigration
     records; records, immigration
Need Help?, 4
New & Coming Soon, 3
newsletters
   Ancestry Daily News, 13, 267
   Ancestry Monthly, 252, 267, 270–71
   Ancestry Weekly Journal, 13, 252, 266,
     267, 269–270
   subscribing to, 4
Newspapers and periodicals
   headlines, 255
   Historical Newspaper Collection,
     255
   obituaries, 146–49
   searching, 144–45

O

obituaries, 146–49

occupation, by surname, 255
OneWorldTree, 54
Order original certificate, 98–99

P

Page Tools, 39–40
panoramic maps, 152
park maps, 152
*Passenger and Immigration Lists Index,
    1590s–1900s*, 128–30
passenger lists, 122–23
password, changing, 3
pedigree chart
    printing, 64
    viewing, 63–65
People I'm Looking For, 8
People tab, 59–62
Periodical Source Index. See PERSI
PERSI, 196–200
    documents, ordering, 198–200
    searching, 197–200
Personal Historian, 278
phone books, British, 181–83
photo book
    creating, 204
photographs
    in family trees, 65–66
    historical, buying in Ancestry Store,
        278
    of immigrant ships, 127
    searching for, 136–42
       by keyword, 136–38
pictures
    searching for, 136–42
       by keyword, 136–38
poster
    creating, 202–03
posts for message boards, creating,
        221–25

preferences, 4, 52, 217
Print and Share tab, 202
printing
    forms, 38, 88
printing (*continued*)
    images, 47–48
    pedigree chart of family tree, 64
    Publish and Print link, 59
    records, 75, 83, 131, 212–213
    with MyCanvas, 201–214
privacy for family trees, 58
probate records, 103, 185–90
professional/trade directories, 174
public profiles, 216–17, 218–25, 251,
        264
public records (United States),
        178–79

Q

Quick Links, 5–6

R

railroad maps, 152
Railroad Retirement, 97
Recent Activity, 8
Recent Buzz, 3
records
    adding comments to, 39
    African-American, 259
    alternatives to census, 173–75
    available on CD, 277–78
    birth, 94, 103–07
    CDs of, buying in Ancestry Store,
        277–78
    cemetery, 95
    census, 69–90
    church, 95
    court, 185–89, 185–94
    death, 94–95

records (*continued*)
divorce, 94
FreeBMD Indexes for Births, Marriages, and Deaths, 104–07
immigration, 121–36
passenger lists, 122–23
land, 185–90
marriage, 94, 101–02
military, 107–20, 259
naturalization, 130–34
obituaries, 95
ordering online from NARA, 189–90
parish and probate, 103
printing, 212–13
probate, 1103, 85–90
public (United States), 178–79
reporting errors in, 75–77
requesting from Social Security Administration, 98–99
Social Security Death Index (SSDI), 95, 96–101
types of, 94–95
viewing, 37–40
Red Book: American State, County, and Town Sources, 194–95
reference books, searching, 191, 194–95
reference databases, searching, 192–96
Reference & Finding Aids Collection, 191–209
registering, 2
relief maps, 152
religious membership rolls, 174
Report an Image Error, 77–78
Report an Image Problem, 39
Revolutionary War records, 109–12
Roots Magic, 278

S
Save This Record, 38
saving images, 48–49
Search
new, 22–24
Search page, 8–9
search results
narrowing, 19–20, 28–29
searching, 7–8, 18–33, 71–73
advanced, 24–25
Card Catalog, 30–32
census records
United States, 71–77
city directories, 175–77
court records, 187–94
exact, 24–26, 28
finding aids, 192–96
immigration records, 123–29
land records, 187–94
message boards, 224–33
probate records, 187–94
reference books, 194–95
refining, 27–29
strategy, 19–22, 32–33
ships, photographs of, 127
Shoebox, 8, 38
slave narratives, 167–69, 259
Social Security Death Index (SSDI), 95, 96–101
software (genealogy), buying in Ancestry Store, 278–79
Soundex, 258
Source: A Guidebook to American Genealogy, The, searchable online, 191, 194–95
source citations, 38
Southern Claims Commission Records, 259
Special Offers, 4

SS-5 form, 98–100
Store tab, 275, 275–82
stories
    adding to Family Trees, 66–67
Stories, Memories & Histories
        collection, 158
    searching, 158–71
stub books, 131
subclade, defined, 243
subject lines for message board posts,
        221–22
subscribing, 2
success stories
    links to, 258
surname facts, 253–56

T

tax lists, 174
telephone directories, 174
thematic maps, 152
thumbnails of images, 45–46
timelines for people in family
        trees, 61–62
Toolbar, Image Viewer, 41–51
    Drag, 42
    Help, 50–51
    Image Number, Previous, and Next,
        47–48
    Image Size, 43–44
    Magnify, 44
    Options, 44
        Image Compression, 45–46
        Image Enhancing, 45
        Image Thumbnail, 45
    Print, 47–48
    Save, 48–49
    Share, 49
    View in Full Page Mode, 42
    Zoom, 42

topographical maps, 153
transportation maps, 153
trees. *See* Family Trees
troubleshooting
    Image Viewer, 50
    reporting image problems, 39, 40

U

UK and U.S. Directories, 1680–1830,
        179–81
United Kingdom
    census records, 80–87
        search, 105
    directories for, 1680–1830,
        174–75, 179–81
    immigration records, 125
    military records, 107
    surname distribution, 254–55
United States
    census records for, 70–80
    directories for, 1680–1830, 179–81
    military records, 109–18
    surname distribution, 255
United States Obituary Collection
    searching, 147–149
U.S. Cemetery Address, searchable
        online, 191
U.S. Colored Troops Records, 259
U.S. Deluxe Membership, 26
username, changing, 27
U.S. Headstone Photos
    contributing to database, 138
using Ancestry.com
    articles, 268
U.S. Public Records Index, 178–79
U.S. School Yearbook database
    collection, 143, 177–79
    searching, 177
    submitting to, 177–78

V

videos, 250–51, 256, 272–73
View blank form link, 37
View Full Content, 80
View Image, 40–41
View original image link, 37
View Record link, 37–38
View Ship Image, 127–29
vital records
  defined, 93
vital statistics
  defined, 93

W

What's Happening at Ancestry.com,
    31
World Deluxe Membership, 26
World War I Draft Registration Cards.
    1917–1918, 113–15, 259
World War II Army Enlistment
    Records, 1938–1946, 115–16
World War II United News Newsreels,
    1942–1946, 144–45

Y

Y chromosome, 238
yearbooks, 174, 177–78

About the Author

George G. Morgan

George G. Morgan has been working on his family history since
he was ten years old in North Carolina, tracing his family from
the southwest to England, Wales, Scotland, and Ireland. He
writes regularly for the *Ancestry Weekly Journal*, the *24/7 Family
Circle* blog, *Eastman's Online Genealogy Newsletter*, and *Digital
Genealogy*. He even had an column for over a year with the now
defunct Chineseroots.com. This publication is his sixth book.

George is also co-host with Drew Smith of "The Genealogy
Guys Podcast" at <www.genealogyguys.com>, the longest
continuously running genealogy podcast on the Internet. He is
a director of the Florida Genealogical Society of Tampa and the
Public Relations and Publicity Director for the Florida State
Genealogical Society. He is president of Aha! Seminars, Inc.,
and teaches distance education seminars for the University
of South Florida (Tampa), Pharos Tutors in London, and
Genealogical Librarian Certification for the National Institute
of Genealogical Studies at the University of Toronto. He lives
in Odessa, Florida, a suburb of Tampa.